Technology and the Historian

TOPICS IN THE DIGITAL HUMANITIES

Humanities computing is redefining basic principles about research and publication. An influx of new, vibrant, and diverse communities of practitioners recognizes that computer applications are subject to continual innovation and reappraisal. This series publishes books that demonstrate the new questions, methods, and results arising in the digital humanities.

Series Editor
Susan Schreibman

Technology and the Historian

Transformations in the Digital Age

ADAM CRYMBLE

UNIVERSITY OF ILLINOIS PRESS
Urbana, Chicago, and Springfield

Library of Congress Cataloging-in-Publication Data
Names: Crymble, Adam, author.
Title: Technology and the historian : transformations in the
    digital age / Adam Crymble.
Description: Urbana : University of Illinois Press, 2021. | Series:
    Topics in the digital humanities | Includes bibliographical
    references and index.
Identifiers: LCCN 2020036208 (print) | LCCN 2020036209
    (ebook) | ISBN 9780252043710 (cloth ; acid-free paper) |
    ISBN 9780252085697 (paperback ; acid-free paper) | ISBN
    9780252052606 (ebook)
Subjects: LCSH: History—Computer network resources. |
    History—Research—Methodology. | Historiography—
    Methodology. | Digital media.
Classification: LCC D16.117 .C79 2021 (print) | LCC D16.117 (ebook)
    | ddc 902.85/4678—dc23
LC record available at https://lccn.loc.gov/2020036208
LC ebook record available at https://lccn.loc.gov/2020036209

To everyone who has contributed to *Programming Historian*

Contents

Acknowledgments   ix

Introduction   1

1 The Origin Myths of Computing in Historical Research   17

2 The Archival Revisionism of Mass Digitization   46

3 Digitizing the History Classroom   79

4 Building the Invisible College   107

5 The Rise and Fall of the Scholarly Blog   137

6 The Digital Past and the Digital Future   161

Appendix: Digital History Syllabus Corpus (2002–2017)   171

Glossary: A New Vocabulary   175

Notes   183

Bibliography   209

Index   237

Acknowledgments

I am grateful to Katrina Navickas, who read through every chapter, to my reviewers and editors, as well as to Sarah Lloyd, James Baker, Michelle Hamilton, Jane Winters, Angela Kedgley, and Ellen Crymble, who provided valuable comments and helped me ground the book more effectively in the existing scholarship.

I also thank those scholars who contributed time, resources, or agreed to be interviewed: Josh Greenberg, Rob MacDougal, Roopika Risam, Amanda French, William J. Turkel, Willard McCarty, Stephen Brier, Steven Mintz, Edward Ayers, Kelly Schrum, Chad Gaffield, Janice Reiff, William Cutler, Harold Short, Tim Hitchcock, Alan MacEachern, John Styles, James Baker, François Dominic Laramée, Sasha Hoffman, Lisa Smith, Bob Nicholson, Sharon Leon, Justin Colson, Arthur Burns, Scott Weingart, Patrick Walsh, Sharon Howard, Alix Green, Ceri Houlbrook, Mills Kelly, the Programming Historian team, and Mike Cosgrave, who gave me a virtual tour of his "digital" teaching space.

Finally, my father, Hugh Crymble, and grandfather Sam Crymble, who introduced me to computers in the 1980s and helped spark a curiosity that inspired this work.

Technology and the Historian

INTRODUCTION

"My purpose here," said Roy Rosenzweig in 1997 is "to remind us that we are engaged in a process that has earlier roots and precedents as well as one that responds—as did these earlier efforts—to particular historical circumstances."[1] A celebrated "digital historian," Rosenzweig sadly passed away during his creative prime. This speech a decade before his death addressed an audience of fellow historians in the United States, asking if and in what ways the U.S. history course should be revised for a new millennium. It seemed fitting that a such an apt statement about the future of the profession from one of digital history's most important voices should find a home here at the beginning of this book, which uncovers how technology has influenced practitioners of historical studies in the information age, reminding us that it too was part of a process with earlier roots and the product of particular historical circumstances.

This is a story that needs telling now because no discipline has invested more energy and thought into making its sources and evidence publicly available, or in engaging publics through digital mediums, or transforming their pedagogic practices with the help of technology. Yet the stereotypical historian still remains resolutely tied to scholarly traditions—dust in the archives rather than bytes in the computer's memory. How then, did a field with some of the most severe barriers to change come to claim a greater piece of the forward-looking digital pie than perhaps any other discipline, and why do the dominant narratives of the profession continue to remember otherwise?[2]

As historians know well, how and what we remember is acutely political. It is not a matter of weaving facts into an objective narrative, but of negotiating between competing perspectives and agendas, including positioning oneself for the future as you would like to see it. By that measure, it would seem that in the many histories and philosophies of the field, historians have chosen not to recognize the transformative role of technology.[3] When it does appear, as in Jerome de Groot's 2008 *Consuming History*, often it feels like an add-on that was dated even before the book reached the shelves. Rather than consider the grubbier mechanics of their tools, from Peter Novick, to F. R. Ankersmit, to Sam Wineburg, historians instead seem to prefer to write about philosophies of scholarship—objectivity versus subjectivity; modernism versus postmodernism—or the various intellectual "turns"—social, cultural, linguistic, archival, and spatial, to name a few.[4] Celebrated public historian Ludmilla Jordanova suggests that greater professional reflection on "the digital" "might help stem the fragmentation of history as a discipline."[5] However, for that to be the case, this preference for the inner world of the mind needs to make room for new stories that build on the old ones. We have a number of books outlining the changing public role of the historian.[6] We even have a call to arms by historians looking for a greater role in public policy.[7] Yet in a field so quick to point out why it is important for us to have a deep knowledge of the past, historians have been slow to recognize how their work and their ideas have not been immune to the transformative rise of the computer, which has brought about the greatest social and cultural transformation the world has perhaps ever seen.

As we increasingly work with computers, computers will increasingly exert their influence on our intellectual agenda, and so we must understand both their strengths and the limits they impose on us. This book challenges our professional blind spot by putting technology at the center of the field's own narrative for the first time, providing a history of technology's impact on historical studies. In doing so, it pulls together the histories and philosophies of the field, with a genre of works including books, articles, and blog posts, that is probably best known as "digital history" scholarship but can better be described as works for historians about computers, intended for immediate consumption.[8]

These books by historians for historians, ranging from Edward Shorter's *The Historian and the Computer: A Practical Guide* (1971), to Peter Denley and Deian Hopkin's *History and Computing* (1987), to Shawn Graham, Ian Milligan, and Scott Weingart's *Exploring Big Historical Data* (2016), were written to summarize the state of a field forging ahead into a bright future. Written by historians, they tended not to speak to the histories and philosophies of the field. Like de Groot's contribution, they often became dated within a few years because they failed to position themselves within a longer history. In many cases, and particularly after about the year 2000, it would seem that their authors were not even all that aware of—certainly not that bothered by—the idea that the computer and the historian had a history together worth remembering. Instead, they spent so much time squinting toward the bright future on the horizon that they forgot to turn around and understand from where they had come and how understanding their intellectual roots could give focus to their energy. The result was a technologically adept group of historians operating in an eternal present, both ignoring and being ignored by the histories of the field of which they should have been a part.

This blind spot of digitally inclined scholars toward their own past has been noticed before. As historian of Latin America Chad Black noted in 2010, practitioners interested in both history and computers too rarely had a sense of the field's trajectory and thus avowed novelty, unaware that the same points may have been debated in the 1980s, if not before.[9] His comment highlights the collective forgetting that happened between the late twentieth century and the new millennium. The same was apparently true of many people in the much wider group of "digital humanists" whose disciplinary background were in fields as diverse as musicology, literary studies, and linguistics. Literary scholar and digital humanist Bethany Nowviskie describes the perennial rehashing of old debates in digital scholarship as an "eternal September." That metaphor draws on the cyclical discussion of old ideas each autumn with a new cohort of students who confuse enthusiasm and *new to me* with original idea.[10]

In a society that has tended to discard old technology rather than celebrate it, old ideas were shed simply because they were old. Teaching in the "digital" history classrooms of the new millennium overwhelmingly turned its back on anything published more than a few years earlier. Many of the typical syllabi of the 2010s were nearly bereft of the scholarly debates from the twentieth century, ensuring that the problem highlighted by Black and Nowviskie would continue into the future. Instead, readings tended to focus on practical matters related to doing work right now.[11] By contrast, it remained an expectation that historians would learn the scholarly literature of their field of expertise, be that sixteenth-century London or the antebellum United States. After all, *Capitalism and Slavery* (1944) by future president of Trinidad and Tobago Eric Williams or *The Making of the English Working Class* (1963) by renowned British socialist historian E. P. Thompson had lost none of their intellectual value more than half a century after they were published and were thus still worthwhile reading. Yet, when it came to technological expertise, it would seem there was less pressure to understand the decades of scholarship that preceded one's own time of study, and instead it was often enough to master the approaches of today.

This digital forgetting had several causes, one of which was the pressure from within the academy to show results and justify expenditure. When asked what real changes all of this "digital" work was bringing about, a number of scholars began to respond defensively with promises that the changes were still to come. In 2016, historian of the nineteenth-century United States Cameron Blevins noticed that many historians frequently described their digital contributions in a "perpetual future tense," looking forward to what would be, rather than backward to what had been.[12] The hype surrounding the field so often implied that the potential of technology was not in the scholarship already printed but in the work just over the horizon. One journalist even suggested that the "power of computers applied to newly digitized texts is literally turning into one-day undergraduate exercises what previously might have been the basis for a doctoral dissertation."[13] It was a field of eternal promise, and technology was the solution. This future-focus mirrored the enthusiasm of space-age Americans who visited Disney's Tomorrowland (1955) or tuned into the futuristic cartoon *The Jetsons* (1962–63) to see a world of flying cars and extra-planetary travel that was about to change everyone's lives forever. If historians had not yet felt the impact of technology, there was the sense that they had simply gone looking too soon.

The forgetting was also linked to a string of tech-focused journals in the early new millennium that ceased publishing and thus fragmented conversations. Starting in 2004, many of the "humanities computing" journals began to close, one after another. This denied newcomers access to the communities that often form around scholarly publications.[14] The first to fall was *Computers and the Humanities* (2004), and the process continued until 2014, when the short-lived *Journal of Digital Humanities* ceased publishing. The latter had been founded by and was edited by historians, making it a unique but brief outlet for the historically minded. New journal repositories arriving after the millennium changed the ways that historians found peer-reviewed research. These single-search-box federated portals such as JSTOR and Google Scholar became increasingly important to scholars. Computational history research suffered because the defunct journals had no advocates ensuring that their articles were made available in these new ways.

Around the same time that these journals began to close, new venues for conversations opened up. Blogging, then social media, became important homes for daily unfiltered and self-referential conversations. It was easy to be engrossed in conversations about digital scholarship without coming across references to published research from those defunct periodicals. Curiously for a group of historians, instead of asking how digital history had come to be, most of the energy went to defining digital historical scholarship in the present tense. The first attempt, "Defining Digital History," appeared in 2002 from Deborah Lines Andersen, an information scientist with a background in library sciences and literature. Andersen summarized the first four years of publication of the *Journal of the Association of History and Computing*, emphasizing the field's near-constant "flux," thus perhaps coming as close as one could get to a sustainable description of what digital historians were up to: it depended on *when* you looked as much as who you asked.[15] More than a decade later, definitions remained an important part of a field in search of its identity, and there was no shortage of venues for sharing one's definition. These definitions were often focused on the much broader field of "digital humanities" of which history was a small part. First launched in 2009, the Day of Digital Humanities was primarily dedicated to asking scholars to self-document what they did on a single day. The implication was that digital scholarship was what digital scholars spent their time doing.

One aspect of the annual virtual event asked participants to offer a concise definition of digital scholarship.[16] Well-intentioned, this was akin to asking scholars operating at or near the center of a large phenomenon to describe what it looked like from the outside. While many definitions were well-thought-through, if limited, because digital work was so far-reaching, involving everything from research, to outreach, to software development, there was no easy way to step back to get a view of the whole. Inevitably practitioners produced definitions that included themselves as part of the in-group, but also that reflected their recent experience. While understandable, this meant any coherent definition was impossible, not least because practitioners came from so many different disciplinary backgrounds and worked on so many different types of projects. Contradictory definitions emerged. Tempers occasionally flared. Frustrated by this lack of progress, by the second decade of the twenty-first century, the problems caused by trying to come up with robust definitions resulted in a backlash against them. "Increasingly, I define DH [digital humanities] with reluctance," quipped book historian Justin Tonra in his 2014 contribution to the Day of Digital Humanities.[17] He was not alone in his refusal to offer a prescriptive definition, with many prominent scholars leaving the question blank. Others avoided it because it tended to lead to quarrels rather than clear delineations. Literary scholar Ted Underwood noted that defining digital humanities was "an enterprise from which I never harvest anything but thorns."[18] The *thorns* grew from a metaphor known as the "big tent" of digital humanities, in which there was room for everyone.

The "big tent" phrase was first used as the theme of the 2011 conference of the Alliance of Digital Humanities Organisations (ADHO), held that year at Stanford University. Under that tent stood self-described digital scholars from every disciplinary background. The result was the gradual disappearance of a distinct "digital history" identity around the same time, as its scholars were absorbed into a broader term, "digital humanities." Where "digital history" remained distinct as an identity, it was to describe the group of digital humanists who also self-identified with the historical professions or activities of interest to historical studies. For some, the virtual community of being "digital" and welcomed into the "big tent" was appealing. To be a digital scholar was to have a place of belonging in an academy that did not quite seem to know where to put you. This feeling of digital scholars being on the proverbial outside was not uncommon. Chad Gaffield, a historian of nineteenth-century Canada, recalled the bemusement of his colleagues when he first put a computer monitor on his desk in the 1980s.[19] Professor of humanities computing, Willard McCarty went so far as to describe having a "stain of computing" that hampered his career in the 1980s, with his colleagues in computing offering a place of belonging that was otherwise absent for him at the time.[20] As an inclusive community, any attempts to define the edges of the big tent would surely leave someone out and thus definitions fell from favor for those happy to be on the inside. The big-tent metaphor was not for everyone, however. Melissa Terras, an engineer turned digital humanist, warned of a poor choice of words to describe an academic movement: "suggesting the field is best described using a big top metaphor, although it may be a bit of fun, is worrying. You don't see many string theorists describing themselves as 'Big Tent Particle Physicists!'"[21] For others, the metaphor just did not work because it was important to exclude certain activities and thus certain people if the field was to have coherence and scholarly rigor. Circa 2010 in the blogosphere, a conversation emerged that came to be characterized as "hack versus yack." It attempted to categorize scholars into those who built software (hack) and those who discussed theory (yack), while implying that one group was making more substantial contributions to scholarship than the other. The "hack versus yack" debate also proved divisive for software developers and researchers, both trying to claim the word "digital" for themselves.[22]

The key problem with the definitions approach was a lack of a common vocabulary and an attempt to apply too many meanings to a single term. This created a crisis of vocabulary, and made it nearly impossible to have meaningful conversations about digital history with other colleagues, let alone with other "digital" scholars. The diverse contributions of historians working with technology were lumped together under a single "digital history" banner, which made it difficult to articulate what "digital historians" do or did. The term covered so many different types of activities conducted by very different types of professionals with very different intellectual aims. From research active academics, to museum practitioners, to a wide array of "#alt-ac" (alternative academic) positions that included software developers and designers as well as project managers, seemingly everyone could be a "digital historian," and there were few ways of articulating which type one meant. When you say "digital history," which digital history do you mean? By contrast, a much richer vocabulary had developed to describe the different types of people who worked on the past. From archivists, to curators, to historical interpreters, to academic historians, to heritage professionals, and public historians, there was a way to describe whom you meant, and thus what they probably did. Not so for digital history. If "digital history" had come to mean everything, then it was no longer fit for purpose.

The challenge of these cross-disciplinary conversations became even more difficult when one realized that discussants were often unaware of the many meanings of "digital history." While many people thought they knew what it meant, they may not have had the same notion of it as the person across the table. Compounding the matter further, individual scholars' understanding of history and technology was often crystallized at the point and place where they first encountered it, leading to many opportunities for conversations to get unwittingly derailed. For example, British and Irish historians who lived through the quantitative history of the 1980s and who decades later found themselves in managerial positions may have expected the young historian in their department to be the direct descendant of those economic and demographic historians who had also used computers. If they instead worked in the U.S. tradition of digital engagement outlined in Dan Cohen and Roy Rosenzweig's *Digital History* (2005), confusion was inevitable because the type of work each was likely to produce was respectively unrecognizable.

These misunderstandings could have a serious impact on individual careers and broader scholarly agendas. Fears about scholars facing incompatible tenure and promotion criteria in U.S. universities led to organizations such as the American Historical Association (2015) stepping in with guidelines for making the process fairer.[23] These high stakes showed that knowing how to distinguish between different digital activities and how to communicate those differences effectively was crucial for practitioners. What *counted* or what was deemed *valuable* was often connected to a wider ecosystem of which these scholars were a part. To navigate that ecosystem, they needed to learn to explain the merits of their contributions in ways that made sense to their colleagues and fulfilled their disciplinary sense of purpose. In this book, I contend that an understanding of the field's history is the best way to develop the vocabulary necessary to lead those conversations and to take the field into the future (see the glossary for the beginnings of that vocabulary). What these earlier attempts demonstrate is that digital history does not need definitions. It needs histories.

By providing a history, *Technology and the Historian* acts as a meeting place between historians who have too long been looking in opposite directions. Even though this space has largely been ignored, I have not had to build from scratch. Instead, this work starts from the article-length foundations laid by scholars on both sides of the Atlantic since the dawn of the twenty-first century. From historian of the U.S. South Edward Ayers's several reflections on the past and future of digital scholarship (2000–2013), to historian of slavery William G. Thomas III's account of history and computing (2004), to historian of British poverty Tim Hitchcock's account of mass digitization in Britain (2015), to Caribbean migration historian Lara Putnam's reflections on how digitization has changed the ways we do historical research (2017), and histories by Chad Gaffield and historian of digital archives Jane Winters (2018), many historians are starting to consider how technology had influenced the trajectory of their careers and the works they created.[24]

These early attempts to survey or describe where digital history had come from had a political purpose within the discipline: to make it possible for digital history to be understood by historians as growing out of and in conversation with theoretical and methodological approaches that preceded the digital turn. It was in some cases to stitch the digital into the fabric of the profession, however uneven the material and weak the thread. As reflections on a movement in progress, some of these works now suffer from time having marched forward and technology having taken the field in directions that the authors were unable to anticipate. This book takes these articles further while staying true to their aims, both by having many years of added hindsight over some of the earlier research, but also by substantially writing technology into the history of historical studies for the first time. This puts history in line with recent trends in other humanities disciplines, which already benefit from histories of technology, including those by library scientist Susan Hockey, computational text analyst Matt Jockers, African American literature scholar Amy Earhart, information studies scholar Julianne Nyhan, and archival scientist Andrew Flinn, or reflections on technology and scholarship such as media scholar Janet Murray's *Hamlet on the Holodeck* or games studies expert Espen Aarseth's *Cybertext*.[25]

A history also forces historians to acknowledge that their field is influenced not only by philosophical shifts and theory, but by each new gadget or piece of software coming out of Silicon Valley. Continuing to pretend otherwise is to miss opportunities to highlight the varied impacts of the field on society and to attract creative talent to the profession and broadly curious students to the lecture theatres. Finally, the book stands as a call to "digital" scholars. Knowing one's own intellectual history is a fundamental precursor to articulating past successes and planning future contributions in context. No longer can the promise be on the horizon if it is not rooted in the past. Doing so will help to ensure that the next generation of "digital" content ages with more grace than the work of the previous generations, and that the profession as a whole can begin to communicate aims and objectives with a common professional vocabulary (see glossary).

One of the key arguments this book makes is that there is not one history of technology and historians but many. This reflects the multifaceted work of historians themselves, who may split their time and energy between the library, the community, the lecture hall, the lab, and the quiet of one's study. Each of these areas of work and many others besides has its own relationship with changing technology. The leaders of change in digitally enabled historical research were not the same as those driving a technological overhaul of the classroom. Neither did the same forces or necessarily the same technologies motivate them to experiment. Thus, while a chronological approach is important, a single overarching narrative is misleading, which is a key reason why no definition of digital work has managed to stick. Instead, *Technology and the Historian* looks at the histories of technology and historical studies, separately considering the history of five aspects of the historian's work that have been substantially influenced by technology since the latter twentieth century.

They are historical research, the archive, the classroom, the self-learning ecosystem, and scholarly communication channels. The topics reflect some of (but by no means all of) the key ways that historians understand their field and the professional divisions within it. I consciously chose this approach, which privileges the understanding of historians over "digital" colleagues, as a means of encouraging scholars to adopt a narrative and vocabulary that allows them to speak productively with each other. To borrow the language of the European Union, the approach intends to encourage an "ever closer union" between all historians. Though few scholars (broadly defined, as they should be) are active in all five of these areas, all five fall under the purview of professionals who care about and work with the past. By exploring the impact of technology on each in turn, this book provides a clear road map of the forces that shaped the various branches of the field in the age of the computer.

This book is aimed at historians and humanists of all levels, from undergraduate students to established scholars, and draws explicitly on the language and approach of the historian, looking forward from the beginning of the field, through each of the key developments and themes as they sculpted the types of contributions made by historians over time. Readers who are too young to have experienced the digital revolutions of the 1980s and '90s will have the most to gain from this historical account, which adds context that has thus far been too thin for newcomers to the field. By adopting a "history" approach, I hope that the book will sit naturally with historians, helping to bridge one of the many divides between the "traditional" and "digital" scholar. This approach makes it possible to consider each type of activity on its own merits and reflects the way that the historical professions are already organized. The contributions of the research active historian writing journal articles and academic books were necessarily distinct from those of the collection manager working with a digital archive from the museum, or the educator trying to find new ways to bring primary sources into the classroom. By arranging the book in this way, it becomes accommodating for use in historiography and historical methods classes, and also helps outline the distinct types of activities that have unhelpfully been lumped together as "digital." This is an opportunity for historians and humanists more broadly to reflect on decades of work in the field and really underline what it is they hope to find over that bright horizon. The pressures of space mean that this book necessarily makes choices about which stories to tell, leading to decisions that may not reflect all local realities. In particular, the book has a strong geographic bias, with most examples consciously taken from the United States, Canada, or the United Kingdom. Having lived and worked in all three of these countries, these practical limitations allowed me to write with confidence from experience. I hope that my broad, if largely

Anglo-centric, international experience has helped me to highlight some of the key regional differences in scholarship that helped history evolve into such a diverse set of activities, and to help readers understand how in their national context technology may have transformed the field in ways that are not representative of the experience of those working elsewhere. What was digital in Los Angeles may not translate into the experiences of those working in Lima, Lagos, or London. Global awareness is as important as historical awareness, and readers are encouraged to explore the many fabulous contributions on global digital scholarship, ranging from Roopika Risam to Dominco Fiormonte, to learn more.[26] Despite the geographic limits of this book, it provides a framework for a wider global discussion about what historical studies has been, is, and can be with the help of technology.

Chapter 1, "The Origin Myths of Computing in Historical Research," looks at two very different ways that scholars used computers for research in the mid- and late twentieth century, and how they contributed to the intellectual landscape of the twenty-first century. In particular, it considers the "Cliometrics" quantitative history inspired by scholars such as historian of the U.S. South Frank Owsley in the 1940s or economic historians Conrad and Meyer in the 1950s, contrasting it with the linguistically focused "Humanities Computing" work of Robert Busa of the same era, which evolved into "digital humanities" by the new millennium. The chapter highlights how each worked with computers but inspired a distinct intellectual movement and provided answers to different types of questions. As this chapter shows, the "digital" historical research of the twenty-first century was inspired by both of these movements but was the direct descendant of neither. Instead, they each provided a diverse toolkit and social infrastructure from which subsequent historians could borrow as they sought to respond to external changes to the research landscape in the 1990s: the rise of the Internet, and the mass digitization of billions of primary sources. This new landscape needed new critical approaches before its practitioners could contribute actively to the existing historiography. Therefore, what we saw of "digital" research in the early new millennium was not new answers to old questions but new answers to interdisciplinary questions that had not been asked previously. Understanding the genealogy of these various movements helps put the different types of historical research reliant on computers into the context of their own intellectual aims and objectives, challenging any assumptions that their time in front of a monitor gave them a common purpose.

Though mass digitization had a tremendous impact on the research landscape of the twenty-first century, the digitization of millions of sources was a story that was in many respects intellectually independent from the research world—particularly in the United States. Chapter 2, "The Archival Revisionism of Mass Digitization," builds a binational understanding of not only how so much of the archive came to be digitized, but also how that process and the motivations behind it differed on both sides of the Atlantic. Considering U.S. desires to bring primary sources into the classroom, and a British impetus to drive research agendas forward, this chapter highlights the importance of national context to the story of digitization. It also extends our understanding of the digitization era by considering the ways the changing technology of the Web and of mobile computing continued to force scholars to evolve their practices. Understanding "users" became as important as understanding the sources in the collection, as scholars—many of them public historians and documentary editors—experimented with new ideas ranging from crowdsourcing to cocreation, and from sonification to mobile computing to virtual reality. Ultimately, they brought the archive out into the "real world," challenging core archival principles such as original order in favor of a new experimental space where the archive or collection could be revised as often and in as many ways as one could imagine.

Chapter 3, "Digitizing the History Classroom," looks at the ways that technology-led teaching made its way into the official curriculum and how that changed over time. Focusing on four distinct waves: quantitative approaches, collection building, big data analysis, and a return to history, through an analysis of more than 130 syllabi the chapter shows that technology repeatedly disrupted practices in history. It challenged everything from the value of the lecture to the wisdom of assigning essays. Heavily influenced by both the quirky offices of Silicon Valley and educational and psychological theorists who advocated for student-centered learning, many of the key innovations were not "digital" at all. Instead, the "digital" classroom was an antiestablishment space that sought to challenge the perceived status quo and to react to new trends and opportunities. The approaches were also uniquely regional, with key differences between Canada and the United States—which placed more emphasis on helping students to become digital storytellers, and the United Kingdom, which retained stronger links to developing student's research skills through new approaches to their sources. This divergence helps demonstrate the international variation within pedagogic practice, and thus the need to understand the different regional narratives.

The vast majority of universities did not provide would-be learners with teaching provision or technical skills opportunities. Chapter 4, "Building the Invisible College," looks at the ways scholars were able to pick up technological skills through informal channels. These informal channels developed to fill voids left within the traditional structures of universities, which were slow to adapt to the growing demand for new skills for historians. It considers in particular the role of the "invisible college," and is based on a study of social media, discussion groups, workshops, summer schools, and online tutorials. This chapter draws on my own experience as a founding editor of the Programming Historian. Because skills provision was not directly controlled by the establishment, it meant that digital historians were increasingly influenced by people operating in other fields, including linguistics, library science, archival science, and computer science. This helped bring new types of approaches to the historical profession. However, practitioners learning these new skills too suffered from the "eternal present" problem of digital history. The expectation to update materials, and the pressure to provide the "best" or "latest" approach, had left newcomers unable to see the skills they were learning in the longer context of the history of digital history, and often made it difficult to know what one needed to learn in the first place.

Chapter 5, "The Rise and Fall of the Scholarly Blog," looks at the history of blogging and digital communication methods among historians. Blogging was one of the key and most obvious technical developments introduced by digitally inclined historians into the historical professions. As a case study, it provides a unique window into the ways that experiments with technology evolved within the digital community before being adopted by mainstream historians. Blogs and changes to scholarly communication practices in the late twentieth and early twenty-first century helped create a community of professionals and amateurs who might not otherwise have had all that much intellectually in common. The blogosphere changed scholarly communication in a very short timeframe. Many of the traditional "digital" journals collapsed just as blogs took off, and without blogging we may never have heard of digital history. It was the pulse of the community in the early new millennium, and this chapter explores its rise and fall as well as the role it played in the scholarly ecosystem.

The research is based on a reading and analysis of blogs from digital scholars, as well as oral interviews. Blogging was once viewed as a risky career move for early career scholars. Passion was its key, which began as a form of protest writing for (often anonymous) graduate students, adjunct professors, and those who felt that spaces were not offered in traditional publishing venues for the conversations that they felt they needed to have. Its astronomical rise in digital scholarship came circa 2005 when more established colleagues joined these conversations, writing openly and enthusiastically about issues affecting higher education and scholarship (but rarely research findings themselves). Blogging helped historians see themselves as "digital humanists" for the first time, and its roots in protest became a defining feature of much "digital" work thereafter. Attempts to preserve these conversations through a model akin to journal publishing ultimately failed because it threatened to install a hierarchy in what had been successful because it had been hierarchy-free. The real story of blogging was social rather than technological, as was the case with many of the so-called technical innovations introduced into historical practices.

The final chapter, "The Digital Past and the Digital Future," considers how this past might suggest pathways into a productive next phase for the field. In particular, it focuses on three key arguments: that historians must reclaim the memory of technology's role within their discipline, that historians must adopt a broader vocabulary to better describe what they consider "digital" work, and that the future will be global. That last issue in particular highlights the importance of understanding the regional variations in this story. While this book focuses largely on the Anglo experience, it does so with the aim of highlighting the fact that there is not one experience that rings true around the world, and that awareness of diversity will help ensure that future solutions consider local needs and local contexts, grounded both in a knowledge of where problems came from and where local partners want to see the field going in their region.

Through each of these chapters, a distinct historical narrative is formed that highlights the fact that the term "digital history," though it has served many people well, might better be expressed as "doing history in the digital age." Instead of referring to a single type of activity, we need to understand the many ways that the "digital era" and the cultural changes it has brought with it have influenced different aspects of the historical professions. Many of the innovations I describe in this book are not "digital" at all, but are instead reflective of the ways that technology has brought about social change to how we work and think about our collective efforts. By understanding the historian who works creatively with computers as someone with an eye on new trends that could solve professional and intellectual problems for the field, it becomes possible to appreciate and support those contributions in appropriate ways. Technology has and is changing the historical professions. But not all technological interventions tried to change aspects of the professions of interest to each and every historian.

To present this history, I have collected private papers, studied blogs and social media, analyzed syllabi, examined archival collections and grant applications, looked at discussion group logs, conducted interviews, and dug deeply into the Internet Archive's Wayback Machine to see the digital traces of this field as it developed. The work also draws extensively on my experience helping to build the globally focused Programming Historian project, a growing suite of more than a hundred tutorials in English, Spanish, and French aimed at teaching historians how to incorporate technology into their research and used by more than a million readers each year.[27] Nearly two decades after "digital historians" took rise, and more than ten years after the first launch of the Programming Historian, this book starts a timely conversation about the future of history that is possible only once the field better understands the roles of technology in its past.

1

The Origin Myths of Computing
in Historical Research

Computing in historical research, according to the historiography, emerged in 1949.[1] But just who was involved and how that took place is a matter of contention. As a result of that contention, just where "digital history" research fit within the field's scholarly traditions remains unclear. William Thomas III argued in 2004 for the centrality of Frank Owsley's 1949 *Plain Folk of the South* as the key text in the genesis of the field.[2] According to Thomas, it was the first history to make use of a computer to sample tax returns and the U.S. census, enabling Owsley to challenge the stereotype that the antebellum U.S. South was a dichotomy of rich slave owners and poor white people. Instead, he put forth a statistically supported argument for a substantial class of small-scale farmers who occupied the middle of the social hierarchy. In the fifty years that followed, the number of quantitative histories blossomed, leading American Historical Association president and colonial U.S. historian Carl Bridenbaugh in 1962 to decry historians' worshiping "at the shrine of that bitch goddess QUANTIFICATION."[3] For those social scientific historians worshiping at the shrine, the computer was a calculator, and scholars such as Owsley proved it could be done. For many historians who were active in the twentieth century in particular, quantification is the obvious predecessor to "digital" work because it was research conducted using a computer.

Yet many of those active in digital history scholarship, including the authors of *The Historian's Macroscope* (2016), overlook that earlier work.[4] Instead, the second story and the one adopted by many "digital historians" of the twenty-first century, puts Jesuit priest Robert Busa at the core of the historical narrative. Busa's work was very different from Owsley's. A linguist by training, he built the Index Thomisticus in collaboration with technology company IBM over many years. The project was a complete lemmatized concordance of the writings of Saint Thomas Aquinas—an index of each root word used. Busa's work started in 1949 and was finally published in the 1970s. It had a profound impact on our society, helping IBM to establish the type of linguistic expertise that would later be applied by the likes of search-engine giants Yahoo! and Google to index the content of the Internet and make it keyword searchable. Few scholars could claim the level of impact that Busa's (mostly female and rarely discussed) team and colleagues like them have been able to impart on our daily lives.[5]

Was it Owsley or Busa who led historians into computing? And did one influence "digital history" more than the other? Some scholars, who focus on the role of technology in the research process, see no difference between the two. Jane Winters (Britain) and Chad Gaffield (Canada) have independently suggested that both branches of research were part of a wider movement of progress that helped take historians from a state of mono- to interdisciplinary research.[6] A progress-focused approach (sometimes referred to as "Whiggish" by historians) is not surprising for scholars writing about technology; in popular culture, machines are often depicted in a utopian (or dystopian) march toward progress.[7] However, this assumption that the computer was the key driver rather than the different sense of scholarly purpose between these two types of research epitomized by Owsley and Busa overemphasized the intellectual similarities for the sake of a simple narrative. In this chapter, I show that both Winters's and Gaffield's approaches were too simple as ways of understanding digital history's roots. Instead, one must understand the intellectual underpinnings that led to the computer's use, rather than what technology a scholar employed in the course of their daily work. Computation in research is not about electricity, but about a way of thinking algorithmically about a problem and applying certain principles of problem solving to evidence, in search of a solution. The groundwork for this algorithmic thinking had been set decades if not centuries before 1949.

This chapter uses the two origin stories of history and computing as the starting point for understanding the different ways that computers have changed the working lives and research landscape of historians. Building a focused understanding of the ways technology has changed approaches to historical research—defined here as an *argument-driven, evidence-based answer to a question about the past*—enables us to explore the power of scholarly experimentation and interdisciplinarity over time. This makes it possible for researchers and sector leaders to develop strategies that most effectively enable different groups of historians to pursue productive experimentation, while also giving scholars a clear understanding of the intellectual origins of their activities and the assumptions that might underpin them. Different groups of scholars have different aims and approaches and therefore require different types of support to flourish. Understanding their respective intellectual points of origin makes supporting them more viable by allowing readers to decipher the traditions in which scholars work and the customs that go along with them.

Looking at the different intellectual underpinnings of the work inspired by Owsley and Busa (and scholars like them), it becomes clear that the social scientific scholars such as Owsley and the linguistically inclined such as Busa were following different purposes. Recognizing this is important because thus far too few historians have done so, with negative consequences for practitioners and research quality. That means that too many people expect digital work to follow in the footsteps of the statisticians of the 1980s, while many practitioners instead see themselves as cultural analytics researchers pursing answers to questions inspired by humanists such as Busa. Without a clear understanding of how these two narratives differ, but also come together in the new millennium, the ability to support digital research remains limited.

Using the history of the field as its evidence, this chapter argues that the "digital history" researchers who emerged in the early new millennium may have been drawn to the Busa narrative, but they were themselves a unique product of their place and time. Unlike the social scientists, who were statistically driven in their work, motivated by a growing interest in history from below, social radicalism, and challenging the traditional political history of their parents' generation, the "digital historians" were most significantly active in work enabled by the mass digitization era of the 1990s, which opened up new possibilities but also different types of research problems. These problems meant that scholars working with technology in the twenty-first century rarely conducted "historical research" and instead pursued a new type of methodological question such as "what to do with a million books" that had not traditionally been of interest to historians, and which did not immediately lead to new understandings of the past.[8] Instead, this methodological research built knowledge of the sources and approaches through which we might know history. This ultimately made it seem like "digital history" was not contributing to research, when instead it was not providing new answers to the same questions, but new answers to new questions.[9] To understand why these two tales diverged, we must start at the beginning: with taxes.

Taxes and the Social Sciences in History

Without taxes we might never have had a need for computers in historical research. The state has been devising new and ever-more efficient means of understanding its financial position since at least the 1086 completion of the Domesday Book.[10] For its time, Domesday provided an impressively comprehensive survey of the private wealth in newly conquered England, giving the crown an overview of everything that might be taxed. In the centuries that followed, the developing of what eighteenth-centuryist John Brewer termed the "fiscal military state" continued to build the paper trail it needed to maintain control and stay solvent.[11] The invention of double-entry bookkeeping in the fourteenth century, and the rise of the printed form, which was entrenched in British bureaucratic processes by the eighteenth century and which spread across the Atlantic and the empire, have left historians with a veritable trove of sources that are uniquely well suited to a structuring and categorizing machine built on a series of 0s and 1s.[12]

From the tables of the censuses, to the thousands of forms recording the outcomes of vagrancy, settlement, or bastardy examinations, to the relatively formulaic trial accounts of criminal courts, these instruments of bureaucracy offered particularly valuable insights into the lives of the common people. Their structured format set them apart from the more verbose, often more personal details available about the lives of the elite. A gentleman's letters and diaries might make compelling evidence for a "great man" biography in a way that a printed form never could for a forgotten pauper. While pauper stories can and have been told through more personal accounts, the historiography is bursting with examples of works about the poor that rely on the bureaucracy as the basis for their argument.[13] Thus the nature of computers and the nature of certain types of sources left by the state and various bureaucratic processes inherently meant that certain types of historical research questions were more aptly pursued with the help of computers. It is no coincidence that economic and social historians took to computers in greater numbers than the political historians of the mid-twentieth century. After all, the archive does not adapt to the needs of the historian. The historian must work with what survives, and many social history sources were apt to come from the state's bureaucracy.

A full understanding of historians' use of computers for research therefore must start with those sources. It must also consider how contemporaries used those materials. Historians were not the first to notice the paper trail, nor did they first put it to use as a pathway to understanding. The people then living too turned their eyes to these new data, and some of them began asking questions about what it could tell them of the society in which they lived. These sociologists, statisticians, and early social scientists devised the methods that historians would later adopt for their own studies. The history of computing in historical research was therefore intimately connected to the much longer history of social science, even if that work did not necessarily involve a computer running on electricity.

The social sciences developed on the basis of a post-Enlightenment European worldview that presumed that if the natural world could be understood in robust, repeatable scientific terms, so too could the human social environment. It was a worldview that slowly proliferated into the seventeenth and eighteenth centuries, and was being widely applied by the Victorian era by scholars and civil servants alike.[14] These social scientists took many forms and worked in many ways. Among their ranks was seventeenth-century English statistician and demographer Gregory King, who in 1688 estimated the number of families in each band of the country's pyramidical social hierarchy.[15] They also included nineteenth-century civil servant and geographer E. G. Ravenstein, whose *Laws of Migration* sought to understand and even predict the movement of groups of people. Both King and Ravenstein relied on the readily structured records of bureaucracy. King's data came from English hearth, poll, window tax, and marriage duty records. Ravenstein turned to the 1861 and 1881 British censuses, looking for patterns of movement between different types of communities.[16] Those efforts of King and Ravenstein and many others like them, put social science methodology within easy grasp of historians who were similarly interested in data—albeit historical.

Ravenstein published his *Laws* in the 1880s, the same time that, according to renowned historian of historical studies Peter Novick, "scientific objectivity" first rose to prominence among U.S. historians. Novick outlined the influence of the German system of higher education and German modernist philosophy, which he argued had caught the attention of U.S. scholars. This resulted in a shift in practice that included Harvard and Yale temporarily changing "seminars" to "labs" to reflect a new scientific outlook toward the past. Though they faced many critics, these objective historians sought to produce an impartial understanding of history that was free of their own agendas and biases, allowing them to sit as would a "disinterested judge" who interpreted evidence and dispassionately presented findings. Numbers seemed like a sufficiently *hard* set of evidence on which to base those dispassionate findings.[17] In light of this, by the 1920s when some of the first quantitatively focused history journals were founded, the idea of counting and structuring was already deeply embedded into historical thought. Among those new journals was the *Economic History Review*, founded in 1927 to provide a more prominent space for scholars seeking to shift the emphasis of historians away from politics and toward the economy. The French Annales school of social history founded *Annales d'histoire économique et sociale* in 1929, and became renowned for long-view, quantitatively driven arguments.[18]

Changing U.S. politics in the 1930s may also have pushed historians toward quantitative history. According to historian of the U.S. South Clement Eaton, the rise of nonelite history in the United States, which began in earnest in the 1930s, was inspired by Roosevelt's New Deal program of social welfare, launched during the Great Depression. In the years that followed, U.S. historians turned with growing interest toward the stories of the common (white) people.[19] As this cohort of nonelite people had left many historical traces but generally few records per person, historians came to realize that their story would be easier to tell through statistical analyses than individual vignettes. Across the Atlantic, British scholars too increasingly found themselves captivated by the lives of the common people. History from below rose to prominence thanks to widely admired works including those of E. P. Thompson and his *Making of the English Working Class* in 1963.[20]

It was in this U.S. post–New Deal era and historiographical tradition of quantification that Frank Owsley's *Plain Folk of the South* appeared in 1949.[21] Thus, it was not the starting point, but a continuation of many decades of thought on the role and approaches of the historian to his or her sources. Though William G. Thomas III suggests that Owsley's work "demanded methods of computational linking," it is unclear if Owsley used an actual computer or meticulously adhered to computational logic while hand-processing the records. This means that the intellectual roots of Owsley's approach was more important than the machine that may or may not have helped facilitate the analysis.[22]

Owsley's work, though criticized by Novick as being motivated by a racist pro-Confederate agenda, inspired a number of other historical works on American slavery that adopted a quantitative methodology.[23] These U.S. historians of slavery perhaps did more than any others to aid the evolution from statistical processing to computational analysis. The next key development came in 1957, when economists Alfred Conrad and John Meyer published two articles that brought together economic theory and statistics, ushering in a "new economic history," sometimes also called "econometrics" and "cliometrics":[24]

"Economic Theory, Statistical Inference and Economic History," *Journal of Economic History* (1957)

"The Economies of Slavery in the *Ante-Bellum* South," *Journal of Political Economy* (1958)

Better remembered than Owsley by quantitative historians, Meyer and Conrad likely did use a computer, thanking the Harvard Foundation for a grant in support of "computational and secretarial assistance" (though accounting for use of the term in the 1950s, the "computer" may have been a person with a deep understanding of mathematics). Like Owsley, their goal was to challenge conventional wisdom about antebellum society. They took particular aim at Confederate scholars C. W. Ramsdell and U. B. Phillips's beliefs about the economics of slavery in the U.S. South (summarized by Conrad and Meyer) that "slavery had reached its natural limits by the 1860s and that it was cumbersome and inefficient and, probably within less than a generation, would have destroyed itself." Using a data-driven econometric approach, Conrad and Meyer put forth a counterargument, showing that slavery had been profitable and that the Civil War had been vital in bringing its downfall.[25]

The approach continued to inspire historians of the U.S. South, leading historians of slavery Robert Fogel and Stanley Engerman, to publish *Time on the Cross: The Economics of American Negro Slavery* in 1974. Though Fogel would be awarded the Nobel Prize in economics for his contributions, *Time on the Cross* proved controversial for historians. A number of reviewers suggested that the authors had pushed the approach too far, blasting them for using statistical analyses to suggest enslavement was perhaps not so bad after all.[26] The approach had taken a question of humanity and tried to apply a mathematical model that was not designed to account for the emotional realities of chattel slavery. It has since become a caricature for statistical approaches to history gone wrong. Peter Novick went so far as to joke that, when asked how they knew that enslaved people "were only moderately exploited," Fogel and Engerman responded:

$$Ex = \frac{B}{\sum_{t=0}^{n} \dfrac{\lambda_t(a_1 P_{ct} Q_t L_t^{-1})}{(1+t)^t}}$$

Not every scholarly use of the computer proved so controversial. Neither did economically focused cliometricians conduct all of this quantitative work. Geographers (and by extension, historical geographers) too began to experiment with computers, using them to produce visual arguments in the form of data-rich maps. The big breakthroughs in computational mapping came in the 1960s when Roger Tomlinson, while working for the Canadian government, pioneered what came to be known as geographic information systems, or GIS.[27] Widely used by the early twenty-first century, GIS maps combined spatial data into "layers" of information that could be added on top of a base map, and which historian of the U.S. West Richard White called a "humble—if demanding and expensive—attempt to do history in a different way."[28]

By the 1970s and '80s, maps built using Tomlinson's pioneering work were widely used in historical studies of spaces. This geometric analysis was as quantitative as the work of the cliometricians, though drew on a different branch of mathematics. A spatial approach allowed historians to answer a range of questions that were difficult or inaccessible otherwise. For example, legal historian Andrew Charlesworth's 1983 *Atlas of Rural Protest in Britain, 1548–1900*, used spatial analysis to argue that food rioters strategies were profoundly regional. Latin Americanist Frank Zephyr used a similar approach to bring the world and experiences of Jeronymo José de Mello, a nineteenth-century artisan living in Rio de Janeiro, back to life. Using a GIS-based approach that included a many-layered map built from a range of sources from the archive, he was even able to suggest where Jeronymo most likely purchased his bread, providing an intimate look at a forgotten life.[29] Early modernist Anna Mitschelle's 2014 mapping of witchcraft trials in Scotland allowed her to show that it was lowland Scots, not their highland counterparts, who instigated accusations against women, and that instability in government during the War of the Three Kingdoms was the key cause of the witch craze.[30] The layered approach to mapping provided the spatial evidence for these historians, in support of their conclusions.

Historical demographers also made great use of mapping, as well as the other computational possibilities of the punch-card era. The most prominent faction was the Cambridge Group for the History of Population and Social Structure, or "Campop," founded in 1964 by Peter Laslett and Tony Wrigley. The most famous effort coming out of Campop was Wrigley and R. S. Schofield's monumental *The Population History of England 1541–1871*, first published in 1981. The work meticulously reconstructed the demographics of the nation, including the years before the first English census of 1801, drawing heavily on parish records.

Social historians too made great strides by collecting data about the people of the past and processing them in search of patterns. A pair of scholars working on British crime in the eighteenth century made particularly heavy use of quantitative history in the 1970s and early 1980s. In 1974, legal historian John Beattie published his statistically driven "The Pattern of Crime in England 1666–1800." Beattie analyzed criminal indictments in two English counties, concluding that growing urbanization had led to a growth in conflict through the eighteenth century—a pattern that was not seen in rural areas.[31] A few years later, in 1982, crime historian Douglas Hay conducted a similar type of analysis, this time of the prevalence of theft cases in a single English county over time, to argue for a correlation between army demobilization and increased petty crime.[32] It was this quantitative-style research that inspired the Social Science History Association, where many social scientists found an intellectual home for many years.[33] Though less controversial than *Time on the Cross*, these quantitative approaches to the history of crime came with warnings from scholars keen to ensure quality did not suffer with the introduction of counting machines. While Hay believed that quantitative work was useful for revealing previously unnoticed relationships in the archive, he also warned that statistics of prosecution rates could not show rates of crime. The difference between the two was what early modern British historian J. A. Sharpe called the "dark figure" of unreported crime, which left no paper trail.[34] Historians needed a deep understanding of the records they wanted to measure to avoid those types of pitfalls. In 1975 J. S. Cockburn warned that early modern criminal records were unreliable documents written by early modern lawyers to settle disputes on behalf of clients and therefore should not be treated as sets of comparable, accurate data. Cockburn chose to single out legal historian and former lawyer Joel Samaha's 1974 *Law and Order in Historical Perspective* as an example of these "bad habits," suggesting the work was "virtually devoid of worthwhile source criticism."[35]

Despite the controversy, quantitative history proved popular for the next several decades. In the United Kingdom, the growth of numerically inclined historians also led to a number of distinct economic and social history departments in the 1970s and '80s, and a feeling among its practitioners that they were fundamentally doing something different. Economic historian Robert Whaples suggested it might in fact have been a youth movement. His 1978 analysis of cliometricians showed that this new way of looking at the past was initiated primarily by young academics, with thirty-five-year-old economic historians dramatically more likely (91 percent) to be cliometricians than their sixty-five-year-old colleagues (33 percent).[36] A cursory look at some key figures in the field reinforced those claims: Conrad and Meyer were in their early thirties when they published their seminal cliometric papers, while thirty-eight-year-old Engerman and forty-eight-year-old Fogel were certainly not aged when they wrote *Time on the Cross*. Tony Wrigley was only thirty-four when he cofounded the Campop group.

These young quantitative scholars found lots to say to one another, but the field became increasingly insular—particularly the economic wing of the quantitative school. In a 2008 interview, British economic historian Martin Daunton reflected on this insularity: "What happened with economic history in the late '70s and '80s was that it became rather introverted. It started to feel it was under threat and under challenge. It became very defensive. . . . Some economic historians felt that historians did not want to listen to what they were doing."[37] Daunton's memory certainly mirrored U.S. economist Douglass North's tone in his 1997 reflection on forty years of cliometrics, in which he gives the impression that he and his fellow economic historians were feeling ignored. Rather than bridge the intellectual gulf, North suggested that the path forward was to further entrench the divide with historians, seeking impact by "widening the horizons of the economist" rather than the historian, politician, or layperson.[38]

By the twenty-first century, nearly all of the splinter departments had been folded back in with history departments; however, this did not lead to the end of quantitative history.[39] U.S. urban historian Margo Anderson outlined a number of publications that continued to publish on quantitative history into the twenty-first century, including *The Historical Methods Newsletter* (1967), which was renamed *Historical Methods* in 1978; the *Journal of Interdisciplinary History* (1970); and *Social Science History* (1976).[40] Far from being defeatist, economist Avner Grief even suggested in 1997 that more powerful computers meant that the potential for cliometrics was growing. He believed that the technological constraints put on earlier quantitative historians would begin to fall by the wayside, allowing them to turn to "larger cross-sectional studies, longer time series, or data sets that could not have been assembled or analyzed before."[41] Despite being written in 1997, the suggestion sounded very similar to the promise of big data in the 2010s.[42]

For these groups of quantitatively inclined, statistically adept scholars, the computer was a tool for conducting analyses in the spirit of social science–based approaches to history. It allowed them to build ever more complex models of past societies, tested through economic theories or theories of migration and societal structure. The computer as a calculator helped generations of young scholars shift the focus of the academy for a few decades at least and has left historians with a library of valuable research findings. Until the late 1990s, these scholars represented the vanguard of historians working computationally, making the most of the types of the available machines, which were essentially calculators.

Their work took on a range of vocabulary over the decades: "quantitative history," "new history," "new economic history," "cliometrics," "econometrics," "social science history," and "history and computing." In the new millennium, quantitative historians continued to publish work that was challenging the historiography with the help of computers. However, they began to draw less attention and were no longer seen as the next big thing by the year 2000. Instead, the focus had changed, in part because technology had done so much to change the world. Personal computing had boomed in the West in the 1980s and '90s, meaning that many more historians were growing up with new skills and confidence with their computers. Meanwhile, advances in file formats saw an explosion of images, video, and audio, in qualities never before possible. This was made even more pronounced by the rise of mass digitization, which brought billions of historical records into machine-readable form. Finally, scholars were left to consider the potential of the relatively recent arrival of the Internet, which was still finding its feet. In this changing world, the term "computing" slowly faded from use as the "e" revolution (e-mail; e-text) briefly had its heyday before everything, including the file formats, became "digital."

Mass digitization in particular helped create opportunities for exploring culture at scale. This was distinct from the earlier attempts to understand the economy or social history. In 2006 when classicist Gregory Crane asked "What do you do with a million books?," it was not the economists that had the answer.[43] These were new problems and required a new approach. Recognizing the importance of the approach rather than the machine, these historians did not turn to their quantitative brethren for inspiration, but to the corners of the historiography best adapted to working with machine-readable texts. They did not read the computing historians of slavery; they built intellectual shrines to Father Busa, the Jesuit priest and linguist who counted words.

The Parallel Rise of Cultural Analytics

Busa's research, and the "humanities computing" work that he inspired, was fundamentally different from the various econometric analyses of antebellum society. For instance, his project told us very little about history, and much about language choice in a historically significant 11-million-word body of writing. Busa was not a historian; instead, he and his humanities computing followers drew heavily on the fields of linguistics and literary scholarship, and made their impact in those fields. Like cliometrics, Australian historian Paul Turnbull highlighted the attraction among younger scholars.[44] Though these scholars too were interested in patterns, their methods were rooted in linguistics. This work included both approaches devised to engage with the existing scholarship (new answers to old questions) and also to provide new means of working with digital texts (new methods and workflows).

In the former category was the first article published in *Literary and Linguistic Computing* in 1986, which sought to prove that authors had unique styles of writing, just as they had unique fingerprints. This style could be measured to attribute authorship of anonymous or disputed works.[45] Authorship attribution methods were a recurring feature in the journal, as were other statistically driven treatments of texts. The conversations were new, but not necessarily appealing to the type of people who viewed themselves as at the center of the literary scholarly world. It led to Canadian novelist Stephen Marche's rant that "literature is not data" and U.S. literary critic Adam Kirsch's claim of "the false promise of the digital humanities"; both of those articles failed to acknowledge that this type of work required a different set of background knowledge and different sense of scholarly purpose than their own research.[46] It also required faith in new algorithms. It was not possible to turn to the primary source archive to prove the conclusions of an unknown authorship inquiry. The algorithm may have done what it purported to do, but it was easy enough to remind scholars that it might not, and one could not be sure.

In the new methods and workflows category were more mechanical approaches that sought to automate a research activity. In 1989, *Literary and Linguistic Computing* ran a special issue on machine translation of texts, raising the question of the continued need for human intervention in this supremely human form of expression, eventually leading to the launch of automated tools such as Google Translate in the new millennium.[47] The automatic translation of digitized texts was a humanities problem, and a major concern of the scholarly editing community, many of whom saw themselves as part of this cohort. For decades, editors had worked meticulously to bring historical texts and primary sources into published volumes, involving a tremendous degree of scholarly knowledge, and an understanding of how best to make and record decisions taken in the transformation of texts from their original to their edited state.[48]

It had long become clear to some scholarly editors of the later twentieth century that computers would open new doors, with the chance to "mark up" a text with tags that could be hidden or displayed depending on the needs of the end user. These intellectual interventions into primary sources were often incredibly detailed, with one paper even suggesting a need to tag at the level of the pen stroke. Others debated the best way to tag spoken language in texts, what to do about the unique challenges of medieval script, and how to manage Old Norse and Icelandic texts.[49] With scholars all around the world using markup in their scholarly editions, it became clear that standardization was needed to ensure work was cross-compatible. This led to the founding of the Text Encoding Initiative (TEI) in 1987, which has become one of the most celebrated contributions of humanities computing.[50]

Of the TEI, information technologist Susan Hockey glowingly remarked in 2004, "If one humanities computing activity is to be highlighted above all others, in my view it must be the TEI. It represents the most significant intellectual advances that have been made in our area."[51] TEI remained a strong organization, and in 2011 launched the *Journal of the Text Encoding Initiative*. However, it had only marginal uptake among historians, who perhaps benefitted indirectly from some of the consortium's work, without ever feeling the need to become deeply involved in its practices.[52] Despite important contributions to TEI by documentary historians such as Kathryn Tomasek and Syd Bauman, whose work on encoding financial records for historical research was an example of the value of markup to particular types of historical research, I suspect few quantitative historians of the late twentieth century would agree with Hockey's assessment of the centrality of TEI.[53]

A lack of zeal for the TEI was not the only thing that separated historians from these "humanities computing" scholars, who rebranded themselves as "digital humanists" circa 2001.[54] Historians simply played a small role in these intellectual spaces—particularly in the official scholarly organizations and journals of the field (see chapter 5 for more on the digital humanities spaces historians *did* colonize). In this light, Susan Hockey's 2004 history of humanities computing was entirely justified in leaving historians out of the picture, without a hint of irony. For her, humanities computing was linked to the activities of literary, linguistic, and scholarly editing colleagues.[55] When scholars wrote biting rebukes of digital humanities, such as Marche's "Literature Is Not Data: Against Digital Humanities" (2012), they were almost exclusively complaining about the ways technology had interfered with their vision of true and proper literary study that involved careful close reading and individual reflection.[56] This was true also of early critiques, including that of U.S. literary theorist Stanley Fish in 1976, who aimed his critical ire at the rising field of stylistics that was catching the attention of the statistically inclined literary scholars of the day.[57]

The place for historians in the official professional organizations and publications of humanities computing and digital humanities was also slight. The chairs of the Steering Committee in the international Alliance of Digital Humanities Organisations (ADHO) traditionally came from literary or linguistic backgrounds, with historians rarely taking up leadership roles in the official organizations. History was such a small player in digital humanities that it led historian of the twentieth-century United States Stephen Robertson to suggest in 2014 that "digital humanities" meant "digital literary studies."[58] Historian of science Scott Weingart's analyses of the applications to the ADHO annual conference (2014–16) reinforced Robertson's claim, highlighting the firm lead textual and literary scholarship had over historians in terms of numbers of submissions.[59] By comparison, large history conferences such as the one held annually by the American Historical Association, had traditionally drawn many historians presenting "digital" or technology-focused papers, suggesting a preference for presenting in history-focused venues and casting doubt on the depth of connection between history and digital humanities research.

Even in one of the humanities computing tribe's preferred journals, *Literary and Linguistic Computing*, founded in 1986, historians seemingly chose not to submit articles. This remained true after a 2015 title change to *Digital Scholarship in the Humanities*, which was an attempt to broaden its appeal. Instead, it was the home of word-focused scholars who had little to say to quantitative historians, and vice versa, with limited cross-citation between the key journals. Even the vocabulary was substantially different. The term "economic history" appeared only four times in *Literary and Linguistic Computing*, and "cliometrics" never. Instead they wrote about "linguistics," and used the term "digital humanities"—though rarely "digital history"—to describe their activities. By contrast, *Economic History Review* had thousands of mentions of "economic history," more than a thousand mentions of the "historiography," and two hundred references to "cliometrics" (table 1). Placed alongside similar counts in the later *Journal of the Association of History and Computing*, it becomes clear that there were many different types of scholars working computationally on the past, and they were each having their own distinct conversations.

Given these intellectual differences and the general apathy by historians toward key humanities computing achievements such as the TEI, it may seem striking that any historical researchers would adopt the Robert Busa linguistic origin myth, and yet they did.[60] That is because what the TEI, scholarly editors, and linguistically inclined researchers did do for historians was to create an appetite for a new type of machine-readable historical text at scale. Writing in 1989, linguist Mark Lieberman noted that research had been "severely hampered" by the dearth of "a large enough body of text on which

Table 1. Number of articles published in a quantitative history, a humanities computing, and a history and computing journal to highlight the thematic differences between them, calculated via the journal website's full text search features.

	Economic History Review (1928–2017)	Literary and Linguistic Computing (1986–2017)	Journal of the Association of History and Computing (1998–2010)
Common in *Economic History Review* only			
Economic history	4,667	4	31
Historiography	1,310	19	31
Cliometrics	240	0	5
Common in *Literary and Linguistics Computing* only			
Digital Humanities	2	1,728	5
Linguistics	113	835	28
Common to more than one publication			
Digital	341	1,751	1,850
Digitise / ize	98	1,759	444
History	4,667	463	5,604
Rare			
Digital History	1	9	98

published results can be replicated or extended by others."[61] Lieberman was trying to drum up interest in his project that would create a 30-million-word shareable corpus, but underlying his wish was a desire for mass digitization and the wide sharing of machine-readable texts. In the next two decades Lieberman would get his wish, fueling a new era of scholarship enthralled by a seemingly endlessly growing body of digitized materials, shared widely via an up-and-coming new network called the Internet.

From Scarcity to Abundance

Historically, the lack of access to a wide enough body of digitized primary sources of interest to historians led Stephen Robertson to conclude that "digital humanities" generally meant "digital literary studies": "[it] lies in the limited availability of machine readable texts: historians more often rely on unpublished sources than literary scholars, and on handwritten records that it is not yet possible to effectively use OCR [optical character recognition] to transform into machine readable text."[62] Robertson was suggesting that historians simply worked from a broader corpus than literary scholars, and therefore were behind their literary cousins in terms of having had the opportunity to fully exploit the fruits of a digitized archive. An intellectual movement in its own right, the history of digitization is covered in greater detail in the next chapter. However, with time, through the 1990s and early 2000s, mass digitization put billions of words, and then millions of images, sounds, videos, and digital objects at the virtual fingertips of historians for the first time. Soon, scholars wanting to work with digitized materials helped promote the idea that machine-readable text was more than a means of reducing the pressure on library shelf space. It allowed researchers to do different things with the books.

Mass digitization's effect on historical research was profound. It had begun to turn a much wider collection of cultural and social history sources into machine-readable text than ever before. Not only was the bureaucracy of the past available, but also the rich literary and cultural artifacts too: newspapers, letters, and literature. These newly reformatted records enticed a new group of scholars who arrived with new questions focused around these new cultural objects. The early questions were not ones that engaged directly with existing scholarly conversations about the history of a time and place ("historical research"). Instead, they included practical debates and proposed solutions for how to work with these new forms of media, as well as high level questions that focused on the cultural objects: the texts, the collections, the corpora, and the creative outputs of human beings ("methodological" or "meta research"). These were not the questions of the social and economic historians of the 1980s. They were instead a blending of the intrigues of the humanities computing scholars, of cultural historians, and of information scientists.

Among these new digital scholars, debates began to emerge about how best to deal with these huge new corpora, and what the research implications were for historians who used them. As mentioned, in 2006, classicist Gregory Crane asked, "What do you do with a million books?," noting that it would take forty lifetimes without a pause to read so much. Literary critic Franco Moretti had suggested what he called "distant reading" as one option.[63] He coined the term in 2000 to describe the process of measuring rather than reading texts. Historians Shawn Graham, Ian Milligan, and Scott Weingart preferred "macroscope"—the opposite of the scientists' microscope. This expression was borrowed from science and technologist Katy Börner, who suggested that "rather than make things larger or smaller, macroscopes let us observe what is at once too great, slow, or complex for the human eye and mind to notice and comprehend."[64]

There was a general excitement among digital historians of new discoveries on the horizon, facilitated by these new digital archives. Historian of humor

Bob Nicholson joked in 2011 that "media historians did things very differently in 2002."[65] Yet, despite the excitement and the awareness that digitized texts had opened up new possibilities for history, very few historians were actually data mining these collections in ways that resulted in published historical research—at least not in the first decade of the millennium. Practical limitations proved challenging and needed to be addressed before historical conclusions could be forthcoming. In other words, the new digital archives were (for the most part) insufficient for rigorous historical research based in data mining. For most scholars, they were approaching digital archives not of their own making, which contained layers of decisions that may or may not have been in the best interests of historical scholarship. Just as Cockburn had warned about the biases and nuances in early modern Assize court records, historians needed to take time to get to know these new sources and how to best work with them. The digital archives had a substantial if under-discussed impact on historical practice.[66] As digital editor Jonathan Blaney showed, historians still pretended to cite paper-based sources, while drawing heavily on new digitized archives, sticking their heads in the sand about any implications of using the digital surrogates.[67] Despite the lack of engagement by many historians, the way these archives had been set up was affecting the way scholars were finding (and not finding) relevant materials. A shift from a culture of browsing and understanding the hierarchy of the archive was quickly swapped for keyword searching.[68] Yet few historians put enough thought into the implications of this swap. Latin Americanist Lara Putnam warned, "when we fish in digitized text, we are fishing in a very particular sea."[69] Historian of gender Michelle Moravec warned of the importance of recognizing how a digital archive often fails to communicate the context of the collection, noting that she never only looked at one item in a folder at the archives, but was routinely forced to do so by the Web-based interfaces historians now interacted with.[70] British cultural historian M. H. Beals pleaded with scholars to "record how you search, not just what you find."[71] Beals hoped to convince historians that one had to be critical and transparent of how digital sources were found so that peer reviewers could be critical of any subsequent historical conclusions.

This was a tough sell. As Lara Putnam noted, most historians preferred to keep their method invisible, noting that she was broadly unaware of historian's research practices, because historians didn't often share them, perhaps for fear of scrutiny.[72] But being critical of search methods was important not only because many historians were not trained to be effective digital searchers, but because the quality of transcriptions in many digital archives was poor. This meant that even good searching could return unsatisfactory results, but if a historian was not savvy, they may not have been aware of the quality of their findings. Poor quality was particularly a problem in collections converted through optical character recognition (OCR) software, which struggled with non-English, archaic fonts, and poorly preserved historical documents.[73] In 2009, curator Rose Holley estimated that Australia's *Trove* digitized newspaper collection had an average of 145 errors per paragraph of text, dramatically reducing keyword matches. Librarian Natalie Binder made a similar criticism of the accuracy of the OCR and the quality of the metadata in the Google Books corpus, which she declared not "ready for prime time."[74] Handwriting only became viable for OCR programs circa 2015 with the EU-funded Transkribus project, and in 2018 was only beginning to make its mark.[75] Historians of different time periods each faced unique challenges with OCR'd texts. For example, scholars searching for texts in the eighteenth century had to contend with the "long S" problem, which was used frequently until about 1820. OCR software in the early 2000s frequently interpreted ſ as an "f," leading to the "suck" versus "fuck" conundrum, in which word-frequency analyses of early modern text seemed to suggest the latter was in heavy use, when in fact this was an artifact of the digitization process.[76]

These types of problems were widespread, yet most commercial publishers were unwilling to acknowledge them for fear it might hurt profits. Despite their silence, the problem can be measured by analyzing the results of targeted keyword searches in the Connected Histories search portal.[77] The search engine queries a copy of the twenty-five digital archives in its collection as they were in 2012, providing a snapshot of OCR quality frozen in time. Words containing ſ were particularly vulnerable to mis-transcription. In certain digital archives containing texts published between 1725 and 1799, the misspelled "yeſterday" was substantially more common than "yesterday" (table 2). A similar search for variations on the word "Irish" highlights the striking variation in spellings resulting from poor OCR processing. Users of some databases could unknowingly expect to miss one in six relevant entries (table 3).

As tables 2 and 3 indicate, the method used for digitizing the resource had a significant impact on the likelihood of transcription errors. Sites that had relied on OCR software had much poorer results. The British Library's eighteenth-century newspapers had the correct spelling of "yesterday" in only 36.7 percent of matches—which was only marginally better than the 43.1 percent rate in the House of Commons Parliamentary Papers collection. That meant that a majority of relevant matches for those words were missed in those collections. By comparison, projects that employed "double

Table 2. Matches of "Yesterday" and "Yefterday" in the Connected Histories database, searching select collections for items published between 1725 and 1799.

	British Newspapers	House of Commons Parliamentary Papers	Nineteenth Century British Pamphlets	British History Online
Transcription Approach	OCR	OCR	OCR	Double rekeying
YESTERDAY	86,370 (36.7%)	2,420 (43.1%)	83 (96.5%)	1,318 (100%)
YEFTERDAY	149,207 (63.3%)	3,189 (56.9%)	3 (3.5%)	0 (0%)

Table 3. Matches of various spellings of the term "Irish" in the Connected Histories database, searching select collections for items published between 1725 and 1799.

	British Newspapers	House of Commons Parliamentary Papers	Nineteenth Century British Pamphlets	British History Online
Transcription Approach	OCR	OCR	OCR	Double rekeying
IRISH	119,603 (84%)	8,626 (83.8%)	1,767 (96.5%)	1,103 (99.6%)
IRIFH	20,342 (14.3%)	1,532 (14.9%)	34 (1.9%)	0 (0%)
I RISH	910 (0.6%)	24 (0.2%)	29 (1.6%)	3 (0.3%)
INFH	399 (0.3%)	48 (0.5%)	1 (0.1%)	0 (0%)
JRISH	379 (0.3%)	24 (0.2%)	0 (0%)	1 (0.1%)
JRIFH	264 (0.2%)	27 (0.3%)	0 (0%)	0 (0%)
INIFH	212 (0.1%)	0 (0%)	0 (0%)	0 (0%)
I RIFH	121 (0.1%)	3 (0%)	0 (0%)	0 (0%)
J RISH	70 (0%)	3 (0%)	0 (0%)	0 (0%)
F RISH	33 (0%)	2 (0%)	0 (0%)	0 (0%)
J RIFH	16 (0%)	0 (0%)	0 (0%)	0 (0%)

rekeying" (two human typists manually transcribing material, checked for discrepancies), had very low error rates. British History Online employed this strategy, and on the "yesterday/yefterday" test returned no instances of the s/f problem.[78]

Despite the better results, double rekeying was not failsafe. My 2013 analysis of transcription accuracy in a 51-million word subset of the Old Bailey Proceedings Online corpus (which claims to be double rekeyed), showed an error about once every 4,000 words. While much better than in the *Trove* newspaper database or some of the collections noted above, the unlikely nature of the errors (nearly 500 cases of a "u" where "n" should be) cast doubt on whether or not the company hired to do the transcription work had in fact double rekeyed the text as instructed.[79]

The poor quality of transcription and the knock-on effects for keyword searching was not the only problem faced by historians using digital archives. A substantial barrier proved to be the business model of commercial scholarly publishers as well as a lack of understanding and foresight at the time into how historians would want to work with digitized materials. Until 2014, commercial scholarly publishers in particular tended to restrict access to the machine-readable text layer of digitized sources, providing instead a search box to query the database before returning a page scan so the user could read the source as if on a microfilm reader. This approach prevented the leaking of the text layer, which was the company's intellectual property and investment. That investment had to be recouped via subscription fees, and given the widespread pirating of music in the early 2000s, these companies were not eager to take risks.[80] The fears were understandable, but the policy was frustrating for scholars who were seeking to data mine the collections.[81]

Not all textual archives protected their machine-readable text. Some academic-led projects including the Old Bailey Proceedings Online (2003) and British History Online (2003) made the machine-readable text available.[82] However, access to some of the most enticing collections for historians, including digitized newspapers, was generally only available to those with the social capital to coerce businesses to hand over the data.[83] Some senior colleagues did have the clout to make such requests, including social historian Tim Hitchcock, historian of crime Robert Shoemaker, and digital archives specialist Jane Winters who in 2011 obtained the text layer behind 3 million pages of digitized British newspapers, as well twenty-four other collections from commercial and library partners when putting together their federated search engine of historical materials, Connected Histories.[84]

Less established scholars, including independent scholars, students, and early career researchers, had to do without. In 2010 the British Library denied my request for access to the machine-readable text of the nineteenth-century newspaper collection for research into attitudes toward Irish communities. Five years later, the library had changed its mind and in 2015 granted media historian Ruth Byrne the data to pursue a similar PhD question.[85] The reason for the library's change of heart was linked to the British Library Labs initiative, launched in 2013, which was responsible for supporting and encouraging innovative uses of digital collections.[86] Others too benefitted from the Library's growing openness. Historian of protest Katrina Navickas's Political Meetings Mapper (2015) was only feasible thanks to the cooperation of British Library Labs.[87] Bob Nicholson's research into Victorian jokes, and M. H. Beals's project on scissors and paste journalism were likewise built on access to the library's digital newspaper collection.[88]

This shift toward openness was not solely the doing of the British Library. It was also a response to wider societal expectations about the potential for data mining. Historians benefitted substantially from the U.K. government's decision to modernize copyright legislation after three centuries, based on the recommendations of the Hargreaves Report (2011). This consultation resulted in a 2014 change that exempted scholarly data mining from U.K. copyright restrictions. Clauses in user agreements that prohibited such use were unenforceable.[89] Commercial companies were forced to adapt, leading to a number of publishers willing to allow scholarly data mining, or offering a separate product to facilitate this work.[90]

These and other similar challenges kept digital historians busy in the years following the mass digitization wave. Scholars struggled to solve issues related to the digital archive that would allow them or others to begin to make research-based discoveries about the past that were rigorous, and much of the conversation was around data cleaning and data quality rather than historical conclusions. Before historical research could be published, there was a need for new infrastructural research or historical "methodology," which importantly validated research approaches in a peer-reviewed format before applying them to historical research questions. There were many such examples in the early twenty-first century. Environmental historian Jim Clifford's collaborative research into how best to identify mentions of tradable commodities in ten million pages of nineteenth-century sources fulfilled that *how to* step between idea for a research project and defensible historical conclusions.[91] Tellingly, Clifford called this work a "digital" approach to history. Tool validation has long been common practice in many applied science and engineering fields where approaches were tested and the results measured before they were put into practice. For example, computational models are increasingly used to study the effects of surgical treatments, but the techniques are validated with experimental data before being tried in patients. These results are then published as a methods paper for the benefit of surgeons who are considering adopting the new technique.[92] This made the validation of a method an integral step in its pathway to application, and many historians were likewise adopting a similar approach to their work in the digital era, particularly when the method involved putting primary-source evidence through a repeatable process or algorithm, as opposed to a mental analysis that occurred in the mind of the scholar.

Culturomics and the Google Books Corpus

Even before digital historians had fully managed to overcome these challenges, a high-profile collaboration involving Google Books made headlines in 2011, seemingly with an answer to Crane's question of what to do with a million books. Geneticist Erez Lieberman Aiden and biologist Jean-Baptiste Michel had been given privileged access to the Google Books corpus and used it to create the Google N-Gram Viewer. The N-Gram Viewer let anyone visualize the relative rise and fall of any word or phrase in the published record in the past two centuries.[93]

Among the many conclusions of the team of fourteen was an assertion that they had measured changes in the way people had become famous. They argued that over time individuals became famous quicker and younger but were forgotten sooner. They called this approach to machine-readable texts from the past culturomics—a play on the word "economics," or the measuring of the economy, adapted for measuring culture.

The published article appeared in *Science* and was launched with widespread publicity. Yet it found few admirers among historians (or humanists). One of the key problems was the fact that none of the article's fourteen authors was a historical researcher. Aiden was a geneticist and Michel an evolutionary biologist. Both had experience working with data at scale, and it would seem it did not occur to them that the work they had done fit within an established scholarly literature in humanities computing and cultural history. President of the American Historical Association and early modernist Anthony Grafton was one of the first historians to witness a presentation of culturomics, and he was critical of the authors' apparent belief that historians did not have the skills to be valuable to the project. Aiden and Michel retorted that several prominent Harvard historians had been consulted and helped steer the project, though their level of contribution did not warrant authorship.[94]

Whether historians were consulted or not, social historian Tim Hitchcock argued that the culturomics team had been on a misguided attempt to "code break" human society. Hitchcock suggested that the culturomics conclusions should instead have been "the evidence put in the appendix in support of a subtle point," rather than conclusions in their own right.[95] Culturomics had found evidence of an interesting phenomenon but had stopped before critically discussing why it was interesting, or even whether it actually represented what it purported to show. Hitchcock's criticisms highlighted the importance of subject specialism and source knowledge for digitally driven research, with the scholar needing to understand the subtleties both of the methods and the primary sources—in this case, millions of books. He accused the culturomics team of misunderstanding what books were or could show, noting that while they had calculated the mentions of physicist Albert Einstein per year, they had failed to prove this represented a level of fame.[96] This failure was precisely the criticism that J. S. Cockburn had made in 1975 of Joe Samaha, who was accused of not understanding the court records across which he sought patterns.[97]

Though the culturomics article has been cited widely, it has not made its way into the historiography. Like the earlier *Time on the Cross*, it has become a caricature for over-exuberance. However, it was a good example of the type of work that became possible from mass digitization, and it showed the ways that this approach to sources was distinct from the types of questions quantitative historians had asked previously. The statistical modeling of the past had moved beyond the countable entities of society and had begun to encroach on the cultural records of the humanities computing scholars.

Culturomics was merely a high-profile example of the emphasis on skills used by or developed by linguists, which was more prudently executed by humanities-minded scholars. These included linguist Magnus Huber's 2007 research that analyzed the speech patterns in tens of thousands of criminal trial accounts from eighteenth- and nineteenth-century London, by political historian Luke Blaxill's 2013 work on the language used in parliamentary speeches in Victorian Britain, and by linguist Anthony McEnery and early modern historian Helen Baker's 2017 book, *Corpus Linguistics and 17th Century Prostitution*.[98] To facilitate this type of work, a growing number of "tools" began to appear in the 2000s, often pegged as "digital" but which were much more accurately described as linguistic software. These tools included linguist Laurence Anthony's AntConc (2004), a concordance program (used for measuring word use), which he originally developed as a classroom tool for language learners, but which made it easy to process keywords in context in texts. The previous year, in 2003, literary scholar Stéfan Sinclair and philosopher Geoffrey Rockwell had released Voyeur (renamed Voyant to avoid untoward connotations), a Web-based text analysis tool that made it easy to measure a textual corpus in various ways.[99] From document length, to vocabulary density, term frequency, and average sentence length, this was linguistic processing. Tellingly, it came with two built-in corpora that users could practice with: Shakespeare's plays and Austin's novels, which show the literary rather than historical background of its creators and assumed audience.

Voyant Tools was part of a major "digging into data" collaborative project with the creators of the Old Bailey Online, which sought to process a corpus of 127-million words of criminal trial accounts from London's seventeenth- to early twentieth-century criminal court. The aim of the Digging into Data challenge (funded jointly by the American, Canadian, and British research councils) was to encourage scholars to see what these newly digitized archives could teach us and to find the promised "new questions." The Datamining with Criminal Intent project, of which the Voyant Tools team was a part, led to much publicity, but relatively little in terms of published research outputs aimed at historians.[100] Instead, its contributions were in the field of digital archives, information management, and what we might call "digital history." The white paper at the end of the project highlighted ways of using the digital archive, rather than historical conclusions derived from an analysis of it.[101] One of the key developments was a "more like this" idea, which built on computational historian William J. Turkel's earlier series of blog posts on using a naive Bayes classifier (a statistical machine learning algorithm) to identify sets of trials that were statistically similar but that might not easily be paired by a human reader.[102] Turkel's approach was about seeking patterns across the archive, which then needed close reading to verify, adding a new step to the research process rather than forming historical conclusions. So while the "new questions" did not have a direct impact on the historical research questions that historians had already been asking, digital history was certainly not bereft of new knowledge.

Far removed from the statistical tabular data of more traditional quantitative historians, this new linguistic work was profoundly interdisciplinary, and built on the ideas of the humanities computing scholars of earlier decades. Increasingly in the second decade of the twenty-first century, digital scholarship became tightly associated with interdisciplinary approaches to digital resources. In 2014, oral historian Penny Johnston suggested that digital research was "an emerging interdisciplinary field of study where digital technologies are incorporated (as method and/or topic) into humanities research practice."[103] That interdisciplinarity took historians far beyond working with text.

Since 2010 a number of projects have developed that bring historians together with experts in other fields. Medievalist William Endres's work explored the way 3-D modeling techniques could build understanding of the materiality of medieval manuscripts. His approach used "reflectance transformation imaging" to take many images of a single manuscript from different angles and under different lighting conditions before using them to build a virtual 3-D model. The approach allowed Endres to model stress points on the parchment where the ink may be under strain and in need of repair. This unique approach to digital materiality pushed the boundary of computers in new ways. Endres was not the only scholar working with imaging. Alejandro Giacometti's 2014 PhD research explored ways that medical imaging technology could recover the text on rolled-up ancient documents that were too fragile to unravel.[104] In both cases, the digitized object was the focus of scholarly intrigue, and the method designed to give new knowledge about that object rather than the history of the society that created it. In that sense, these were studies into material culture.

Space too has become a promising new venue for the digital historian, both through the astronomic rise of digital mapping described above (an evolution of historical geography), but also through innovative work that takes advantage of virtual environments. Scholar of seventeenth-century literature John Wall was the principal investigator of the Virtual St. Paul's Cathedral Project, an initiative that digitally reconstructed London's lost medieval St. Paul's Cathedral.[105] St. Paul's was London's most important early modern church, but it burned down in the 1666 Great Fire of London, meaning that no one alive has ever experienced a sermon in that destroyed and now substantially changed landscape. No one knows what it was like to hear the powerful oratory of renowned preachers such as John Colet or John Donne. The experience of early modern churchgoing has an extensive scholarly literature. Historians including church historian Christopher Marsh have considered the ways space was used within the church: who had the right to sit where, and what effect did that have on the social hierarchy of the community?[106] This intellectual exploration of churches as spaces of meeting and listening was incredibly insightful; however, the Virtual St. Paul's Cathedral Project has once again made it possible to experience a sermon in a representation of the old churchyard. They did this by inserting a virtual clergyman voiced by an actor into the virtual space that they built in a computer, to deliver an actual sermon that they know was given on 5 November 1622. Sound engineers modeled the virtual space so that the voices echo properly off the surrounding surfaces. Viewers can choose where in the churchyard they want to stand and listen, discovering what it was like to hear the oratory from pride of place on the stage itself or from the back of the buzzing crowd. This was interdisciplinary research, drawing together the fields of sound engineering, 3D virtual modeling, ecclesiastical history, and dramatic performance into a new way of knowing history that was based on the digitization of a long-lost building.[107]

Meanwhile the Web itself has begun to be an object of study. Historian of the Internet Ian Milligan's ongoing work on the history of the Canadian social Web in the 1990s takes historians into new territory and a born-digital set of resources. To do his research, Milligan had to deploy a range of skills not usually found in the historian's toolkit, including programming skills to automatically download thousands of websites.[108] Thus, many of the contributions made by "digital history" researchers are best described as methods or meta research. The former validated approaches to historical research, while the later reflected on the scholarly practices of historians or audiences of history. These studies were important for the field as it sought to understand and make the most of new opportunities or challenges created by the digital age, yet despite filling an important need they were not necessarily having an easily measurable effect on the scholarly literature of "historical research" where many historians were used to looking for impactful work. Measured in this way, digital history seemed to fail to live up to the expectations and promises. More optimistically, it opened up new areas of knowledge for those seeking to understand the past.

Conclusion

By the 2010s, "digital" work was not confined to the study of words. But even when words gave way to images, videos, and virtual objects, many still saw Busa as their intellectual "father," because it was he and the humanities computing scholars who had inspired the study of human cultural relics en masse. This made the digital historian's sources and therefore their questions distinct from the scholars of the 1970s, '80s, and '90s who had focused heavily on the records of the bureaucracy. These newly available machine-readable text archives had not been part of the toolkit of the quantitative historians of the twentieth century but were instead the purview of the humanities computing scholars. Thus, the social scientists and digital historians simply operated in different spheres of intellectual interest. They used the same computers but in different ways and for different purposes.

The genealogy of historical research and technology was therefore not a linear progression from the quantitative historians of the previous generation as Winters and Gaffield implied.[109] Instead it was one that was heavily influenced by the literary-inclined humanities computing scholars who had more experience working with digital textual objects and corpora, and by the rise of mass digitization in the late 1990s. When the term "digital history" began to emerge in the early new millennium, it brought with it promises of new questions. New media scholar Andrea Horbinski called it a "means of asking old questions in new ways, identifying new questions, and introducing new questions to the field that can only be asked through collaboration both among individual scholars and between scholars and software applications."[110] Despite the promises, a decade and a half later, there has rightfully been concern about the lack of engagement between digital historians and the traditional historical published scholarship. Unlike the generations of quantitative historians before them, there are still only a few influential digital history research papers in mainstream history journals. This led historian Tom Scheinfeldt to ask in 2010 "Where's the Beef?" In 2017 his former colleagues at the Center for History and New Media hosted a workshop, "Arguing with Digital History: Workshop to Address a Central Problem in Digital History," and the Programming Historian put out a call for more lessons that would result in publishable argument-driven research.[111]

However, as showcased in this chapter, there were new questions and new arguments being developed, and historians working on digital research did change the field, but not necessarily the historiography. As historian of science Scott Weingart has remarked, "new types of questions that are too different from previous types are no longer legitimately within the discipline of history, even if they are intrinsically about human history."[112] Digital history was about working with the newly digital archive and understanding how or if it would facilitate new historical knowledge. The production of that historical knowledge was not necessarily the prime objective, whether practitioners realized it or not. The new questions were not necessarily connected to the old ones, meaning the highly esteemed history journals were not necessarily the right venues for the new conversations. That was in part because the subject-specialists did not speak (or did not want to speak) the new interdisciplinary language of digital scholarship, which facilitated dialogue between and across disciplines in combinations that were atypical of historians. Nor were they particularly interested in reading the "methodology" papers that digital history proved better suited to. These methods papers were not part of the traditional conversations historians had with one another. Instead, new conversations took place between different parties than before. They were between historians and literary scholars, historians and linguists, historians and librarians and archivists.

As J. S. Cockburn warned of the early modern courtroom records, and as Tim Hitchcock pointed out of the culturomics paper, good research was founded on a deep understanding of the nature of the records one studies. Since the mass digitization of records had fundamentally changed the records, adding in layers of new decisions that had to be understood, as well as throwing out the notion of original order in the archives, the questions were different from the ones that came before. Gregory Crane's query "What do you do with a million books?" did not fit in the historiographical narrative because it was a question that historians had never asked before. Many of the digital historians engaged in research that helped to provide new answers to Crane's question, while subconsciously keeping the warnings of Cockburn and Hitchcock in their minds. Thus, they paved the way for a new generation of scholars to start turning back to those historical questions using these better-understood digital archives and objects. We are just now starting to see the fruits of their research as it comes to engage with the traditional historiography. When the history of their contributions is written, I suspect we will not call *those* scholars digital historians, just as we should not confuse the digital historians with the quantitative historians or the humanities computing scholars. The history of historical research and technology makes it clear that if we are to understand the different scholarly traditions of these distinct groups of scholars and reap the benefits of the different types of work that they can contribute to the profession, we must get our vocabulary straight (table 4). These groups may have shared an interest in the potential of computers for their work, but that does not mean that the computer was the most important element in those stories, nor should it be used as the basis of a Whiggish narrative of progress.

This takes us back to the two origin stories: Frank Owsley's quantitative approaches and Robert Busa's linguistic processing. While neither is sufficient to understand the historical development of these different movements, they are symbolic of the different approaches and inspirations that led to historians

Table 4. Terminology used over the years to describe the three distinct groups of research scholars.

Quantitative History	Humanities Computing	Digital History
New history	Literary computing	No widely used synonyms
New economic history	Digital humanities	
Cliometrics		
Econometrics		
Social science history		
History and computing		

Source: Thomas, "Computing and the Historical Imagination"; Winters, "Digital History."

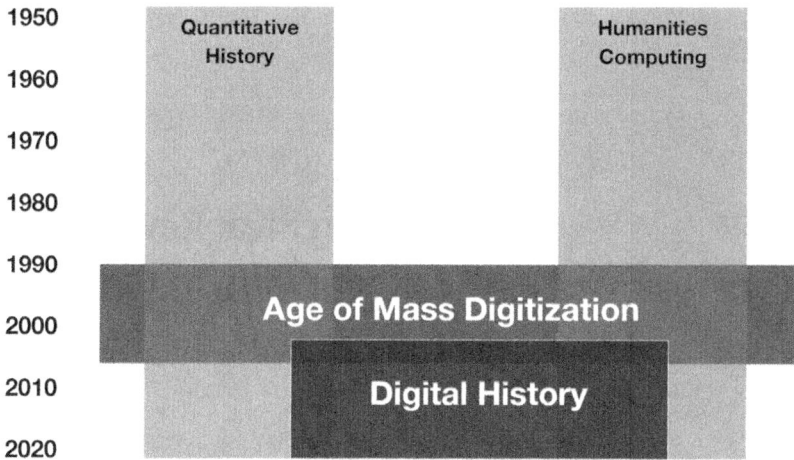

Figure 1. The simplified conceptual place of research-oriented digital history in the quantitative history and humanities computing movements, bursting forth from the age of mass digitization in the 1990s and early 2000s.

adopting computers in the service of historical research. The more recent research movement, "digital history," was *not* intellectually the brainchild of the quantitative movement led by "computing and history" scholars. However, neither was it solely the product of humanities computing. It was best described as the child of both, looking more like humanities computing, and conceived in a hazy and unplanned experiment in the 1990s that led to the mass digitization of billions of words of historical texts (fig. 1). Knowing this allows the historical profession to foster the types of research that each group is best suited to, and to harness it to best serve the needs of scholarship.

2

The Archival Revisionism
of Mass Digitization

In 1840, inventor Samuel Morse patented his now-famous "code," providing a format for encoding the letters of the alphabet into a schema of dots and dashes, kick-starting the telecommunications era.[1] This foundational work provided the intellectual infrastructure needed to store the twenty-six letters of the English language in the memory of the not-yet-invented binary-based machines we call computers. The dots and dashes could be mapped onto a series of 1s and 0s—the basic building blocks of all digital memory. Without such a system, computers would have been limited to simple counting machines, able to work solely with numbers.

In the years that followed, the range of encoded characters expanded. In 1963, the American Standards Association (now the American National Standards Institute, or ANSI) published the American Standard Code for Information Interchange (ASCII), a set of guidelines for managing upper- and lowercase letters in the Latin alphabet, as well as punctuation common in English.[2] Subsequent work by the International Standards Organization (ISO) and the Unicode Consortium, which developed the Unicode Transformation Format (UTF), have helped internationalize the systems, making it easier to store and share accented characters and non-Latin alphabets.[3] These mechanisms were some of the key foundations for what would become digitization. However, encoding was only one of a number of advances that established the preconditions for the digitized archive. The history of digitization is part of a longer narrative of adaptive storage solutions, including early microfilming and microfiching efforts, as well as advances in software development, database design, digital imaging, CD-ROMs, and the rise of the Internet.[4] It was also built on the archival turn and changing understandings of the historian's relationship with the archive, including conversations about the historian as an "unintended reader" of documents as in Carolyn Steedman's *Dust*, the archive as a colonial form of control as in Ann Laura Stoler's *Along the Archival Grain*, or the historian as the sculptor of memory as in Michel-Rolph Trouillot's *Silencing the Past*.

While many scholars and technologists, including public historians, contributed to the development of these technologies and social changes within collection management circles, these advances primarily occurred in either the commercial or public sectors. In hindsight, the role of the historian was principally to wait until the technologies presented a new opportunity, and then to seize it. Michael Hart was just such an opportunistic scholar. In 1971 he was given free computing time from the Materials Research Lab at the University of Illinois. Believing that the potential for computers was in storage rather than calculation, Hart used his time in the lab to transcribe and store a copy of the U.S. Declaration of Independence. It has since been recognized as the first digitized historical document, and the first text in what would become Project Gutenberg, which would come to hold machine-readable versions of more than 50,000 public domain works.[5]

Over the next two decades, a number of similar initiatives on both sides of the Atlantic sought to bring together collections of digital texts, including the Oxford Text Archive (1972), the Perseus Digital Library (1987), and the Women Writers Project (1988), the former representing the old canon, while the latter was a product of rising interest in women's history at that time, and a glimpse into early priorities.[6] The scale and ambition of digitization initiatives accelerated. By the second decade of the twenty-first century, billions of sources were accessible remotely, coming from a wide range of original formats including but not limited to text, sound, video, material, and spatial information. Many historians were actively involved in this unprecedented reimagining and reformatting of the archive. Thus, the way scholars conducted research was not the only change to historical practice linked to technology. Mass digitization was one of the most substantial shifts in the historical profession ever to occur, ushering in new possibilities and challenges. While many of the most technically robust digitization initiatives began in libraries and archives, led by practitioners better trained and equipped for the task, many too were conceived of and executed by practicing historians. The result was hundreds of what public historian Serge Noiret called "invented archives," or what U.S. historian Edward Ayers referred to as "intentional archives," creating a collection that did not exist in any one place but instead brought together materials into something new.[7]

Understanding this archival revisionism and the history of mass digitization is fundamental to understanding the environment of historians in the late twentieth and early twenty-first centuries, as well as one of the key ways that historians applied computers to their cause. It not only revolutionized historical research in ways discussed in the previous chapter, but it gave historians a new relationship with collections, putting a privileged few in control of their new shape and allowing them to set the agenda for the next generation of scholarship. It also led to creative experiments into what a collection could be, moving far beyond the traditional notion of an archive as a bricks-and-mortar institution, becoming something that could be accessed first from home and then in the streets.

The material they chose to work with was not free of selection bias. As American cultural historian Ben Schmidt noted, U.S. copyright restrictions designed to protect Mickey Mouse had resulted in a "copyright black hole," with all texts created after 1922 largely undigitized.[8] That same phenomenon made older historical texts safe for experimentation by commercial and public-sector initiatives and was a boon for historians studying the pre-twentieth century. Nevertheless, despite promises in early discussions of digitization that there would be a branching out beyond the well-worn path of the literary canon of famous works, this did not materialize. Given the difficulties of attracting funding for this work, as archivist Abby Smith Rumsey noted in 2001, special collections were often the first sets of records that a library or archive was able to undertake.[9] While many of these contained new voices, the new digitized collections tended to promote famous works at the expense of more diverse perspectives. Shakespeare was more likely to be digitized than women, people of color, or less well-known authors. London was more likely to receive attention than Montevideo or Montréal.[10] The lack of spread and representativeness in the digitized material was exaggerated by the fact that printed books proved easier to digitize than manuscripts or ephemera, and the literary canon was more likely to be printed. Digitization thus perpetuated earlier decisions about what was worth reading.

This led many in the archival sector to begin conversations about critical archival studies—a collective self-reflection on what it was archivists were collecting and preserving, and what those decisions meant for those whose voices were too rarely heard in society. Michelle Caswell and other archivists led the way in encouraging archivists to stand up and change their practices rather than perpetuate old wrongs.[11] Meanwhile, Ann Laura Stoler reminded her colleagues that colonial archives in particular were both the products of and creators of the state, by producing paper trails of power and agency for some at the expense of others.[12] These important conversations within archival sciences have helped lead the field to be more conscious of the nature of archives, power, and voice.

Some historians, including those interested in gender, ethnography, and sexuality, had long also been involved in those conversations. However, many of those focused on the digital sphere had a different set of initial priorities and a new set of skills to learn if they were going to play leading roles in these new digitization initiatives. Moving into the realm of collection management meant learning to become masters of user experience and user engagement to a greater degree than ever before. This subsequently led to a rise in what might be called user studies—a branch of meta research that studied the scholarly practices of historians or audiences of history, and snowballed into a new role for early adopting historians as a vanguard of product testers on behalf of the profession. What began as a foray into redesigning the archive became a beta testing ground for everything from crowdsourcing to augmented reality.

These seemingly disparate areas of work were all fundamentally linked to a reenvisioning of the archive and of collections and the ways that people could engage with them. By the twenty-first century, these historian-led digitized collections and the meta research they inspired were being discussed as contributions to "digital history," thanks in large part to American historian of science Dan Cohen and labor historian Roy Rosenzweig's 2005 *Digital History: A Guide to Gathering, Preserving, and Presenting the Past on the Web*. The book promoted an audience-focused approach to history that leveraged the power of the Web to engage new and more people with the past, rather than discussion of new types of computer-aided research mentioned in the previous chapter. For Cohen and Rosenzweig, digital history was distinct from research activity. This vision was rooted in their own experiments in new media in the digital age.

As the term "digital history" became more popular in the years that followed, it came to refer to many different types of activities involving computers and historians. This explained why digital archives historian Jane Winters decided to fold research and digitization into a single narrative in her 2018 history of the field.[13] Many of the definitions offered during the annual Day of Digital Humanities suggested the same. This was one of the causes behind the "what is digital history?" debates of the 2010s in which everyone insisted it was whatever *they* were working on. Some scholars, including public historian

Serge Noiret and socialist historian Steve Brier, were more careful to specify which form of digital history they meant, but this was rare.[14]

This chapter breaks free from the existing broad-strokes historiography of "digital" history by looking specifically at the process and effects of digitization and the reenvisioned archives and collections on historical practices. It does so by exploring them in their own context as distinct from historical research. This is important for a number of reasons. Namely, in most cases the scholars involved in mass digitization were *not* the same as those pushing the boundaries of research methodology shifts discussed in the previous chapter. There were a few exceptions to this, including Edward Ayers in the United States and Tim Hitchcock in the United Kingdom. However, it was rare to be heavily involved in both computer-led research and the mass digitization movement.

Second, while mass digitization had many international elements to it, different national contexts and agendas meant that each country experienced digitization differently. Digitization projects relied heavily on government and nonprofit or charitable granting bodies, meaning that historians were responding to, or perhaps even at the mercy of the agendas of these (often) national bodies. Thus, Tim Hitchcock's "Digitising British History since 1980" provides a useful history of the institutional factors influencing digitization in the United Kingdom, but makes no pretense to accounting for the stronger pedagogical drivers behind much of the U.S. digitization work in the same period, which were present but not as dominant in British circles.

The first two sections of this chapter correct these historiographical issues by providing a historical account of digitization that considers some of the differences and similarities between the U.S. and British approaches in particular. While limited to the experiences of two countries, their starkly different approaches show that the story of digitization must be understood at the local level to be understood at all. These different approaches led to the digitized collections that scholars have access to today. Understanding the contexts in which those collections were produced lays bare their limits and any oversights of their creators. Those might include everything from reinforcing colonial structures to privileging certain types of research questions because of the way the sources were organized and presented. As I show, particularly in the United States, digitization was seen as an opportunity to shake up the history curriculum. Inspired by British socialist historians such as E. P. Thompson, a generation of American historians began using digitization to tell a U.S. history from below. By contrast, the British experience was rooted more firmly in the idea that one's research and by extension one's research area, could benefit from wider access to some of the relevant primary sources in digital form.

The next two sections also make room in the history for some of the newer ways that historians and public memory organizations have begun to restructure the archive, and which were inspired by the activities of an earlier generation. From the archive as a physical collection held in a bricks-and-mortar building, to a digitized collection held in the memory of the computer, that same material began to find its way out onto the streets in the new millennium. This occurred first through the shrinking of computers over the past seventy years into powerful machines that fit into the palm of one's hand and that were equipped with ubiquitous access to the Internet. In a process that started in the late 1970s, by the 2010s the situation had evolved to the point where objects in the so-called real world were becoming part of the global archive of human memory. From love locks linked to databases that held details of alleged enduring love, to historic sites using virtual spaces to reclaim lost viewpoints, digitization changed the way we engaged with and understood history as well as the archive and the collection material it contained. These developments would have been impossible if not for the creative push of historians and software developers working hard to explore this new space. This chapter thus explores the evolution of the mass digitization movement, considering its influences and key turning points in its development, starting with the crucial role of English historian E. P. Thompson.

U.S. Socialism and Multimedia

The key inspiration for the mass digitization movement among many U.S. historians may well have been E. P. Thompson, author of *The Making of the English Working Class* (1963). American historians who I interviewed for this book and who were involved in digitization overwhelmingly professed admiration for Thompson's work.[15] Thompson was never directly involved in a digitization initiative. Instead, he was known as a radical socialist campaigner and Marxist historian. He was an important early proponent of the "history from below" movement of the 1960s that convinced many historians to shift their gaze away from the stories of the elite.

By the 1970s, the type of left-leaning history written by Thompson and historians like him was becoming more embedded in U.S. scholarship. Some historians even took their radical history into the community, including labor historians Herbert Gutman and Steve Brier who hosted a summer workshop in New York City in 1979 to spread new labor history to the public through an adult education initiative aimed at working-class Americans. Quickly realizing that these in-person workshops had limited reach, they looked for new alternatives to expand their audiences. In 1981 Gutman helped to found the American Working Class History Project at the City University of New York.[16] The project would later become the American Social History Project, which continues at the time of this writing. Brier, who was director of the project for many years, credited Thompson, as well as other British socialist historians, including Eric Hobsbawm and George Rudé, for the intellectual inspiration for the initiative.[17]

For Gutman and Brier, primary sources would be the key to challenging the traditional elite narrative of U.S. history. By giving people access to the right sources, they could showcase the stories of the common people through the traces that they left behind, or that were left behind about them. In the late twentieth century, primary source anthologies were one of the only practical ways to get these materials into the hands of students and interested publics, at scale. It was no surprise then that the team's earliest attempts included a series of textbooks called *Who Built America?*, aimed at high school and undergraduate students, which provided opportunities to include primary source examples.[18] By adopting the textbook model, the American Social History Project was drawing on what was already accepted in education circles at the time, and what was technologically feasible as well as economically viable. New, however, was the argument of the text, which put forth a view that the United States had been built by the workers rather than by the elite, and it quickly made socialist and radical history accessible to students and members of the public.[19]

Despite their success, the textbooks had not yet reached their potential with the public. Luckily, advances in digital media elsewhere were opening new doors for those seeking to break free from the limits of traditional textbooks and print-based media in order to bring primary sources to the masses. A big boost to the multimedia history genre came in September 1990, when 50 million Americans watched filmmaker Ken Burns's nine-part documentary series, *The Civil War*, which aired on PBS. The series prompted a growing interest in the nation's Civil War, and also a number of critical responses from historians. Its reception and extraordinary audience figures led U.S. historian Kenneth Williams to proclaim director Ken Burns "one of the most successful historians of all time."[20]

The documentary's popularity was in part due to Burns's story-telling ability and to its engagement with historical primary sources, beamed into

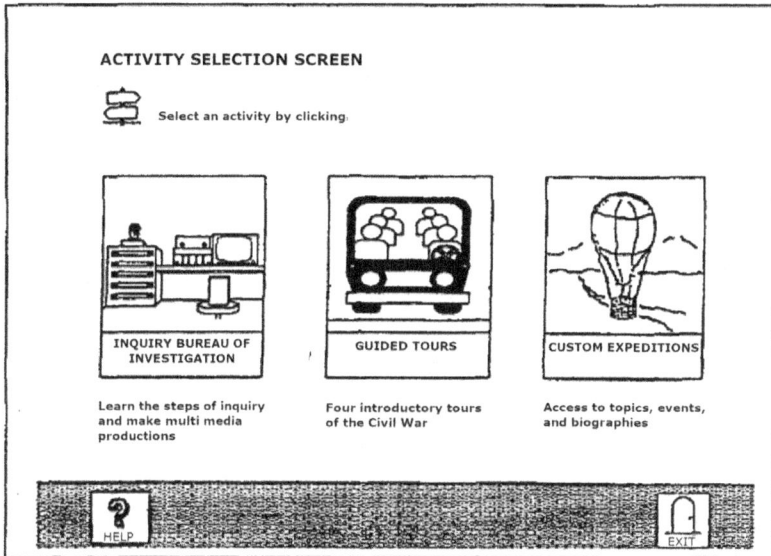

Figure 2. Screenshot of *The Civil War Hypermedia Project* CD-ROM in Cates, Fontana, and White, "Designing an Interactive Multimedia Instructional Environment" (8).

the living rooms of the nation. Using his characteristic approach of zooming and panning the camera over historical photographs to give a sense of movement, Burns enlivened otherwise static Civil War imagery.[21] By bringing primary sources out of the archives so people could engage with them, Burns was achieving on the small screen what many educators of the late twentieth century had long wanted to do with their textbooks.

Building on the success of their documentary series, Burns's team was one of the early adopters of new media opportunities for history. They partnered in 1990 with scholars at the George Mason University Center for Interactive Educational Technology to experiment with the latest multimedia tools. With $100,000 of support from PBS, the team produced a now-forgotten videodisc, *The Civil War Hypermedia Project*, as part of a wider engagement strategy that included a number of spin-off products such as a separate coffee table book.[22] Using the strengths of the multimedia format to their advantage, the videodisc was distinct from the television series in one important way: it encouraged fairly basic interaction. This was a key theme of digitization and multimedia experiments by historians that set them apart from passively consuming expert narratives in academic history books. While the technology was not yet at the level to allow high-quality images to be included (as fig. 2

makes clear), users of *The Civil War Hypermedia Project* had the option of going on "guided tours" of selected themes in order to learn more about the history. The "Inquiry Bureau of Investigation" section was aimed at students, encouraging them to act the part of the historian and do some digging in the virtual archives, which included simple digitized primary sources.[23] Though still a fairly controlled experience, the disc had helped creators take a small step toward the "ergodic" nonlinear texts literary theorist Espen Aarseth devoted his research to and which put readers or players in control of decisions that would affect their experience, be that a book or a video game.[24] It was also reflective of the discussions of dynamic "hypertexts" or "cybertexts" that were enthusing so many scholars in the 1980s and 1990s.[25]

Despite the obviously historical content, historians did not lead *The Civil War Hypermedia Project*. The PBS lead, Lynn Fontana, had studied history at undergraduate level, but her academic background was in pedagogy, specifically curriculum and instruction.[26] Wayne P. Thomas, the project leader at the Center for Interactive Educational Technology, was a science and mathematics teacher by training, with an interest in digital pedagogy.[27] Although these two were eminently qualified to lead the project, this cutting-edge multimedia work apparently did not require the input of historians. Much of the early historical production of the 1990s lacked historical rigor, and historians did not overlook this. A disk released in the mid-'90s about the Korean War included what historian Roy Rosenzweig called "a startling admission from the author/publisher that until 'a few months ago,' he was only dimly aware that the U.S. had fought a war in Korea in the 1950s." In 1995, librarian Thomas Corbett noted, "much of the current multimedia CD-ROM products on the market are more flash than substance."[28] In 1999, political scientist Melvin Dubnick also took a similar shot at multimedia history: "these CDs are high on glitz and low on substance."[29]

The multimedia version of *The Civil War* never reached anything near the level of publicity of the original series. The discs are presumably no longer functional, and may well not exist in their physical form. No entry for the disc appears either in WorldCat or the Library of Congress. It seems that no one felt that they were worth keeping. Projects like *The Civil War Hypermedia Project* struggled to withstand the test of time, in part because technological obsolescence reared its head and the discs stopped working on new operating systems. They also often found themselves discarded by owners who lost interest once the experiences began to look dated. Where a book might have survived on the shelf, the disc did not hold the same gravitas. Nevertheless, the project did help by engaging in one of the early experiments that brought history and multimedia together, and helped lay some of the intellectual groundwork for projects such as the *Who Built America?* textbooks to go multimedia.

The shift into the multimedia space was not inevitable for *Who Built America?* Doing so required a substantial capital investment and technical expertise that few people possessed in the early 1990s. That chance would come for the project through good fortune and being in the right bookstore at the right time. In 1991 a multimedia pioneer and cofounder of the Voyager Company, Bob Stein was in the airport in Boston, looking for a book to read on his flight back to California. He purchased a copy of *Who Built America?*, and somewhere over the plains he became convinced that he had found his next endeavor.[30] Stein, who specialized in multimedia laserdiscs, approached coauthors Stephen Brier, Roy Rosenzweig, and Josh Brown who had recently published updated editions of the textbooks to reflect new scholarship. He convinced them to sign on, and together they converted *Who Built America?* into a CD-ROM, published in 1993.

The CD had all of the advantages of an interactive hypertext, including information not available in the original textbooks. The team had taken advantage of the multimedia format to include more images than could be printed in the textbooks, as well as video and audio that was of course incompatible with a print edition. Like *The Civil War Hypermedia Project*, they also provided users with two hundred "excursions," which made it possible to divert from the main text to explore certain themes in greater detail.[31] Unlike *The Civil War Hypermedia Project*, however, this CD was arguably more influential than the original book—at least for a time. This was due to the fact that Stein managed to get the CD bundled as the history offering in the educational CD-ROM package distributed with every Apple computer sold to U.S. educational institutions. Despite failed efforts by the socially conservative Moral Majority to have it removed for its primary sources about homosexuality and abortion, the project found its way into nearly every school in the country, selling more than 100,000 copies to Apple alone.[32] Its success was also enabled by the fact that the team had a clear plan to target and engage with high school educators.[33] The distribution strategy made it one of the most widely available historical texts and a pioneer of academic history on CD-ROM. It became the impetus for the founding of the Center for History and New Media in 1994, to build on the initial partnership with the American Social History Project by focusing on "all the ways that *new media* are prompting historians to reconsider their modes of researching, writing, and teaching about the past" (added emphasis).[34]

While the project was a huge success, it was not without irony that the creation of the *Who Built America?* CD-ROM was steeped in privilege. Especially considering E. P. Thompson's socialist influences on the authors, as well as their own desire to challenge an elite American narrative. CD-ROMs were expensive to produce, meaning that the very fact that a scholar had the opportunity to make one was a matter of unequal opportunity. The multimedia field also became very U.S.-centric. Roy Rosenzweig conducted a scholarly review of sixteen historically themed CD-ROMs in 1995, each focused on an American topic. Even those that were not obviously linked to U.S. history, such as an interactive version of the anti-Holocaust cartoon *Maus*, had U.S. connections, the work of an American cartoonist Art Spiegelman. Meanwhile, the project on the fall of the Berlin Wall, *Seven Days in August*, was intimately linked to U.S. Cold War politics. The remaining entries included four distinct projects about the history of U.S. film or music, which took advantage of the possibility of including audio and video on this new medium. Three others were about U.S. presidents, two about wars involving the United States, and two about African American history.[35] These were but a taste; by 1997 more than eighty U.S. history–themed CD-ROMs were on the market.[36]

Not only were they expensive—averaging nearly $110 each in 1995, compared to the typical $15 price tag for a music album at the time—but these projects gave a very narrow view of history that focused on the United States. I suspect Rosenzweig would have struggled to find sixteen projects of equivalent quality about Canadian history topics.[37] Comments appearing on discussion boards in the 1990s suggested that the U.S.-centric problem was widespread, and that many felt left out of these new expensive digital narratives. In 1994, historian Rich Slatta complained nothing of suitable quality was available for those working on Latin American history.[38] Meanwhile, French-Canadian historian of the United States Isabelle Lehuu at the Université du Québec à Montréal longed for a translation of *Who Built America?* for her francophone students, which would never materialize.[39] Though there were a number of CD-ROMs focusing on African American history, it would take many years for some of the other groups to get exposure in these multimedia spaces.

While far from ideal, these pedagogically focused multimedia projects were an important series of first steps, taken on behalf of the profession. Pioneers were needed because historians were not known for being early adopters of technology, leading medieval historian James Brodman to predict in 1994 that most would not even bother to buy a CD-ROM drive until there was evidence that it would make a lasting impact on the field.[40] He was right that a majority of historians would never enter this space; instead it was an enthusiastic minority that would act as multimedia's torchbearers in the historical professions. The experimenters included some big names: by 1993, the Smithsonian Institution was already on the lookout for librarians with experience working with CD-ROM, keen to ensure they had experts in house who could advise on this new form of creative output.[41] And despite being a minority, there were many enthusiastic voices. In early 1994, when improved digital video formats were released, Joseph Fusco Jr. reported with glee that "IT WAS INCREDIBLE," even believing rather condescendingly that "a child could spot the difference."[42] Thanks to the enthusiasm of these and other historians, the profession developed examples of interactive media that might not otherwise have emerged.

Yet, this was a brief encounter. CD-ROMs would soon fade. The format died an unceremonious death within a decade thanks to the rise of the Web. Here too historians played a valuable role. Not far away, at about the same time that Rosenzweig and Brier were producing their CD-ROM, a historian of the nineteenth-century U.S. South named Edward Ayers was in a meeting at the University of Virginia that would result in one of the first major forays by a historian into the brand-new space that was the World Wide Web.

The "Intentional Archive" of the Appalachian Valley

Ayers had built his scholarly reputation and received his tenure on the back of a social-science history of crime and justice in the nineteenth-century U.S. South published in 1984.[43] No stranger to the computer lab, his first book included hard number crunching, and by his own reckoning, about a year and a half in the engineering department borrowing their computers and pestering them for statistical knowledge. By 1990 he recalled with a laugh "it was clear that the '90s were not going to be a time when computers were important," so he had begun to envision a project that would take an "archival dust under my fingernails sort of approach." He planned to conduct a comparative analysis of life in two communities on the leeward side of the Appalachian mountains straddling the Shenandoah Valley in Virginia, into the Cumberland Valley of Pennsylvania. The inhabitants of these two regions fought on opposite sides of the Civil War. The purpose of the project was to understand what he saw as a failure of human logic: "How it could be how Americans living in the same valley, separated just by a line on the ground, same ethnicity, same soil, same climate, same crops and religious faiths, could in six months be persuaded to kill each other?" Despite his skepticism about the future of computers and scholarship, he agreed to sit on a university-wide computing committee at the University of Virginia, where he was the only humanities representative. The university had recently received a generous donation and decided to invest it in computing. Recognizing that his own humanities colleagues were not an obvious destination for that funding, and despite being uninterested in the money for his own work, the charismatic Ayers put in a pitch on behalf of humanists. Not entirely sure what humanities scholars might do with computers, the chair asked Ayers for an example of how he might use it in his own scholarship. Shaking his head, Ayers insisted that his computing days were over, and instead described the comparative valley project that he was about to embark on. He reaffirmed his plan to get into the dust of the archives, where he would collect records from both communities before turning to his interpretation. Yet that process of describing his plan to the committee helped him to realize, even as he was speaking, that he was talking about building a database. And so Ayers's computing days were not over after all. He was given the $100,000 donation, which bought six 17-inch color monitors and computers with 1-gigabyte hard drives, and he set about collecting.[44]

These materials did not just come from a single archive; the two counties of his case study crossed state lines (one was in Pennsylvania and the other in Virginia) and represented combatant regions in the Civil War. Those facts, along with the state-based or community-based nature of many archives in the United States, meant that the materials were held in different locations and thus needed to come together virtually into an invented, or as Ayers called it, an "intentional" collection. He and his team went looking for materials wherever they existed, rather than where they had been traditionally kept. They collected newspapers, maps, church records, letters and diaries, census and tax records, as well as soldier's records.[45] They also appealed to the people in those two communities, hosting a "History Harvest" in Augusta County, Virginia, inviting people to look in their attics for relics or documents that could be added to the collection.[46] Once completed, the project ultimately allowed Ayers to make some substantial new claims about the reasons these communities were divided. One of those came through an analysis of the language used in the newspapers of each county. He was able to show that the people of these two counties belonged to distinct "linguistic communities," using "the same words as one another and not speaking in the same terms as the other side."[47] One might even suggest that interdisciplinary foray into linguistics was the type of "digital" research that fit comfortably with the work described in the previous chapter. The award-winning book he wrote on the back of the collection was titled *In the Presence of Mine Enemies*, which he called "the first book that was ever published that is based on an entirely transparent archive."[48]

In addition to the value the project had for Ayers's own research agenda, he quickly also came to see its value as a pedagogical tool. This may have been an honest realization for a scholar engaged in both scholarship and teaching, or it may have been influenced by the 1996 creation of a new funding category at the National Endowment of the Humanities called "Teaching and Technology," under which the project would find support.[49] While still used for scholarly research, the project was reframed as a "research library in a box" for students, enabling them access to a large and relevant collection, where they could learn to do the same kind of research as professional historians."[50]

That library in a box was about to get much easier to access thanks to some good advice the team had received from some library colleagues in their earliest days. They had been convinced to use a markup format for their textual content called standard general markup language (SGML). Their goal, as with most multimedia projects of the day, was to produce a hypertext collection that was accessible via CD-ROM. Those plans quickly changed in 1993 when a computer scientist friend pulled Ayers into his office to show him Mosaic, the first Web browser with a graphical interface. He explained that these new "sites" were built with hypertext markup language (HTML), which he called a "baby version of SGML." Their decision to adopt SGML thus meant that the step to the Web was a small one, and with a few tweaks *The Valley of the Shadow* became one of the first substantial historical invented archives on the Internet.[51] No longer needing to wait for the release of a CD-ROM, this allowed the project to be "shared even as we gathered it."[52] The project quickly gained national attention, with stories appearing in *American Heritage*, *Wired*, and the *New York Times*.[53]

The Valley of the Shadow was followed online in short succession by a slew of new digitized collections. The American Memory project, launched by the Library of Congress in 1994, was one of the first to take advantage of the newly improved digital image capabilities, paving the way for combined initiatives that included both an image of the original text (photo or page scan) and a machine-readable text layer.[54] These were joined by a number of others, including pedagogically focused sites such as Digital History in the mid 1990s, produced by U.S. historians Steven Mintz and Sara McNeil as a clearinghouse of U.S. history sources brought together to help educate a new generation that was more critical than the last, by providing them access to the sources behind the narratives they learned in class, and educational scholar Pennee Bender's *History Matters* in 1998, which styled itself a "U.S. Survey Course on the Web," rooted in access to primary sources curated by the project team, along with contextual guides to help students understand how best to use and analyze those sources.[55] Both of these projects found large user bases thanks to good historical work and teams of talented Web developers supporting them. Digital History attracted 150,000 visitors a week, while History Matters too counted its visitors in the millions per year.[56] These were some of the most important of a growing number of U.S. history websites available by the late 1990s, with a list circulated in 1997 by the American Social History Project containing 223 sites identified as worthwhile.[57]

The Web was bringing the U.S. history textbook and the archive together in a new way and transforming the nation's classrooms as a result. The U.S. pedagogical focus was in part connected to funding priorities such as the Teaching and Technology grants already mentioned, but also nearly a billion dollars of U.S. Department of Education money dedicated to Teaching American History grants. These grants brought together higher education historians and public school history educators across the country, giving historians interested in pedagogy access to seemingly endless funding just at the moment that personal computing was taking off.[58]

While U.S. federal government support was instrumental to many of these early digital collections, so too were private trusts and nonprofits, not all of which were as focused on classroom teaching. The forward thinking of granting agencies is too often overlooked in the development of the field, which prefers to remember the brilliant ideas of the historians who propose projects, rather than the brilliant minds who thought it worth putting out a call in the first place. One of the most important early supporters of digitization work was the Andrew W. Mellon Foundation, with the organization's president, William G. Bowen, noting in 1997 that the foundation was committed to "support[ing] projects intended to test the effectiveness of electronic technologies in providing libraries and others with scholarly materials in formats that are easier to use and viable financially."[59] Between 1994 and 1998 alone, they funded at least thirty-five digitization and digital library projects, to a tune of $9,980,350.[60] Many of these initiatives were international. Among the important digital archives supported by Mellon were JSTOR, Electronic Beowulf, Early Canadiana Online, the Shakespeare Electronic Archive Project, the Renaissance Women's Writer's Project, and the Latin American 19th Century Newspapers Project. The historians, librarians, archivists, and other humanities scholars involved had significant agency regarding what to digitize.

Private enterprise also found a role to play, often basing their business model on subscription fees and viewing digitization as an investment. Genealogy companies such as Ancestry.com, which came online in 1996, built vast resources, targeted at people seeking records related to their family history.[61] The public appetite for family history materials was huge. When the Church of Jesus Christ of Latter-day Saints put many of its genealogical databases online in 1999, they were recording at least 40 million visitors per day, with an estimated 60 million others unable to get through to their servers.[62] The appetite continues to grow. In 2014 alone, Ancestry digitized 900 million new records from twenty-seven countries, aimed at genealogists but ripe for the picking for academic historians.[63]

The materials these companies digitized were the types of social history records (censuses, parish records) that had attracted the earlier quantitative historians. Others sought to partner with cultural heritage organizations to target other markets, including that of the classroom. University libraries were the principal intended clients of many of these digitized collections, and thus materials were assembled into combinations that were thought to be appealing to educators, and thus profitable. There were many examples in the United Kingdom in particular of these public-private partnerships, despite early attempts in the late 1990s in which the British Library shut down a planned private-sector partnership after failing to find enough common ground.[64] A decade later, the situation had changed sufficiently for the library's liking. Gale Cengage teamed up with the library to digitize millions of pages from the latter's newspaper collection, starting with the eighteenth-century Burney Collection, before moving on to nineteenth-century material.[65] ProQuest similarly partnered with the University of Michigan Library in 2000, resulting in the Early English Books Online project. And Google vowed to digitize all of the world's 129 million books when it launched the Google Books project in 2004.[66]

In the United Kingdom, much of the support came from national funding agencies. The Arts and Humanities Research Board (AHRB) launched a New Opportunities Fund (1998–2006) and a Resource Enhancement scheme (2000–2009), both of which supported digitization work. The Joint Information Systems Committee (JISC) also supported a number of digitization projects between 1998 and 2011. Digital archives specialist Alastair Dunning compiled a full list of all 486 U.K.-based projects funded under these schemes, at a cost of £119,803,577, many of which involved historians.[67] To that could be added the support of the United Kingdom's Heritage Lottery Fund, which received its money from the national lottery, and which in turn funded a number of digitization initiatives.

Many of these digital resources disappeared from the Web due to poor sustainability planning, leading to a number of discussions, particularly in the information science communities, about how best to sustain them long-term. In 2002 the Alfred P. Sloan foundation invested in the Council on Library and Information Resources (CLIR) in Washington, D.C., commissioning a study on how libraries could best sustain digital resources.[68] CLIR became an important source of reports and advice in the coming decade, with Abby Smith leading the way. Despite many mistakes made during the digitization era, a number of these projects went on to transform British scholarship in particular, and society more broadly. One of the most successful was the Old Bailey Online project produced by British historians Tim Hitchcock, Robert Shoemaker, and Clive Emsley, with the first phase launched in 2002. The archive was a straightforward textual digitization project, converting the 127 million words of the *Old Bailey Proceedings* into a searchable database, covering the period from the late seventeenth century to the start of the First World War. The *Proceedings* were courtroom reports of trials held in London's Old Bailey criminal courthouse. The reports included details of what was said and by whom during the trial. The team worked from earlier microfilms, and with the help of transcribers in India, created a resource that, according to the project creators, "represent the largest single source of information about non-elite lives and behaviour ever published."[69]

Like Ayers's *Valley of the Shadow,* the Old Bailey Online too was an invented archive. Though the *Proceedings* were published as a series, no institutional archive held a complete run, meaning that the digital collection brought the records together for the first time. As a result of coming online, the project attracted much academic attention, and transformed the *Old Bailey Proceedings* from a relatively underused set of sources accessible only via patient microfilm users, into one of the most overused primary source collections of British social historians. Between 2003 and 2017, the team counted 188 academic books, 431 academic articles, and 13 PhD dissertations that cited the collection. To this, they could add a number of prominent cultural impacts of the project. These included an award-winning BBC1 television series, *Garrow's Law,* a popular BBC4 radio series, and a vital resource for the editors of the *Oxford English Dictionary* when sourcing legal terminology.[70] The project was ranked "4*" (i.e., A+) in the government's 2014 Research Excellence Framework—the highest possible rating for research impact.

The Old Bailey Online's influence on the cultural sphere was tremendous, and though an interest in pedagogy did not inspire the creation of that digital archive in the first place, as it had done for some earlier U.S. projects, the classroom was never far from the minds of the team behind it. Like in the United States, some of the funding schemes available to U.K.-based scholars had focused on pedagogy. These included the Technology in Learning and Teaching Programme and the New Opportunities Fund for the Digitisation of Learning Materials—both of which funded the project team at various times. The former had funded Hitchcock and Shoemaker to produce a CD-ROM in 1994 on British history in the eighteenth century. The latter helped expand the Old Bailey Online archive by bringing in educational expert and one of the authors of the English national history curriculum, Peter D'Sena, to advise on and produce educational resources for the classroom based on the materials. Aware of the site's pedagogical potential, Hitchcock and Shoemaker described the project as a chance to "promote life-long learning and reskilling in both history and information technology by attracting a wide range of users to the source, including those from diverse communities, non-elite backgrounds, and with little experience of ICT [information and communications technology]."[71]

Yet in many respects, the Old Bailey Online team was unusual within the British scholarly ecosystem. Perhaps the project's emphasis on an E. P. Thompson history from below put it in the same league as some of those earlier U.S. initiatives that sought to revolutionize the classroom. However, many of the British projects funded during the mass digitization era were research or even family history focused, perhaps driven by the UK system's continued emphasis on the printed monograph above all others as a symbol of scholarly prestige. Archives ranging from the Clergy of the Church of England Database to British History Online tended to focus on the needs of their perceived users—be they historians of the church, or genealogists— rather than the potential to transform the classrooms of the nation.[72] Thus, what was digitized and by whom was intimately tied to the funding schemes that enabled that work, and by the national scholarly contexts that placed differing emphases on research and teaching. To understand digitization as an internationally coherent movement is to miss this nuance.

While the complete digitization of the world's cultural heritage has yet to come to pass, we seem to be getting closer. The Million Book Project, launched in 2002 with the aim of digitizing a million books, surpassed its goal five years later, reaching 1.5 million volumes.[73] The Hathi Trust, founded by thirteen research libraries in 2008, made available the works scanned by

Google Books from their collections. In 2008, Europeana launched a pan-European platform for European cultural heritage organizations seeking to share their digitized collections through a single portal. And in 2009, the Australian National Library launched its much-lauded Trove newspaper database.[74] By 2010 there were billions of words of historic text from all around the world available online, in addition to millions of historic images and a growing body of more complex formats. Building on Europeana's federated search box model, the Connected Histories portal, which brought together twenty-five of these databases into a single searchable portal, allowed users to search more than two billion words of historical material related to early modern Britain alone.[75]

From the CD-ROMs of the previous generation to these newer federated search portals of millions of sources, history was experiencing a technological moment in the early new millennium that was changing the nature of the archive as well as the way we engaged with it. However, this was not a matter of a single change—from paper to digital. Instead, this ecosystem was constantly evolving. One of the most important of those evolutions occurred around a decade after the Web first appeared, when it was no longer enough to provide access to sources. Instead, the people increasingly wanted to participate in the creation of the Web, and historians had to find ways to quench that desire.

The Rise of the Participatory Web

The public had long been partners in national memory making. After the attack on Pearl Harbor in 1941, a number of oral histories were recorded, which are now kept in the Library of Congress.[76] Preserving memories was one of the key functions of historians, who had experience not only interpreting the archive, but in building it with the voices of witnesses to important events. This function is one that continued throughout the twentieth century, and even began to take advantage of the Internet. For example, in 1998, scholars at George Mason University used the Web to track down people affected by blackouts in the U.S. Northeast in 1965 and 1977 so that their stories could be collected over the telephone.[77] Saving memories after a tragedy had thus long been an important function of public memory institutions, and it was known quite early that the Internet would be key to that process. With some key changes to the technologies behind websites circa 2000, the potential to collect memories was about to get easier, making it possible to quench the public's thirst for getting involved with history and the Web.

The change happened quickly. In 2004 publisher Tim O'Reilly of O'Reilly Media popularized the term "Web 2.0."[78] With it, he encapsulated the recent changes to the status quo on the Internet. This was a recognition that the Internet had evolved into a space where people not only could but were expected to be able to contribute. This principle was fundamental in many nondigital projects in public history, making the rise of Web 2.0 a perfect opportunity for public historians. Web 2.0 replaced an Internet of static sites with user-generated, collaborative online communities of up-voting, liking, tagging, and commenting. The next generation of the Web was not about creating content for readers to consume, but about enabling others to create their own or contribute to yours. Only two years later, in 2006, *Time* magazine named "You" the person of the year, reflecting the influence Web 2.0 had already begun to exert on the world.[79]

Just as with the CD-ROM before it, the Web 2.0 era needed intrepid historians to explore the potentials for the discipline. The 9/11 attacks on the United States in 2001 were a horrible tragedy, but were also one of the turning points for Web 2.0, because the events left so many people with so much to say about what had happened. They also left an acute information problem, which Deborah Lines Andersen described as a "dilemma for information specialists and for historians."[80] The deluge of information that came out in the days and weeks following the attacks risked permanent loss if collection managers did not act quickly. Websites changed rapidly as new information and conspiracies came to light. To fully understand the history of 9/11, Web archivists were needed. One of the first key players on the scene was the Internet Archive, which managed to collect an impressive archive of television footage about the events, and save it in the Understanding 9/11 archive (2001, 2007, and 2011) that they have since dedicated to the victims and preserved so that others can learn about the tragedies.[81]

Historians too got involved in their own attempts to bring together the Web and history in the making. Rosenzweig and his colleague Joshua Brown were convinced that there was an opportunity for digital history to play an important role in the nation's process of coming to terms with the tragedies. To serve this need, they established the September 11 Digital Archive only four months after the Twin Towers fell.[82] The digital collection was unique, because rather than present expertly curated material to users, it invited the public to help build the resource from scratch. By 2004, more than thirty thousand individuals had added memories or photos. By late 2016 the site provided open access to nearly seventy thousand digital items.[83] Through the words of ordinary people, those saved memories in their various forms helped to capture the process of national grieving. Contributions came from emergency workers who responded to the scene, family members, friends of victims, and shocked or angry people of every faith and background. This collection was of course one of many ways that the nation came to terms with the tragedies. Outbursts of solidarity and community appeared across the country as people united against terrorism. Those with more personal losses to deal with were also included in these acts of solidarity. Some who lost family members in the collapsing Twin Towers were given ashes from Ground Zero, a well-meaning but insufficient substitute for their loved ones.[84]

From a practitioner's perspective, perhaps the most interesting thing about this digital memory archive was the role of historians. Writing in 1990, public historian Michael Frische talked about the idea of "shared authority," in which the historical expert and the participant came together to produce something neither could do on their own.[85] In the September 11 Digital Archive, the expert had almost no role apart from recognizing the need for a space where memories could be collected. A set of planned, expertly written, contextual essays was dropped when the project received less funding than it had requested. Faced with this shortage, the team felt that the real potential for the initiative was in the crowd rather than the expert, and so let go of the academic essays.[86] Instead, the historian's role was as collection managers and public historians who understood the importance of public engagement, memory, and effective strategies for organizing and cataloging digital objects. By standing back and letting the community take a lead on content creation, the team avoided what library scientists Noah Lenstra and Abdul Alkalimat would call the "build it and they will come" trap, in which expert-curated collections can have "negative ramifications in terms of the community's reception and sense of ownership over the project."[87]

The project team partnered with scholars at the University of New Orleans in 2005 and repeated the model to collect memories of Hurricane Katrina, which destroyed huge swathes of Louisiana and upended hundreds of thousands of lives. The Hurricane Digital Memory Bank amassed a 14,000-item collection that included images, videos, oral histories, and stories from people affected by the tragedy. The project's mission was to "foster some positive legacies by allowing the people affected by these storms to tell their stories in their own words," which would then form part of the historical record for future generations.[88] The historian's role was therefore to use the Web to help the people create the records that would tell this history in the future. Theirs was not the only such initiative, nor was it the most creative attempt to preserve memories of Katrina. Artist Francesco di Santis played his own part, producing roughly two thousand hand-drawn portraits of the people he met on the streets in the storm's aftermath. Each subject was then invited to scrawl their story on the same page, producing what he called the *Post-Katrina Portraits: Written and Narrated by Hundreds* (2007)—an analog and emotional companion piece to the digital collection, created in the same spirit, and equally part of the historical record of the tragedy.[89]

By adopting the format of the traditional book of remembrance, and opening it online to the world, Rosenzweig's own take on invented digital archives became digital spaces for actively remembering. They represented successful early examples of digital community engagement in participatory history projects, and captured the ethos of what has since come to be called the "attention economy," in which eyeballs, clicks, and comments rather than citations were the measures of success. As Abby Smith Rumsey noted, technology had given the team an opportunity to do something that would have been impossible when knowledge was shared in books alone. The virtual format allowed them to produce what she called a "deep collaboration between the public and scholars."[90]

One of the most notable outcomes of these types of projects was the staggering amount of work members of the public were willing to put into creating them. Or to put that another way: how much *free labor* could be extracted from the crowd. The term "crowdsourcing" first gained popularity circa 2006 when it appeared in a *Wired* article by journalist Jeff Howe.[91] Howe merely gave a name to a much older practice. As U.S. historian Jason Heppler and U.K. historian Gabriel Wolfenstein pointed out, in the nineteenth century the *Oxford English Dictionary* solicited words for inclusion from its readership.[92] Even in 1982, the Indian Space Research Organisation Satellite Centre Library in Bengaluru had been crowdsourcing (thought they did not use that term). The library expressed disappointment when its attempts to crowdsource acquisition requests for the library collection were met with only few suggestions.[93] By the early new millennium, crowdsourcing found more success transforming a number of creative industries in particular. For example, when a Canadian stock photography website called iStockPhoto was launched in 2000, it revolutionized the way people bought and paid for stock imagery. The site let anyone register as a supplier, opening the stock photography market to everybody with a camera. The photos were then advertised and sold on the site for as little as a dollar. iStockPhoto provided a platform that allowed people to take advantage of the newly modestly priced but high-quality digital cameras. But it came at a dramatic cost to professional photographers, who found the site was able to undercut their prices by 99 percent.[94]

While bad news for photographers, crowdsourcing seemed to provide opportunities for thrifty businesses and ambitious but funding-strapped historians. The many digital archives of historical materials produced during the era of mass digitization in the late 1990s and early 2000s created just the type of work that the crowd might be willing to do. As chapter 1 notes, the quality of transcriptions within these collections was generally poor. Some contained such inaccurate text that effective keyword searching was impossible. Even those collections were exceptionally good in the grand scheme of things because at least they had been transcribed in the first place. Millions of other historical sources were handwritten, and in the early 2000s, converting handwriting into machine-readable text was well beyond the means of computer automation. Thus most historical records remained completely untranscribed and unsearchable. Faced with these labor-intensive challenges, many collection managers looked for new cost-effective means of making improvements.

Help was on the way. In 2007 a team of computer scientists led by Luis von Ahn demonstrated the proof of principle for crowdsourced transcription correction with a project called reCAPTCHA. For about a decade afterward, reCAPTCHAs were a popular antispam security feature on millions of websites, which attempted to ensure that only human users were accessing online services. To prove they were human, a user had to transcribe two partially distorted words shown in an image. At the time this was difficult for machines but fairly easy for most sighted Internet users. Rather than use randomly generated words, von Ahn had the idea of populating the images with one known word and one mistranscribed word from the New York Times archive. If users got the known word correct, they passed the test. Meanwhile their interpretation of the mistranscribed word was used to improve the quality of the New York Times archive. Using the tool, which was already on millions of websites providing antispam services, they tapped into a free workforce of more than 100-million unwitting daily transcribers. According to van Ahn, approximately 10 percent of the planet's inhabitants had taken part, making it one of the most successful collaborative endeavors ever.[95]

Like many organizations, the National Library of Australia found itself with a similar transcription quality problem, but without access to the vast reCAPTCHA audience. The library had millions of pages of digitized newspapers that suffered from poor-quality machine transcriptions. In 2009, they decided to tap into the potential of the crowd to solve the problem by launching their own platform for transcription correction, which they called Trove. The site allowed members of the public to correct mistakes in the digitized copies of the national newspaper collection through an intuitive online interface. By 2013, it had become the most popular feature on the library's website, and more than a hundred thousand registered users had helped to correct over 100 million lines of transcribed text.[96] Often forgotten in these endeavors is the hard work of creative software developers working to create the systems that enabled these amazing feats. All of the projects described in this chapter benefitted from their efforts, as well as those of the crowd who engaged with these new tools.

The British Library (2013) too used crowdsourcing, but in a very different way, opting to try to get the public to help geo-reference its old map collection.[97] Geo-referencing was the process of figuring out the longitude and latitude coordinates represented on a paper map so that they could each be linked to the appropriate place on the globe. To facilitate this, the library digitized 2,700 maps and developed an online tool that let users click corresponding points on both the old map and modern digital street map. After a few points had been identified, the software was then able to geolocate the map, and even to warp it to fit on the virtual surface of the earth. Whether by accident or design, the library caught onto an activity that people really enjoyed. Within a matter of weeks, the entire collection of 2,700 maps had been completed and the library had to go back to digitize 50,000 more.[98]

Not all activities proved as addictive as the geo-referencer. Perhaps by bringing in visual objects in the form of maps, the British Library had tapped into the crowd's enthusiasm for an activity that moved beyond text. For textual transcription projects like Trove to be successful, their creators increasingly realized that they could not just rely on the good will of participants. They had to provide an engaging experience that would keep people coming back to do more work. If contributors were not going to be paid, they had to be incentivized. The crowdsourcing world quickly became a space for coercive psychological experiments that were far beyond the traditional scope of expertise of historians and collection managers, but which were crucial to operating successfully in these digital spaces. The Trove project attempted to keep participants interested through a leader board of registered users' contributions. It seemed to have worked for one user in particular whose username was "JohnWarren," and was still active and comfortably ahead of his nearest competitor by more than two million unique contributions when this book went to press. One might suggest he has comfortably won, even if he ruined any incentive the leader board may have given to anyone else.[99] Old Weather (2010) also used principles of gamification for that project, which sought to make it fun for users to provide transcriptions of weather readings in old ships' logs. In addition to a leader board, they introduced naval officer titles for contributors, inviting them to "get promoted" as they worked their way up from cadet to captain. The team behind the project knew that a playful title would not draw in everyone, recognizing that many of their users were motivated by their desire to help scientists rather than to *win*. To address this, the site included a clear explanation of "why your contributions are vital" to the future of climate change research, as well as a number of videos to demonstrate the research value of the volunteers' work.[100] The importance some volunteers placed on helping scientists was a lesson the project team had learned to apply from an earlier astronomy crowdsourcing project, Galaxy Zoo (2007), which invited "citizen scientists" to help classify more than 100 million images of galaxies.[101]

Historians too were researching and writing about their users as never before. These "users" rather than "collaborators" emphasized the degree to which this work was about the uses of history rather than the process of understanding the past. Transcribe Bentham (2010) sought the help of volunteers to transcribe the collected handwritten works of philosopher Jeremy Bentham. By late 2017 they had successfully solicited transcriptions of more than 18,000 manuscript pages.[102] To fully understand their volunteers, they also conducted some meta research, digging into the factors that got them interested and kept them transcribing. Their findings showed that motivations ranged from an interest in history or philosophy, to a desire to be part of something collaborative.[103] This meshed very well with the findings of the Galaxy Zoo team about what motivated their own astronomy-inclined audience.[104] It was no longer just the history that was the focus of study, but the people engaging with it. That made crowdsourcing meta research not only an area of interest to historians, but also a truly interdisciplinary space where scholars from around the academy could come together to learn strategies for engaging with digital volunteers.

Many of these well-designed projects resulted in valuable work that would otherwise have gone beyond the limited budgets of collection managers. Temporarily leaving the morality of free labor aside, 100 million lines of corrected newspaper transcriptions, 18,000 handwritten manuscripts, and 50,000 geo-referenced old maps was not bad. Happily, the fruits of that labor remained available for anyone to use, and so could be viewed as a contribution to the greater good. However, not every project proved as successful as one might have hoped. Public historian Fien Danniau recounted that only one-third of entries contributed by members of the public to the Children of the Lodz Ghetto project were judged by the historians on the team to be good enough for inclusion in the project.[105] Other projects too faced similar problems. The Transcribe Bentham research assistants calculated that had they focused their own efforts purely on transcription instead of community management and checking the quality of the work of the crowd, they could have transcribed approximately two-and-a-half times as many manuscripts as the project achieved.[106] This perhaps suggests that the writings of Jeremy Bentham were not sufficiently enthralling to a wide audience to hold their attention. This in turn suggests that many of these projects needed to be shaped around the interests of the crowd, rather than the needs of historians or historical understanding. Recognizing this, when protest historian Katrina Navickas needed to correct the transcriptions of newspapers for her Political Meetings Mapper project, she realized that it would be cheaper to hire research assistants than to rely on the free labor of the crowd, and so proceeded accordingly.[107]

Despite the valuable contributions the crowd made to a number of heritage and history projects, crowdsourcing has perhaps seen its day. Cultural shifts have started to challenge this type of use of human effort. It raised the ire of some who felt it was exploitative, akin to a "digital sweatshop."[108] Meanwhile there was a shift in the language, toward the much more collaborative-sounding "cocreation" and "coproduction" and the positive connotations of partnership that those terms implied.[109] The Social Science and Humanities Research Council in Canada had adopted this more inclusive language by the mid-noughts, encouraging scholars to see their work with communities in terms of partnerships rather than "subjects" in a study.[110] Historians were thereafter expected to work with self-defined communities who declared themselves stakeholders rather than leverage the labor of the crowd. It was a reminder of who served whom within the history sphere.

Perhaps more importantly, bleeding-edge technology again shifted. Just as technology had facilitated crowdsourcing through online platforms that made it easy to contribute, so too had it increasingly made the crowd's efforts unnecessary. Machine learning in particular made possible what was very recently only a pipe dream. The handwritten manuscripts that were impenetrable to OCR software in 2010, were by 2017 being pumped through a new machine-learning tool called Transkribus, which was making impressively short work of them.[111] Machine learning was a game changer, and a change that came about quickly. Faced in 2015 with a collection of 1 million digitized but unclassified historical images in the British Library collection, I worked with the library and amateur video game developers to create a series of games that would make classifying fun.[112] A year later, a group of computer scientists would work with the library to tackle the same set of images with a machine-learning approach to complete the task automatically. With a change of strategy, they had rendered the purpose of our games moot, and left the crowd on the sidelines.[113]

The Web in Your Pocket

Web 2.0 principles changed the Internet and the ways scholars engaged with stakeholders and communities. It was not the only technological development catching the attention of historians in the decades between the 1980s and the late 2010s. Computers had been shrinking since the 1960s at a rate described by Moore's Law, which predicted that the density of transistors on a microchip would double every two years. Thanks to the efforts of those working in the microchip industry, computing underwent an extraordinary transformation, freeing users from their desktops and letting them take technology out into the world.

The revolution started in 1979, when Sony released its portable cassette player, the Walkman. Not really computers at all, these electronic personal audio players brought recorded music outdoors as never before. Thirty years later, playing music was only one of the functions of the new smartphones carried around by millions and then billions of people. What had been an iPod audio player in 2001 could by 2007 play audio and video, gained messaging capability, was connected to the Internet via satellites, granted access to global positioning systems (GPSs), and was soon fitted with an accelerometer and gyroscope that could reorient the screen so that the image always faced "up." The fact that these smartphones could also be used to make telephone calls was almost inconsequential. These were not telephones, but personal multifunctional mobile computers that changed the way many people lived their lives.

By 2016, "wearables" were too making headlines. These included smartwatches, or exercised-focused Fitbit bracelets that acted as both step counter and sleep monitor, or the heads-up display of Google Glass eyeglasses. A growing number of people were not only passively collecting data about their lives, but able to access just about any information, no matter where they were. With so much power at one's fingertips, it was perhaps not surprising that one anonymous Reddit contributor joked in 2013 that not everyone was putting these devices to their full potential: "I possess a device, in my pocket, that is capable of accessing the entirety of information known to man. I use it to look at pictures of cats and get in arguments with strangers."[114]

Used effectively or not, since the 1980s, technology had come increasingly out into the public sphere. Properly harnessed, that *had* to hold promise for history. Small groups of historians, computer scientists, and entrepreneurs began independently and diversely exploring new ways of applying portable technology in the service of the past. One of the earliest creative attempts took place in the world of theatre, and was inspired by the Walkman, which drama expert Chris Hardman imagined in 1983 was the key to a future of custom theatrical performances: "Your pretaped intervoice asks you to step through a red door and start walking down a hall. . . . Suddenly a man bursts in with a drawn knife. You are given the choice: join or fight. Your decision determines your play."[115] The encounter had an air of *Westworld* to it, the 1973 film about a historical theme park populated by in-character androids with which visitors could play out their historical fantasies.[116] Typical of a Michael Crichton thriller, everything in the story quickly goes very wrong and the robots start killing the guests. While violence was nothing a museum would ever wish on a visitor, this ability to customize their experience did resonate with the aims of museums and galleries. Throughout the late twentieth century, many were experimenting with ways that technology could add that personal touch. While not quite as interactive as Hardman envisioned, by 1985 the Metropolitan Museum of Art in New York was already offering portable audio guides to visitors. Curator Laurence Libin was the voice of the museum's audio guide about U.S. musical instruments. While visitors were awash with his expert thoughts on the collection through their headphones, Libin was presumably at his desk, freed by technology to both inform the visitors, and get to work on other things.[117] In 1989, James Sheldon noted that "roughly half" of museum-goers "have an audio guide playing in their ears."[118] These walkie-talkie-like devices became ubiquitous in many major museums and tourist sites, offering multilingual tours that visitors could opt into if they chose. Some sites, including Framlingham Castle in the East of England, even created multiple narratives so that parents and their children could hear content pitched at an appropriate level, ensuring everyone was intellectually engaged by the visit.[119] These audio guides did not quite offer a degree of personalization to the extent envisioned by Hardman, but it was moving in that direction.

The audio guide went one step further thanks to computer scientist Benjamin Bederson, who while riding the New York City subway in 1995 came up with an idea to apply location sensors to the devices. Typically, before the audio would play, visitors had to locate a number that was associated with an object in the collection, often located on a sticker nearby on the wall. Once input into the handheld device, the information would play on the speakers. Recognizing an opportunity for an upgrade, Bederson built a prototype that applied location sensors so that the audio would play automatically as soon as a visitor came within range of a relevant object.[120] This same concept would later be applied to the subways and buses of the world, automatically announcing upcoming stops.

This place-based computing resonated with computational historian William J. Turkel's environmental history research, in which he sought to bring together the landscape and the historical record to tell a new type of story.[121] Turkel saw potential for Bederson's idea not just within the museum, but outside on the streets or in the woods. In 2007, he asked the readers of his blog to "imagine walking around outside with an iPod-like device that is playing an electronic soundtrack. The music changes as you move, reflecting the historical land use patterns of the area that you are exploring." Turkel chose music rather than readings from primary sources or an expert narration: "You may choose to represent patches of original forest with a flute, a dairy farm with bass viol and cow bells, a factory with a percussion ensemble, a slaughterhouse with discordant horns. As you walk towards the site of an old factory, the sounds of percussion rise in volume to dominate the music."[122] This was an example of sonification—using abstract but meaningful sounds to convey knowledge about how the space and the archive were connected, and made the wanderer the composer of the musical story coming from the earphones. This device was possible thanks to inexpensive Arduino microcontrollers about the size of the palm of one's hand, which could be programmed to control electronics including GPS enabled devices. Turkel also experimented with Phidgets, a Canadian-based supplier of inexpensive programmable sensors that could register anything from movement, to distance, to temperature.[123] These elements of physical computing were part of Turkel's efforts in his Lab for Humanistic Fabrication, which uniquely among historians sought to build custom electronic devices that took advantage of these newly available tools, and applied them to matters of concern to historians. For the Geo-DJ, Turkel connected an Arduino microcontroller, a GPS sensor, and a small audio player with some custom code. In producing it he freed the user from the confines of the museum and took digital history outside.

A number of projects followed suit, but few took Turkel's approach of designing a custom device. Now that so many people owned their own smartphones, the emphasis shifted toward taking advantage of the computer in our pockets. These mobile devices meant that historians could build on Turkel's work and engage with audiences out-of-doors. Drawing on the participatory principles of Web 2.0 as well as Turkel's idea to connect spaces with the surviving archival material, Historypin launched in 2010.[124] The interface allowed users to virtually "pin" historic photographs in situ on Google Streetview so that the viewer could see the image in its original context and see how the area had changed since it was taken. The Museum of London went a step further the same year, launching an app called Street Museum, which directed users to certain spots around the city of London.[125] Using their mobile device as a virtual window into the past, as if by magic the app would display geolocated historic images overlaid onto the live video feed of their phone's camera and visible on their screen. This app helped bring the objects in the museum collection back out into the spaces depicted in the paintings. London was the museum, rather than the exhibition rooms.

Public historian Mark Tebeau attempted a similar initiative in Cleveland, producing a mobile app to geolocate eight hundred oral history interviews. The original plan had been to share the stories via fixed kiosks in Cleveland, but the release of the iPhone provided a quick change in strategy, and a much more cost-effective solution for the historian.[126] A number of commercial initiatives soon made it possible for anyone to leave traces of digital evidence out in the built environment. Though motivated by profit rather than history, starting in 2014, a German company called SmartLoveLock began selling padlocks featuring a quick response (QR) code and a near-field communication (NFC) chip.[127] Starting in the 1990s, love locks, attached to bridges before tossing the key, had become a popular way to anonymously express enduring romantic love. The SmartLoveLock innovated on this expression by allowing passersby to use their smartphone to scan the lock's QR code or NFC chip in order to access the story or photos that the besotted couple had linked to their lock. This brought the digital archive to someone interacting with the physical object deposited out in the world. As the combined weight of love locks have caused considerable structural damage to bridges, the hyperlink presumably also provides local governments with an idea of who should receive the bill for damages. Like many public history initiatives, SmartLoveLock facilitated the telling of a particular type of history, but it started out on the streets rather than in the museum or on the Web. Similar initiatives have brought QR to the memorial industry, with Living Headstones and Qeepr just two of the companies helping bereaved families share the stories of their loved ones with anyone with a smartphone who comes across their headstone.[128] Like the SmartLoveLock, the headstone includes a link to a Web archive of the person's life, reinforcing the link between the physical environment and the archive.

Lack of physical objects did not stop everyone from bringing digital stories out into the streets. The idea also caught the attention of scholarly video game maker and computer scientist Mads Haahr at Trinity College Dublin. Haahr founded Haunted Planet Studios in 2010, and has since helped produce a number of mobile virtual reality games set in Ireland that use Irish landscapes as the setting for historic ghost hunts. One game, Bram Stoker's Vampires, takes place on the grounds of Trinity College itself, asking players to search for clues with their phones, while avoiding unsuspecting students, buildings, and other hazards of the natural environment.[129] Stoker was a former student at Trinity College Dublin, which meant that the historical connection between the site of the game and the story's iconic creator was meaningful. While limited to people physically in Dublin, it demonstrated a principle that could be applied to any historic site seeking a way to engage audiences while on the grounds. A number of historic sites have since followed suit. In 2015, the Fort York National Historic Site in Toronto hired a virtual reality company to produce immersive experiences for visitors that took advantage of new virtual reality headsets. Using the headsets, visitors could experience the space as it was before European settlement, or as it underwent an attack by a U.S. Navy ship during the War of 1812.[130] Fort York was particularly well-suited to a virtual reality experience because it has since become swallowed by the urban sprawl of the city of Toronto. Though a protected site, what was once a lakeside fort guarding the people of Upper Canada was by 2015 nestled under a busy elevated highway, and lost its view of Lake Ontario due to a high-rise development in the late twentieth century. Virtual reality thus helped this urban historic site reclaim the experience of the past by digitally erasing twentieth-century urban growth and inviting the visitor to imagine what it might once have been like.

Conclusion

This chapter shows how changes in technology enabled historians to revise the nature of the archive, first by bringing primary sources into the classroom, and then into the streets. This work, whether conducted in a museum, a history department, or the offices of a Fortune 500 company, transformed the way users and the scholarly public engaged with the past. Like the digital research of the previous chapter, this was both an interdisciplinary and applied space. It was interdisciplinary because it required the talents of the technologist, of the collection management specialist, of the historian, and in some cases of the sociologist, psychologist, or educational theorist who could help them understand the needs and desires of the crowds that they worked with, worked for, or studied. It was an applied space because each of these projects represented a digital *moment*. Often for no more than five or so years, a new technological trend would attract the intense attention of adventurous historians who explored its potential for the field, and who then moved on.

The CD-ROM really only kept historians interested for the decade between about 1985 and 1995. It was unceremoniously killed by the rise of the Web. The Web too evolved rapidly, and by 2005 Web 2.0 was everywhere. People now expected to be able to participate in the Internet, not just consume it. Historians thus had to adapt. The devices we used were also changing rapidly. Within a decade, computers on our desks shifted into computers on our laps, and finally into devices in our pockets or on our person. Suddenly, everything had to be designed for mobile devices. This was a fast-paced world of bleeding-edge technologists who were passionate about the past. During each of these digital moments, it was up to them to find ways to apply these new ideas to the archive quickly and effectively.

Importantly, this was a public-facing space that for many early projects in particular was inspired by a desire to transform education. The role of historians of below such as E. P. Thompson has been thus far overlooked by the historiography of technology and historical studies, yet his approach to a democratizing history was the foundation for many historian-led digitization initiatives. As the pedagogically driven historians gave way to a generation of scholars dabbling first in Web collection management, and then in mobile computing, the work changed, as did the products that were produced. "Users" became a unit of study in their own right, with a number of historians having to become experts on user experiences, needs, and expectations. This work was intensely valuable because it opened up and continues to open new doors for people to build their own niches as historians engaging the public with the archive. It has allowed collections to reach wider audiences than ever before, and arranged in combinations as never before. With virtual reality and 3-D printing only just coming into their own, and linked data and machine learning continuing to break down barriers, the promise for more developments remains on the horizon. With each new trend in technology comes a new opportunity for historians, but we must not forget the many ways that technology has already changed the archive.

As this chapter shows, our current memory of the era of digitization itself needs revision. Tim Hitchcock's narrative of digitizing British history since 1980 provided a solid history within the British context, but it was not intended to capture the motives behind more pedagogically driven U.S. colleagues, let alone the unique circumstances of other countries.[131] Meanwhile, Cohen and Rosenzweig's *Digital History*, the best-known proponent of encouraging historians to build digital archives, was published too early (2005) to see the coming of many of the key technological changes that have helped historians' archival revisionism come into the streets.

No longer bound by the limits of the brick-and-mortar repositories, collections that had never existed, from the *Valley of the Shadow* to the digitized archive of the *Old Bailey Proceedings*, came to be used by millions of people around the world, reaching audiences that no traditional archive could. This revisionism does not replace but augments the work of collection managers, providing new opportunities to experiment without risking the original materials or principles of archival science. As highlighted, these experiments were principally driven by external factors: an evolving Web (the rise of Web 2.0), by changes to computers (the rise of mobile devices), and by increased access to mobile data when on the move. However, changes also came from within the profession. The drive of many U.S. historians in particular to get more primary sources into their classrooms and to challenge the elite narrative of U.S. history is vital to the story of digitization and historical studies.

3

Digitizing the History Classroom

The classroom is not a static space, but it is one rooted deeply in traditions that stretch back centuries. In particular, the lecture, the cornerstone of historical higher education pedagogy, saw its rise at the pulpit of Protestant churches. The men who would stand at those pulpits in the centuries following the Reformation received their training at universities, where it became a core part of the learning environment—particularly in humanities subjects.[1] This was not the only model of education. Socrates, Western culture's most famous teacher, did not lecture. Instead, he prompted the student with questions meant to encourage a dialogue of self-discovery. This was the Socratic method, as it came to be known, and perhaps closer in style to the seminar than the lecture. Conversely, vocational skills were learned on the job via the apprenticeship model that had been in place since the medieval era, and through which people learned a skill over the course of a seven-year hands-on training program.[2]

Lectures are still a dominant mode of teaching history at the university level. However, their supremacy is perhaps not what it had been. For some, their measured decline in historical studies has become symbolic of the impact of "digital" teaching. This is because the lecture was one of the first symbols of "traditional" teaching to come under question when computers first started to appear in classrooms in the 1980s. Many of the humanists working at the intersection of computing and history at the time began to ask questions about the role of the teacher in the classroom. The conversation was perhaps prompted by a change of the teaching rooms themselves. Just as the pews faced the pulpit, lecture halls had been arranged so that students' bodies faced the lecturer. In the 1980s, teachers were given access to a new type of teaching room: the "computer lab," which by their very design turned the students bodies away from a central focal point and toward a personal one.

Interrupted sight lines in these labs made group discussions impractical. The flicker of each student's monitor proved a distraction for anyone trying to lecture. It was clear that strategies needed to adapt. This led many to ask what type of teaching was most appropriate in these new spaces. The conversations would endure for decades. In 2013 and as a result of the dynamics these labs created, historian and Web designer Jeremy Boggs would describe the instructor as part role model, part tech support, and part cheerleader.[3] However, the matter emerged very early as one of the first key themes in a conference about teaching computing in the humanities, held at the University of Southampton in 1988, where it was raised in a number of papers. Summarizing the event, text encoding expert Lou Burnard and literature scholar Judith Proud wrote that "with or without the presence of a computer terminal in a classroom, teaching methods in tertiary education must move away from the traditional master/disciple roles which the availability of hypertext systems and videodiscs are beginning to expose and challenge."[4] They suggested that "the chief effect of the introduction of computing had been to provoke a re-evaluation of the methods and priorities of teaching methods in the humanities, quite independent of any technological considerations." This move toward what would later be called student-centered learning would have been quite an important pedagogical intervention for the humanities had the ideas actually originated with these computational scholars. However, technologically adept teachers were simply on trend with the wider discussions in higher education, whether they realized it or not. The leaders of those trends were not computing scholars working in history, but psychologists and educational theorists who had begun studying how humans learned and whose conclusions threw the value of the lecture into question. A few key studies from the latter twentieth century stood out as pedagogically groundbreaking in this regard. Educational theorist David Kolb challenged the wisdom of lecturing in 1976 by suggesting that real learning involved a four-part process of doing, thinking, consolidating, and applying new concepts.[5] The lecture on its own was therefore, apparently insufficient. Others built on this foundation. In 1983, educational scientist Keith Purvis suggested that the teacher could find a more effective role by stepping into the position of moderator, in an attempt to encourage what he called "interactional learning."[6] A decade later, Alison King's influential pedagogy article criticized the "sage on the stage," ushering in a new era of "guides on the side," in what became a powerful wave of student-centered teaching that remained influential more than two decades after that.[7]

Also in 1993, psychologist Howard Gardner's *Multiple Intelligences* put forth an argument that we are each a unique combination of aptitudes, which makes it easier for each of us to learn certain types of knowledge than others. Gardner suggested that these intelligences—musical, bodily-kinesthetic, logical-mathematical, linguistic, spatial, interpersonal, and intrapersonal— makes us who we are. A person with a high bodily-kinesthetic intelligence might learn a lot on an archaeological dig, or in a hands-on session about conserving artefacts, but might find learning in a lecture hall less effective. Educational expert Neil Fleming's "I'm Different; Not Dumb" (1995) suggested the method of delivery was the key factor in learning success, noting that we learn better through our own uniquely combined preference for visual, auditory, writing/reading, or kinesthetic approaches—which he condensed to the acronym VARK. According to Fleming's VARK model, only auditory learners will be able to take full advantage of a lecture. A subsequent study by Annette Vincent and Dianne Ross showed that auditory learners made up between 40 and 50 percent of university students, meaning half of the students could learn more effectively through other means.[8]

The late twentieth century was thus an era during which great energy was expended on the theory and practice of teaching. The new pedagogical research clearly suggested that the history classroom was ripe for revision. Energy from historical educators too showed a profession willing to change. As U.S. politicians and educators battled over the contents of the history curriculum in the early 1990s, great teachers fought to overturn old views that the purpose of historical studies was to teach names and dates in the accepted national narrative, and instead sought to usher in an era in which it was viewed as a pathway to acquiring critical thinking skills.[9] Likewise in England, the introduction of the country's first-ever national history curriculum around the same time had historians across the country debating the purpose of a historical education.[10] The late twentieth century was an energized time for history pedagogy. Since 1971, the Committee on History in the Classroom's newsletter provided a means of keeping history educators in touch, and talking about their pedagogical aims.[11] Organizations such as the American Association for Higher Education, the Carnegie Foundation for the Advancement of Teaching, and the National History Education Network gave U.S. scholars in the 1990s opportunities to come together to discuss their teaching strategies as never before.[12]

There were some obvious changes to practice brought about by technology. As educationalist and historian William Cutler noted, a U.S. movement in the 1990s encouraged scholars to remove the veil of secrecy from their classrooms, and to instead think about their teaching publicly and for the benefit of other colleagues. He called this "making teaching a public activity," and it encouraged a generation of historians by circa 2004 to not only produce teaching portfolios, but also to post thousands of course syllabi online where conversations about pedagogy could push the classroom experience forward in productive ways.[13] In another practical development, business historian Janice Reiff noted that the advent of e-mail gave students more opportunities to correspond with their tutors than through office hours alone.[14] A number of scholars interested in computing also found themselves engaged in the conversations about how historical education might evolve. Conferences focused on pedagogy and computers began to appear across Canada, the United Kingdom, and the United States. In addition to that Southampton conference, between 1986 and 2001, drama scholar and pedagogue Brett Hirsch charted a dozen substantial English-language events, starting with a Teaching Computers and the Humanities Courses series at Vassar College in 1986, including a number of U.K.-based events, "Computers and Teaching in the Humanities" (1987–95), and culminating with a major (and well-documented) conference at Malaspina University College (now Vancouver Island University) in Canada in 2001.[15] These events highlighted the passion many people had as they sought to identify the potential of digitally inflected teaching in history departments, and they provide valuable insight into the types of conversations people were having, as well as the wider impacts that were influencing their ideas.

Drawing on the archives left behind from pedagogical conferences, syllabi, blogs, interviews, personal papers, and even virtual tours, this chapter charts some of the key ways that the history curriculum and teaching practices changed between the 1980s and 2010s as a result of so-called digital influences. The chapter builds on the existing history-focused contributions by teaching and learning in history specialists Mills Kelly, Alan Booth, and Paul Hyland, and on the wider "digital humanities" scholarship, including the edited collection of Brett Hirsch.[16] It focuses chiefly on courses that included an intensive focus on technology, rather than on some of the more mundane ways technology crept into the curriculum (the gradual shift to word-processing essays, for example). It does so by taking a historical approach, analyzing the impact of technology on history pedagogy in "waves," highlighting the degree to which teachers were responding to challenges faced by the discipline, or being influenced by outside trends. It has the added benefit of a few years extra hindsight over Kelly's contribution on digital history teaching, which focused heavily on the benefits of a newly digitized archive in the early 2000s, and necessarily was a reflection on the key moments of his own career and that of his colleagues. As such, it formed an important chapter in a wider story stretching back much earlier and continuing after he set his words to the page. The longer historically focused analysis presented here sets Kelly's work and others like it into the context of a classroom that began to see the influence of computers in the pre-Internet era of the 1980s, and which continued to evolve past the trends he highlighted in his book.

Kelly's approach therefore needs to be understood as an innovative product of its time, reacting to the opportunities of the Internet era. But it was not the only approach. Before came a generation of educators who focused their student's attention on spreadsheets and databases; after came a new generation who were keen to impart the skills of big data analysis. More recently still, many digital skills have been imparted on students in dribs and drabs through more traditional historically focused courses with a few digital innovations thrown in. There was no overarching plan for a digital transformation of the historical classroom. Instead, it was a reactive intellectual space led by a few passionate individuals and largely ignored by the rest of the profession.

These passionate few were not pushing a coherent agenda. Instead, they can be categorized into a number of fairly well-defined cliques that seldom interacted with one another, quickly forgot what came before them, but left a substantial mark on the pedagogical landscape of historical studies nonetheless. Whether that was always a good thing is another matter. Understanding how those siloed approaches to technology and teaching came together (or did not) provides a roadmap for how the profession can harness change moving forward, with the needs of students and the interests of historical studies always in mind. Given the previous lack of a plan, this path moving forward is one that should continue to be guided by passion, but would be well served if supported more actively by professional bodies such as the American Historical Association, Canadian Historical Association, and Royal Historical Society, which include the input of a wider cross section of historians, to ensure a more coherent future of history education. The profession can no longer afford to ignore the role technology will continue to have on education; this chapter sets the historical context for starting that global conversation.

The First Wave: Teaching Historians to Count and Code

When computing first came into the history classroom is difficult to pinpoint. The acknowledgment sections of many computational histories written in the punch-card era make it clear that many graduate students experienced computing as early as the 1960s as part of their scholarly apprenticeship, whether formally or informally.[17] By the 1980s, "microcomputers" had dramatically reduced the cost of computing and lowered the intellectual barrier to entry for those wanting to use them; a growth in more user-friendly software meant that it was feasible to bring microcomputers into the history curriculum as never before. With few examples of how to do so effectively, these early historians had tremendous power over the nature of the computing curriculum. This meant a great degree of local variation in what was offered and how it was delivered. Three courses taught in several English universities between 1987 and 1993 and discussed below highlight that variation but also a degree of consistency in England with approaches to computing and historical research at the time, with its emphasis on counting and measuring.

Many ideas came from outside of historical studies, from colleagues in adjacent disciplines. In fact, they may have been responsible for some of the models that were eventually adopted. That was certainly the case in the English southwest. In 1987, sociologist Jonathan Gershuny and research methods scholar Alan Lewis at the University of Bath set an assignment for their students that drew on Gershuny's research interest in contemporary "time use." Today, that same question using the same data would be history rather than sociology: "Young and Willmott claim that the roles of husbands and wives are becoming more 'symmetrical.' Husbands do more housework, wives more paid work. Does the 1983/4 Time Budget survey give us grounds for thinking that the symmetrical family has arrived in Britain in the 1980s?"[18] Before being set loose on the question, students were given research skills. To begin, they spent two weeks in the computer lab learning how to use the school's microcomputers. They were taught relevant commands and software. Then came a grueling multi-week dose of statistics: indicators of central tendency and dispersion, making defensible inferences about a population, and determining "expected values" in a population to understand when data was unusual or otherwise worth a closer look. To acquire this high-level knowledge, they were taught how to conduct practical statistical tests: everything from standard deviation, to chi-squared tests, to analysis of variance. The computers acted as their calculators, allowing them to conduct tests that their predecessors had to do longhand. Primed with everything they needed to succeed, they had to apply those skills to the Time Budget data before offering a conclusion to the above research question. Students were not taught skills for their own sake, but to allow them to be better sociological researchers.

The syllabus for this course was among the private papers of crime historian John Styles, who had moved from Bath to the University of Bristol. It was interspersed in a folder of documents related to a course he and economic historian Roger Middleton were planning that same year for a cohort of Bristol undergraduate history students. Its survival among those papers highlights one of the ways scholars interested in technology were sharing teaching ideas in the 1980s, even across disciplines. It also serves as a useful comparator for the course that a young Styles and Middleton eventually delivered to that group of history undergraduates back in 1987. From a structural perspective, the history course was nearly identical. Styles chose a historical case study connected to his research interests (eighteenth-century crime). There was a dataset: a published notebook of a Wiltshire magistrate named William Hunt (written between 1744 and 1749) that gave both quantifiable information about crime cases and qualitative notes and private thoughts from the judicial bench. From this, students were expected to answer research questions, including this one: "What can the evidence of the Hunt notebook tell the historian about the nature of and reasons for differences in criminal behaviour between men and women?"[19] As at Bath, students spent the first few weeks in the computer lab, learning basic commands and trouble-shooting tips. The course ended with several weeks on statistics tailored to the specific needs of historians and historical data: measures of central tendency (mode, median, mean, variance, standard deviation), and measures of association (contingency tables, cross-tabulation, chi-square).[20]

However, Styles and Middleton added their own historical touches to the course and interspersed lab sessions with traditional seminar-style discussions of relevant historical research, opting not to take the learning environment too far away from what students would find familiar. Styles also included two weeks on "information in history" and "dealing with data," including a discussion on the pitfalls of working with historical datasets.[21] He warned his class of "the importance for the historian of establishing the process by which data comes to be collected and recorded" before jumping in and starting to measure or look for trends.[22] Students were also taught about the "dark figure" of unreported crime and how it acted as a confounding factor in any attempts to quantify criminal activity. Cockburn's 1975 warning about the limits of data found in early modern Assize court records was particularly pertinent for students being challenged to work quantitatively with historical data.[23] The result of Styles's and Middleton's interventions on data quality was a course in which students were being taught simultaneously to count and to be critical of quantitative approaches. It was a very narrowly focused pedagogical intervention that dealt with relevant issues very thoroughly.

Just how widespread courses like this were is difficult to say. First, they were expensive. To be able to teach a mere twenty students per year, Middleton requested a princely £33,269 (£1,663.45 per student) from the history department to build a computer lab and purchase requisite software. That total amount was more than three times the average British salary in 1987, making it a substantial request from the department.[24] There were of course other models for acquiring equipment for higher education. Dartmouth College in New Hampshire asked humanities students by the end of the 1980s to spend up to $2,400 to buy their own personal computer for use with their studies.[25] It was a signal of a major commitment to computer-inflected teaching led by the faculty at Dartmouth, but it transferred the cost to the students directly. No matter who paid, computing was expensive and thus had to be justified.

In order to secure the investment in his lab, Middleton presented it as phase one in the development of a more integrated program that would put computing at its heart. It would not only enable the department to bring economic history in-house (at the time it was taught by the Department of Economics), but would also let students learn "marketable!" computer skills.[26] This course and the ideas behind it were also an experiment that the pair hoped would "teach economic theory in a way that is interesting and relevant for economic and social historians."[27] Just why the computer lab would make a course more "interesting" or "relevant" is never explained in the surviving papers, but it is indicative of a belief among some that technology was going to be a big part of the future of the history classroom and that students would like it. Yet, at Bristol at least, the effect was temporary. In part because John Styles moved on shortly thereafter to a career spent principally at the Victoria and Albert Museum. Digital teaching at Bristol lay dormant until 2015 when the department advertised for a "Digital Historian" and hired a historian of twentieth-century politics, James Freeman, to pick up where his predecessors had left off nearly thirty years before. This loss of computerized teaching at Bristol highlighted the importance of passionate individuals for building and sustaining technology-led pedagogy in the history curriculum.

Elsewhere in England in the late 1980s and early '90s, other pockets of computer-led teaching sprung up in history departments. Starting in 1990 at

King's College London, the team in the Humanities and Information Group of the Faculty of Arts and Music (former BBC producer Harold Short, archaeologist Susan Kruse, and technologist Gordon Gallagher) were tasked with developing and delivering an applied computing minor to students in the faculty. Despite the fact that Short's team had been and continued offering popular week-long computing training to historians, he claimed that the history department leadership at the time was one of a small number of groups in the college who refused to participate in the applied computing minor, insisting instead on a monodisciplinary focus for their students. Undeterred and spearheaded by archaeologist Kruse, they collaborated with a pair of historians (medievalist Janet "Jinty" Nelson and historian of institutions Arthur Burns) to put together and deliver a two-semester optional noncredit course in computing for the college's history students.[28]

For Short, the buy-in of the historians legitimized the activity and helped attract the students as well as maintain their interest throughout the course. As their colleagues at Bristol had done, the King's course also adopted historical case studies. These covered a range of periods, from the Anglo-Saxon era to the eighteenth and nineteenth centuries. Unlike at Bristol, they were not limited to economic history approaches only; given the organizers' experience working with departments across the faculty, they were able to offer historians a wider range of interdisciplinary options. Basic statistics was on the menu, but so too was textual analysis, database use, and spreadsheet analysis.[29] Short's broad approach was in sharp contrast to Styles's focused method, highlighting the diversity of experience students could expect, depending on whose class they happened to take.

Ten minutes north of King's College by tube, a young historian of poverty named Tim Hitchcock was planning his own computational course for his students at the University of North London. The course first ran in 1993, a full decade before Hitchcock would help bring the Old Bailey Online to the world, along with its 127 million words of transcribed criminal trial accounts. Yet, he was already well-versed in the value of databases, and the approach of his course included a focus on them as a tool for helping students to structure historical evidence meaningfully so that they could conduct historical analyses. Their three-part assignment required them to create a database, to suggest an appropriate research question that could make use of that structured information, and then to answer that question.[30] This brought a new technological tool into the classroom while maintaining the historical focus of the class. Keeping with Styles's critical approach, students faced an exam in which they were asked to design a database schema for a primary source, but also to be critical of how their decisions would both improve the historian's options for analysis, and result in lost information.[31]

Hitchcock too was acutely aware of the importance of appealing to students, though he seems to have had a more negative view than Middleton at Bristol, remarking that "any teacher who has been involved in running an introductory computing course will know the difficulty entailed in trying to convince undergraduates of its intellectual importance," noting that instead they do a degree in the humanities because of their passion for the subject, rather than its value as a skill set that might be marketable to employers.[32] With this in mind, he too structured his teaching around historical themes: "Poverty and Poor Relief in England, 1500–1834" in one case. This was the same topic he wrote on for much of his career, highlighting the connection between a historian who studies a topic that left a deep paper trail of quantifiable forms, and an interest in computers. Like at Bristol, he too used both traditional seminars and computer workshops. These familiar features, he hoped, would appeal to students, while the computational approach to research could lead to quite different essays than in the typical classroom. It was a blending of the old and the new. The result, according to external examiner John Morrell of the University of Cambridge, was student work that was "superior to anything I have encountered as external [examiner] to three universities (let alone the antediluvian teaching approaches at Cambridge)."[33]

These three examples of how English history students encountered technology in the classroom highlight some differences (choices of technological focus; for credit or extracurricular) as well as similarities (use of a historical case study, a shift from the lecture hall to the computer lab, retention of seminar discussions, an emphasis on being critical of historical data, an emphasis on answering research questions). These were not part of a solely English approach to teaching in the computer lab. Similar trends had appeared across the Atlantic, with textual editing scholar Murray McGillivray's students at the University of Calgary challenged to produce what he called an "end product" that brought together the skills and technologies they had learned and that echoed many of the features of the English courses.[34] There was a clear sense that this was an evolution from what was being offered in other history classrooms along the same corridors; but it was not to last. Within a few years, the emphasis had shifted to multimedia and the Internet, with little memory of what had come before. This second wave of computing history teachers would fundamentally challenge what constituted a "historical" skill set.

The Second Wave: Silicon Valley and "Cool" Teaching

With the rise of the Web in the 1990s, geeky suddenly became cool. An increasingly graphically oriented "world wide web" replaced talk of the spreadsheets and databases of the previous generation. If Microsoft's Bill Gates had dominated the 1980s and '90s with his business solutions, the future belonged to the charismatic Steve Jobs of Apple and Mark Zuckerberg, the founder of Facebook who would champion an era of sharing and creating that changed the way people lived their everyday lives. Computers were no longer seen as tools for computing but pathways into building social networks and social capital. Content was king. Attention was short. "Likes" on social media became the new currency of many people's self-worth.

The world's relationship with the newly networked computers had changed so much in such a short time span; thus, it was only natural for the history classroom to adapt to the new way of thinking about technology. Given the obvious influence of Silicon Valley on this great social upheaval, it was perhaps not surprising that one of the first universities to apply this new media-intensive history in the classroom was just down the road at Stanford. While most history students at the time still learned their history through lectures and seminars, in 2002 students in science, technology, and society scholar Michael John Gorman's "The Wired Historian" class were busy learning the basics of hypertext markup language (HTML)—the building blocks of a website, and a curious skill for a historian at the time.[35] This was probably not the first such group to learn about building websites, as Mark Fitzgerald had hosted a 1997 workshop in New York City called "Web Page Construction 101: Teaching Your Students How to Create a Web Page."[36] However, Gorman's students were on the leading edge of the wave that would all but sweep away the memory of "computing." This was the "digital" era.

Making the leap from "computing" to "digital" was easy for the next generation of history educators in the new millennium. Many of them had not learned the statistics that underpinned the strategies of their forbearers and were therefore not equipped to teach their classes in the same way. Instead, they were avid users of the new gadgets (iPods, iPads) and visited the new social media sites (WordPress, Facebook, Twitter) just as voraciously as their students, if not more so. Always looking for new markets, and probably convinced of the social and cultural value of their products, the giants of Silicon Valley were only too happy to foster relationships with these self-professed nerds of higher education. In 2003, Duke University was part of an Apple-sponsored pilot that provided all students with an iPod audio player and challenged them to think of ways the device could be used in their studies. Apple was after product ideas, and the students benefited from what was (at the time) a new and sought-after piece of technology.[37] This was an extension of the Apple University Consortium of the 1980s, in which the company partnered with select universities to bring Apple technology into the classroom, not only to build a market but also to understand how their computers and software could better serve the needs of experimental educators.[38] The chance to experiment with technology without clear ideas of an end goal was not limited to the digital classrooms of historians. Historian of slavery Caleb McDaniel, a key proponent of digital history, claimed he first learned HTML in a horticulture class, and though he was not clear how website building would make him a better horticulturist, it taught him "to be willing to learn something even before its utility was immediately clear."[39]

Increasingly, and where students had enough expendable income to afford it, the iPod that those students at Duke were given was one of a growing number of content consumption devices that came on the market in the early new millennium. Designed for listening or viewing rather than creating, they generated a market for endless new content and a belief among some historians that students were now "digital natives" who did not need to be taught technology.[40] It was as creators that students would be encouraged to take advantage of the changes in technology, thinking and learning in public like never before. U.S. historian Jeff McClurken and public historian Marc Tebeau both described it as a chance to get students out of their comfort zone where they could get off of autopilot and really start to learn in a way that did not happen when they wrote only for their teachers.[41]

Slowly at first, a handful of educators, predominantly in the United States and Canada, built audience-focused classes that took advantage of new media and the Internet. Increasingly, these types of classes became associated with "digital" teaching in history. One of the key developments was student blogging, which probably first appeared in 2004 in historian Josh Greenberg's undergraduate course at Cornell University, spreading to dozens of digital history courses before beginning to fade in about 2013. In a sample of eighty-five unique self-described "digital" history courses from 2002 to 2017 (appendix), just over half included blogging.[42] The practice rarely found its way into more traditional courses, despite the fact that blogging was not inherently a "digital" idea. Computational historian William Turkel was one of a growing number of historians assigning blogging in the early new millennium; he credited philosopher Donald Schön's *The Reflective Practitioner* (1983) as the pedagogical basis for the activity, suggesting that it would help his MA students build their skills quicker if they took the time to reflect on their learning process.[43]

Blogging also proved a novel means of exposing students to each other's writing as never before, with some courses requiring active commenting on the blog posts of colleagues.[44] Digital archaeologist Shawn Graham at Carleton University in Ottawa even set aside 20 percent of his undergraduate student's grade to "active, value-added community-building by participation in the discussion(s), across multiple media and platforms."[45] Students were thus marked for their contributions to a community of learning. In a very few cases, those communities even stretched across institutions. In 2014 Andrew Torget (University of North Texas) and Caleb McDaniel (Rice University), historians of the nineteenth-century United States, taught their digital history courses together but separate, opting for a common theme of the history of runaways during the era of slavery, and sharing findings in progress with students at the other university.[46] These virtual pen pals were breaking down traditional social and practical barriers that had kept students from working on interuniversity projects, and they challenged the notion that learning was something that occurred only through an exchange between the individual student and the professor. These new communities that developed in some classrooms reinforced the shift from "sage on the stage" to "guide on the side." In a discipline associated with solo study in the library, these virtual communities could also help foster a real sense of camaraderie. To commemorate and celebrate the time they spent together in the classroom, students in Mills Kelly's Clio Wired course in 2005 even designed and ordered class T-shirts.[47]

This rise in public-facing history teaching was boosted significantly by two developments in the Center for History and New Media at George Mason University. The first was the publication of Dan Cohen and Roy Rosenzweig's *Digital History: A Guide to Gathering, Preserving, and Presenting the Past on the Web* (2005). The second was the release of Omeka (2008), a user-friendly website-building platform targeted at historians and museum professionals. These two initiatives provided some key infrastructure aimed at historians, enabling students studying the past to take full advantage of the Web.

The former was an influential call to arms for historians, who Cohen and Rosenzweig entreated to take advantage of the great potential of the Internet as a venue for sharing history. The book contained a lot of practical advice in an era where such detail in accessible prose, targeted at historians, was nonexistent. It quickly became *the* textbook of the field, whose practitioners adopted the title of the book to describe themselves henceforth as "digital historians." Courses influenced by the "digital history" model did not focus on answering research questions about the past, as in the courses of the previous generation. Instead, they were about using the Web to present history or engage with audiences who might have been interested in historical content. These were new media courses aimed at historians, and inspired by many of the early digitization initiatives described in chapter 2, which allowed primary sources to come into the classroom as never before.[48] It was a chance to take advantage of the changing new media landscape, as described by media scholar Janet Murray in *Hamlet on the Holodeck*, acknowledging that the essay was not the only nor necessarily the best way of expressing historical thinking, but that nonlinear and multisensory storytelling was too an option worth considering. Between 2002 and 2014, this public-facing approach effectively *was* "digital history" teaching. Courses belonging to this genre were characterized by their emphasis on building public-facing "projects" rather than writing essays, and on building archives or digital collections of primary sources. This was in line with the increasing professional pressure many academics felt to brush up on their storytelling skills, in an effort to raise the impact potential of their research with both publics and policy makers. Starting in 2013 in Canada, the Social Science and Humanities Research Council began hosting an annual "Storytelling" competition that celebrated the very skills that were foregrounded in these "digital history" classes of the previous decade.[49]

In the latter, teachers were helped substantially by the first release of Omeka in 2008. The software was a content management system, designed to give historians and collection managers a free and easy-to-use but also robust tool for building websites of historical materials. Omeka made it viable for educators to ask students to build or contribute to high-quality virtual archives for the first time. No specialist technical knowledge was necessary, freeing up time for students to think about the story they wanted to tell with their collection. A number of courses began assigning digital archives as the class project, using Omeka or other website-building packages such as WordPress or Drupal. Historian Jeff McClurken and educationalist Jerry Slezak saw these websites as a good opportunity for students to engage with wider audiences, but also a good chance to learn a new skill not available elsewhere in the curriculum.[50]

One of the most common approaches was to encourage students to build websites about the history of the local area. This seems to have been more popular than a course based on the research interests of the instructor. In some cases, students were encouraged to stay very close to home. Historians of the U.S. West Douglas Seefeldt (2009), the U.S. South Jeff McClurken (2012), and of U.S. national parks Anne Mitchell Whisnant (2014) had students research the history of their own university. Whisnant's digitally focused public history class challenged students to dig deeply into the white male personas after which the campus buildings had been named, as a way of encouraging them to question the origins of the status quo of their community.[51] Many others also kept it local. Public historian Leslie Madsen-Brooks's class at Boise State University was asked to work on the local history of the Central Rim neighborhood in Boise—an approach that was strikingly similar to the theme of curator Adina Langer's Atlanta Beltline project for students at Georgia State University and of medievalist Fred Gibbs's digital history of Albuquerque, assigned to his students the same year he arrived to take up a post at the University of New Mexico.[52]

Others put their pedagogical emphasis in slightly different skills, while maintaining a focus on storytelling. The most innovative was historian of Eastern Europe Mills Kelly, who focused on how to tell a good lie—not a typical skill taught to history students. His Lying about the Past (2008) course taught students to be critical consumers of the Web by teaching them *why* their teachers were so bothered about Wikipedia, which had become a bogeyman in history classrooms of the day.[53] Instructors regularly told students not to use the online encyclopedia in their essays without necessarily helping students understand why the site was problematic. Instead of a blanket ban, Kelly opted instead to show his students why. To do so, they researched an elaborate historical hoax involving a fake American pirate and created an accompanying Wikipedia article. A decade before "fake news" became the phrase of the year, the students sent the phony story out into the world and successfully fooled at least one journalist.[54] In the process they managed to "really, really, really annoy" Wikipedia cofounder, Jimmy Wales. They also learned the important lesson that they must be as critical of Web-based sources as they had come to be of any other historical materials.[55]

Storytelling was also key to historian of the family Paula Petrik's course, but she placed her emphasis in a very different set of skills. In particular, she had evolved her pedagogy to ensure that students had a solid grounding in Web design principles and theory, recognizing that a beautiful website was one that might attract a larger audience, and a good historian would know how to build one.[56] Computational historian William J. Turkel too took a very different tack in his aptly named master's-level course Interactive Exhibit Design, which taught students about physical computing so that they could build exhibits that beeped, moved, or lit up.[57] I suspect that few of his history students had held a soldering iron or knew how to interpret the color bands on electrical resistors prior to taking his class.

In these and many other cases, the technical skills needed to tell new types of stories in new forms of media were emphasized over learning historical content. A lack of historical content was one of the most notable elements of digital history classes in the early twenty-first century. Nearly half of the eighty-five courses in the sample collected in the appendix had no content that would obviously be viewed as historical by a typical historian—that is, no history of a time, place, or theme. Historiographical readings (journal articles and scholarly monographs) were rare, appearing in only a quarter of those courses. Instead, students read blog posts and technical guidance and were being taught implicitly that digital history did not speak to traditional historians. In 2013, William J. Turkel's digital humanities programming class appeared to have foregone readings all together, opting instead for a series of tutorials.[58] While it is possible that the readings appeared elsewhere on a course management system, this appeared to be a dramatic shift away from the traditional literary emphasis of the history classroom and instead adopted a practical learning approach more akin to some science, technology, engineering, and medicine (STEM) programs.

For students to be able to create cutting-edge digital content, they needed cutting-edge equipment, leading to the development of some of the most advanced digital history hacking spaces, replete with the latest gadgets. The most extreme example was William J. Turkel's Fab Lab at Western University in Ontario.[59] "Fab," short for "fabrication," certainly implied a connection to "fabulousness" and the notion that digital work was somehow *cool*. When the lab launched in 2008, it boasted 3-D printing and scanning equipment, as well as remote sensing equipment such as motion sensors, a wide array of electronics components, soldering irons, and workbenches. The equipment was so sensitive that Angela Kedgley, an engineering PhD student used the 3-D scanner for her research because it outperformed anything owned by the school of engineering at the time.[60] It also proved fundamental for Devon Elliott's PhD research on nineteenth-century stage magic, which applied fabrication and physical computing as a means for re-creating and understanding these long-lost performances without having to build full-scale models of what had been theater-sized illusions.[61]

Though the space has now grown to include teaching rooms, in its earliest iteration, the Fab Lab (or Lab of Humanistic Fabrication, as it was then called) was not really about people. It was about the technology. Turkel described it as "the best-equipped such space in the world," and it has since become a fundamental part of his teaching on interactive exhibits, based in the department's public history master's program.[62] Turkel's version of digital history was very maker-culture focused, with students encouraged to build physical objects that people could interact with. They learned to make, and build, and solder, and code in the service of history. His unique approach to digital history resulted in a lab with a strong emphasis on stuff and technology.

The Digital Humanities Lab (2015) at the University of Sussex adapted this tech-first approach. Historian of poverty Tim Hitchcock, one of Turkel's collaborators, had recently taken a leading role in Sussex's new digital humanities center, and the team set to work building a new "digital" space for their work.[63] The webpage for their shared lab space heavily emphasized the technology available in the room, noting the following among its long list of tech: a 7:1 Mayer sound system (audio), 4K Smart 3D LED TV (audio/video), Enttec DMX USB PRO Mk2 lighting control (lighting), Estimote Beacons Network (location sensors), and NS GoPro Hero 4 4K cameras (images/video). The space had to serve many masters, including historians, media scholars, film studies scholars, musicians, art historians, philosophers, and education and social work scholars. That meant it had to be more flexible than Turkel's Fab Lab, built exclusively for the history department. Much of the equipment in the Digital Humanities Lab was perhaps not designed for use by historians, including much of the lighting and rigging that was presumably for the principal use of the scholars researching on the "digital performance" strand of the center's research themes.

However, more interesting than the technology was the space. Fundamentally they had created a flexible room that could comfortably accommodate about thirty people, with furniture on wheels, nice access to natural light (including an outdoor patio), and a minimalist decor that left the room open to a quick mood change as needed. In a sense, they were masquerading as an advanced lab, when in fact they had created a very effective "yack," or human interaction space where people could work together.

This type of collaborative working space was pioneered in higher education by a group of physicists at North Carolina State University in 2000. The team began working with the university to experiment with a classroom layout that would promote active learning, whereby students would much more frequently be *doing* than *listening*. They came up with a model that they called SCALE-UP, short for student-centered active learning environment with upside-down pedagogies.[64] They built on the notion of the flipped classroom in which classroom time was set aside for what had traditionally

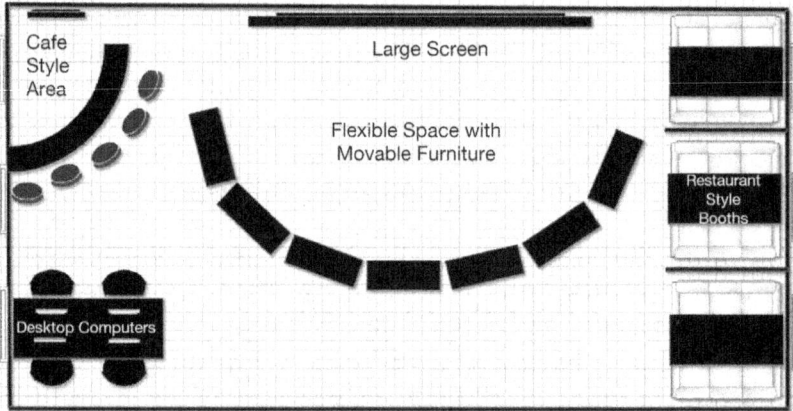

Figure 3. University College Cork flexible digital learning space 2017, floor plan (with thanks to Mike Cosgrave). (Cosgrave, [@mikecosgrave], Twitter [13 March 2017, 3:10pm], twitter.com/mikecosgrave/status/841305479192158208 [IA: 22/01/2018].)

been homework. Their new space eschewed an obvious visual focal point from which a lecturer might stand to deliver content, instead embracing small round tables scattered about the room for handfuls of students to sit together.[65] This was a deliberate challenge to the traditional "chalk and talk" arrangement, and put other students in the line of sight of each other, physically positioning their bodies to make it clear that they were there to interact with fellow students rather than the teacher.

These new SCALE-UP-style spaces were clearly about working and learning together and fostering a learning community.[66] This notion of working together was an important one in the project-centric approach of many digital history classes. Unlike the tech-heavy approach of Turkel's Fab Lab, the digital humanities team at University College Cork opted for a people-focused space when they converted a seventy-seat lecture hall into a digital learning environment, drawing on many of the principles of the SCALE-UP classroom.[67] The room included tech—namely a number of large-screen Apple desktop computer workstations and wireless device syncing—but it was also designed to encourage flexible use. Their new room included a large central space with movable furniture, a corner of the room that looked not unlike a tavern or café for a more focused discussion, a series of computer stations, a segregated digitization suite, and series of restaurant-style booths for small-group work (fig. 3).

This room privileged human interaction above human-technology interaction, and drew on the radical rethink of office spaces around the world, led in many respects by Google and the Silicon Valley giants. Google was renowned for its funky offices and attempts to build creative spaces that were regularly covered by the glossy magazine industry. Magazine writers found much to write about the quirky features of these offices, including playground-style slides and fire station poles instead of stairs.[68] This was a challenge to long-held modernist views of office design that sought to maximize the efficiency of space through the much-maligned open-plan office, which the tech world has rebranded as a space to encourage creativity and serendipitous collaboration by decorating it with some funky posters, an exotic plant or two, and beanbag chairs.[69] Funky spaces of course are not necessarily productive ones. Recent research by management strategy scholar Gemma Louise Irving suggested that social factors were key to whether or not people actually *do* use these open spaces to work together, noting that they have to *want* to and need to be working on similar areas where collaboration would benefit their work.[70] Whether these new spaces worked to boost productivity was thus still up for debate. Nevertheless, they were undeniably different.

The Google approach to office design had clearly rubbed off on digital learning spaces, which have aimed to distance themselves from the traditional classroom. Just down the road from Google, at Stanford University's Center for Spatial and Textual Analysis, by 2017 there was a clear Silicon Valley influence in their room design. The main workspace was split clearly in two, with half the room devoted to a large table covered in computer workstations, and the other set aside for what could best be described as a living room, outfitted with a beanbag chair and comfortable furniture (fig. 4). It suggested an attempt to create a space that invited both work and relaxation. It also implied that the former would be improved with a little of the latter. Fun was often built into the digital space in a way that would just feel strange in a traditional adult learning environment. This approach was not limited to California. At the Center for History and New Media in Virginia in 2008, the software developers building Omeka regularly played short bursts of Mario Kart on a Nintendo Wii video game system brought in as a means of recharging their creative energy after a long coding session. It was Silicon Valley meets ivy tower, and the more influential partner was clearly the former.

In such an unfamiliar and experimental environment, students understandably expressed concerns about how these new tech-inspired classes would impact their final grade. Risk management became a key design feature

Figure 4. Gabriel K. Wolfenstein, Center for Spatial and Textual Analysis, 2017. ("Center for Spatial and Textual Analysis," *Stanford University* [n.d.], cesta.stanford.edu. [IA: 11/03/2017].)

of many digital history classes. This included a new emphasis on developing students' soft skills. More group work in digital classes meant that students who had spent their academic careers forging ahead on the strength of their individual skills suddenly found themselves having to learn how to work together. History students had long resisted this type of collaborative activity for fear of having to carry the burden of less studious colleagues.[71] These soft skills, not traditionally part of the history curriculum, became fundamental to effective "digital" teaching, and references to it began to appear in a number of courses in the new millennium. Some educators were very proactive. Recognizing that collaborating could be taught, Jeff McClurken gave students effective strategies by encouraging them to outline a plan for working together and resolving conflicts, which they documented as part of a collaborator's contract that could be used to mediate disputes throughout the term, if needed.[72] Others, including contemporary historian Marten Düring, addressed the issue by sidestepping it, encouraging groups but allowing students to opt to work solo if they preferred.[73] In both cases, it was about managing the feeling of risk students felt in these unfamiliar "digital" classrooms.

It was clear that students faced a new way of working in the new millennium's digital history classrooms. The influence of the Silicon Valley–led "digital" age could clearly be seen as educators adopted elements from the culture of the tech start-up world in an effort to introduce their students to a new connected and content-driven way of engaging with the past where creativity, experimentation, and storytelling were king. But not for long; this creative heyday began to evolve into something all together different from circa 2010, when digital history pedagogy took another turn to take advantage of a new buzz phrase: "big data."

The Third Wave: Method without Math

The challenges of getting content online in 2000 had, within a few years, become trivial. Improvements in digital cameras and the ubiquity of smartphones among undergraduate students in many Western countries made everyone a creator. Students began to inhabit a world dominated by visual creations on social media sites such as Instagram (2010) and Snapchat (2011) as never before. They began curating their own lives, natively picking up skills of storytelling that only a few years earlier needed to be taught. The collapse of global financial markets starting in 2008 also changed priorities in the West, with indebted students increasingly looking for reassurances that their humanities degrees would help them get jobs on the outside. A number of "digital" history courses began to appear that drew on the promises of "big data" to give students yet another set of skills. These classes began to place their faith in data analysis, research methods, and research "tool" use rather than audiences and archives.

For those involved, this was not neoliberalism taking over the humanities degree; it was about the exciting potential of answering new types of research questions. Finding an existing scholarly catalyst to credit with the shift was easy enough. Literary critic Franco Moretti's phrase "distant reading," coined in 2000, was found increasingly on the lips and fingertips of "digital" scholars by the second decade of the twenty-first century.[74] The mass digitization era, short on new funding by the 2010s, had left historians with billions of pages of materials to be studied and analyzed with interdisciplinary approaches that drew on fields as diverse as linguistics, geography, and machine learning. Slowly at first, a number of courses began adopting a hybrid approach to teaching digital history. Seasoned veterans helped lead the shift, with Dan Cohen updating his Clio Wired class in 2010 class to include both public-facing history and research methods.[75]

Others dove in with both feet, adopting one of two approaches, both of which involved using software (frequently referred to as "tools") that involved analyzing data through a predefined algorithm:

- Teaching students to build tools (programming)
- Teaching students to use tools (applying software to historical data)

Using the same sample of syllabi from the appendix, one-third of courses between 2013 and 2017 took the programming approach. This was despite the fact that building software was a tall order for a student, requiring both a practical grasp of programming and the logic behind it, as well as an understanding of what a "tool" was for a historian. Despite a growing number of resources for learning to code, including the Programming Historian and Codecademy, the learning curve was still steep. Seemingly undeterred by these challenges, programming was reasonably prolific on the syllabi of the 2010s. This was evidence of a clear rejection of linguist and computer scientist Nancy Ide's claim in 2001 that programming was "no longer necessary."[76]

Where it appeared, programming tended to fill a subject-neutral space, rather than one deeply connected to history. It was treated akin to the foreign-language component—something one had to learn in order to do history better, rather than something learned in a way that was integrated with history. William Turkel's approach to programming in the classroom dropped history entirely and was offered as a digital humanities class meant to appeal across the humanities curriculum. It was so far divorced from history that the examples and exercises included building a yellow, googly-eyed smiley face that could be manipulated with code.[77] His approach involved in-class demos of each activity before sending students away to try it themselves.[78] The subject-neutral approach allowed educators to teach students with a wide range of interests, but it meant that digital history courses increasingly sat uncomfortably alongside the rest of the history curriculum.

Recognizing the difficulty of teaching students to code, a 2016 course at Umeå University in Sweden instead focused students on critiquing other people's projects and the decisions that had gone into making them in the form that they took—not all together different from the exam question set by Tim Hitchcock in 1993.[79] This kept students critically engaged and aware of the role of technology, without requiring them to master the specifics of debugging a digital project that they were expected to build themselves. Historian of religion Lincoln Mullen at George Mason University tried a much more technical approach. Mullen asked students to jump into programming whole heartedly. He ambitiously promised students that they would be familiar with "R, Javascript, Ruby, and PHP," each of which was used for different purposes ranging from data crunching to website enhancing, and each had different rules that had to be mastered, or at least fumbled through. This polyglot approach to four different programming languages was perhaps overambitious for a single semester, as it appears to have run only once. With so much to learn, this intensive programming course left little room for the students to actually consider anything historical. Yet the goal was not programming for its own sake, but programming in the service of history. To emphasize the importance of serving the historical profession, Mullen's students were required to produce a "programming tutorial that meets the submission guidelines for the *Programming Historian*."[80] While laudable, none of these was ever submitted for publication, suggesting perhaps that the students either were unable to produce work to the level required or were not sufficiently enthused by the idea to pursue it.

The second approach, using software to conduct data analysis, was more popular, appearing in just over half of the sampled courses between 2013 and 2017.[81] The preference for data analysis over programming was probably due to the more gradual learning curve needed to become adept with a piece of software, than to become competent with a completely new language and way of thinking. Introducing students to "tools" had its own challenges, especially since analyzing sources at scale was quite a distinct activity from the sort they were exposed to in other history classes. These courses included a plethora of skills that reflected the interests of the teacher and what was popular at the time. They ranged from conducting concordance analyses of texts, to topic modeling, to sentiment analysis, to digital mapping.

Conspicuously absent from these courses was mathematical training. Despite obvious parallels between "data analysis" and the statistically driven pedagogy of the 1980s, history educators in digital classrooms of the 2010s overwhelmingly had turned their back on mathematics. Even when present on syllabi, it had become almost tokenistic by the 2010s. In one of the "good" examples, mathematical training went no further than including the statistically oriented *History by Numbers* by economic historian Pat Hudson on the reading list. In another, students worked through a fairly simple session on how to use a spreadsheet to create a column graph of provided historical data.[82] Far be it from a criticism of these educators, these two were among the most rigorous uses of numerical skills I was able to find among examples of twenty-first-century digital teaching. The greatest depth evident from a syllabus was from cultural historian Matthew Friedman at Rutgers University, who included an entire week on quantitative analysis in 2017.[83] Of 127 other syllabi that I examined, none included any mention of quantitative skills training. This was a complete break from the cliometrics of the first-wave classrooms of the 1980s. The reason mathematics was so rare may have been down to a belief that students did not want to learn it, or that few digital historians were qualified to do this type of teaching, falling into the trap software developer Rebecca Koeser suggested of "trusting others to do the math" by blindly using software to calculate for you.[84]

The new "data analysis" approach to digital teaching never fully displaced the earlier audience-focused teaching. From 2013 to 2017 a hybrid approach to digital history teaching was the norm in the sampled syllabi, appearing in nearly six in ten courses inspected, meaning courses tended to include both some form of storytelling or collecting work and some form of data analysis. Despite offering unprecedented levels of choice to students, it could mean a lack of clear learning objectives. The most extreme example of student choice was perhaps historian of the Internet Ian Milligan's 2014 digital history students at the University of Waterloo in Canada; for their final project, Milligan allowed them to choose the type of digital history of greatest interest to them: produce a historical website, conduct a textual analysis, or create a tool using Python.[85] It was not unusual for a syllabus of this sort to offer digitization skills one week, programming the next, and image analysis shortly thereafter, with no common narrative to tie them together.[86] Literature scholar Andrew Goldstone warned against the pedagogical pitfalls of this "field coverage principle" of peppering students with a range of technical skills that did not appear elsewhere in the history curriculum, but which the (usually lone) digital scholar had taken on him- or herself to include in the student's learning agenda.[87] This was but one of many failed pedagogical attempts that had been recounted as bad ideas by the blogosphere. Among the others, higher education journalist Marc Parry noted that students "yawn at the field's arcane issues, like how to evaluate digital work in tenure decisions."[88] Textual scholar Ryan Cordell taught us how "not to teach digital humanities" in his 2015 keynote address, in which he warned against focusing on the "what is digital humanities?" question that seemed to have drawn so much attention in recent years.[89] The fact that there were warnings that educators should *not* teach these topics suggested that some people were attempting to do so.

The Fourth Wave: A Return to History

Despite the occasional lack of coherence in a syllabus, one of the most important things these tool-based classes provided was a bridge back to the type of historical analysis approach that had been suggested by John Styles and his colleagues back in the 1980s. It was not the same economic theory and social science statistics, but it was a return to historical research that had been absent in many digital history classrooms for two decades. With this came classes that started to look distinctly more like history courses. Historian of the nineteenth-century United States Cameron Blevins's course at Stanford University in 2012 was the first self-described "digital" course that I found to have a clear historical focus. Though the course was called the Digital Historian's Toolkit, Blevins's students spent the entire course learning the history of the U.S. West through a series of computer-enabled approaches, each of which gave the students a new way of understanding that time and place. Topics ranged from mapping to textual analysis, network analysis, and thinking about power and space. Blevins noted he hoped "by pairing traditional forms of historical analysis with cutting-edge technological tools, the class will explore how competing visions of the West played out in the mental maps of nineteenth-century Westerners and non-Westerners."[90] Moving toward a loose theme happened with greater regularity after 2012, and may be read as an indication that history students needed to be wooed with the topic that had drawn their passion. This middle way helped students wear both a historical and a digital hat at the same time, or alternatively as required.

Though still rare, a more acute history-first approach rapidly began to proliferate, and at the time of this writing has begun to push out the hybrid classes of the previous wave. In 2017, *every* new digital history course from the United Kingdom in the sample of syllabi opted for this form of teaching digital skills. Historian of humor Bob Nicholson at Edge Hill University in England integrated digital research into what he called conventional modules on the history of journalism and crime, working in a computer lab but emphasizing the historical teaching. Many of these new history-first classes had titles that looked very much at home in a history department but which incorporated a range of digital skills or assignments. Food and medical historian Lisa Smith at the University of Essex offered courses titled the Digital Recipe Book Project and Supernatural Worlds, both of which taught digital history through a thematic approach that appealed to students' interest in the past rather than their curiosity of method. Twenty-eight years after he supported Harold Short's efforts to bring computational teaching to students in King's College London's history department, historian of institutions Arthur Burns returned to digital teaching, launching a class that introduced his students to the newly digitized *Georgian Papers Archive* of materials from the Royal Collection. As his younger English colleagues had done, Burns emphasized the history of Georgian Britain, but his method was to introduce students to ways they could understand that time and place through a digitized archive. This practice extended beyond the borders of English-speaking nations. Medievalist Mathieu Caesar at the University of Geneva offered a Digital History of Religious Wars class, which taught enough digital methodology for students to interrogate the historical theme under review.[91]

The reason that educators in England in particular increasingly shifted to a history-first approach may have been linked to student demand. English and Welsh students living in what many called an "age of austerity" in the 2010s faced incredible pressure to get good grades. Degree classifications (getting a 2:i or a "first"—the equivalent of a B or above) was often projected to students as the difference between a bright future and doom, meaning they may have been unwilling to try classes that looked particularly outside of the norm.[92] This pressure began early for these English students, many of whom specialized in adolescence as they went through the General Certificate of Secondary Education (GCSE) and A-Level systems of high school that encouraged them to stick with subjects they were already doing well in.[93] Students embarking on the shorter three-year English degrees, typically consisting of only four courses per term (twenty-four total) have fewer opportunities to learn history than their Canadian counterparts who do a four-year, five-course-per-term degree (forty total). As many schools required students to take at least one course in historiography or method, a competing class in digital methods may have looked more like an additional dose of medicine than an exciting new opportunity. By digitizing the curriculum through a digital assignment or interspersing some digital readings among more traditional historiographical readings, students were able to benefit from digital history without stepping away from what made them passionate about historical studies in the first place, and the pressures put on English students may help explain why this approach became increasingly popular for educators.

This bringing digital and history back together in England also fit with the ethos of the "Digital History" seminar at the Institute of Historical Research in London, whose convenors comprised a substantial portion of those teaching digital history in the country. The seminar was aimed at research scholars: "we are looking for papers that focus on why the research has made a difference to how we understand the past, rather than a technical description of your software architecture."[94] This meshed with the needs of the United Kingdom's Research Excellence Framework, the semi-regular measuring of the quality of every scholar's research, in which books and articles were generally regarded as the key to a good score and thus funding for one's university. With careers and career progression at stake, a history-first approach to digital teaching in England appealed to students' insecurities, and to the pressures on researchers themselves to publish or perish. It is also good for history, acting as a bridge back to the parent discipline, acknowledging the need for technology to serve the study of the past, not be driven by advancement for its own sake.

Conclusion

Having in many respects come full circle in the thirty intervening years between John Styles and Roger Middleton (1987) and Bob Nicholson or Lisa Smith (2017), the classroom was still unmistakably transformed. In the process, historians had tried out an extraordinarily diverse range of ideas, few of which survived more than a couple of years without having to evolve further or be dropped all together. From a data-centric history course in the late 1980s and early '90s, to an audience-focused multimedia creation lab in the early 2000s, to an emphasis on data analysis with a curious rejection of mathematics in the 2010s, and finally a return to history with some digital approaches thrown in, this was a classroom that was ever-evolving and often shedding unwanted or failed earlier experiments in favor of something new.

This chapter is the first attempt to bring these different approaches and experiments together into a coherent timeline. Not only does it provide a chronological look at the influences exerting themselves on the curriculum over time (the rise of the Internet; the "big data" tidal wave, etc.), but also it provides historians with an accessible shopping list of what has been tried and what has been forgotten. Particularly in "digital" classrooms, historians have tended to look to the future for ideas; now they have the opportunity to look to the past as well, to produce courses that provide students with carefully selected skills and experiences, and a clear understanding of how they fit within a wider intellectual ecosystem of options.

The analysis presented here also means that we must revisit our understanding of digital teaching as described in the scholarly literature. Mills Kelly's *Teaching History in the Digital Age* remains important reading; but it must now be seen in the context of a longer narrative of innovation that stretches both before and after Kelly's own time in the classroom, and also beyond the U.S. national context in which he taught and wrote. The differences in the education systems on both sides of the Atlantic meant that educators were both responding to local and global events when designing these new courses. Being aware of what was happening abroad can only enrich classrooms around the world, and so I encourage readers to look for examples that go beyond the geographic limitations of this book.

Admittedly, historians working with technology were not the only scholars innovating in history classrooms. Booth's wonderful examples of historians thinking creatively and reflecting on practice make that plain.[95] However, the technology-inflected history classroom was one of the most obvious spaces for experimentation with the history curriculum. Over the years, it became a chance to help test everything from student-centered learning, to new skills, and even to rearranging the classroom furniture. As such, it should not be overlooked by those with oversight over programs, recruitment, and student experience who are striving to provide a better education for their cohorts of students. For historians designing courses, understanding this experimental past is crucial for making informed choices moving forward, and the examples in this chapter stand as a reminder of how historical pedagogy fits within a wider scholarship of learning and teaching that includes psychologists and educational theorists which should not be forgotten. Students too should have an understanding of how their own education may have been very different had they studied elsewhere. This provides an easy guide for understanding where one's own education or skill set may need further development, or perhaps where one was subject to an experiment gone wrong.

It is probably fair to call many of these digital history classes a reaction against perceived gaps in teaching provision. Yet, despite their good intentions, they were not all offering coherent learning experiences. For every comprehensive course that built week-upon-week, there was one that sought to offer students everything they were not getting elsewhere. The result may have better served the agenda of the scholar than of the student, with "digital" at times becoming a catchall for things that someone felt should be in the curriculum, but were not. Of course, even those who suffered through a *bad* digital experience could consider themselves privileged. Few scholars ever had the chance to take a class in computational or digital history. For most who were interested, it was a matter of struggling along in the self-learning market and all of the frustrations that came with it. Luckily, there were many historians working to make that a more welcoming space.

4

Building the Invisible College

In 1971 the thirty-year-old historian of medicine Edward Shorter of the University of Toronto published *The Historian and the Computer: A Practical Guide*, noting that "nothing exists at present for the historian who wants to use a computer but has not the slightest idea how to proceed." The book took the reader step by step through the process of designing, implementing, and interpreting the results of a quantitative historical study that took advantage of the IBM mainframe computers of the day. Shorter demystified what computers were and could do, and was the first to put it all in the context of the historical profession. Like many after him, he also encouraged the development and application of soft skills, if only for manipulating junior colleagues: "a winning smile will persuade some lounging graduate student to abandon his Coke bottle long enough to demonstrate how all this is done." The back cover described the book as one derived from "the author's own trial-and-error experience."[1] Shorter was not alone as a self-taught computational scholar.

Self-learning resources that aimed to teach computing and technological skills filled an important continuing professional development niche for the historical profession, as few historians had access to formal training in these nontraditional skills. Even decades after Shorter published his guide, a 2011–12 survey of four-year U.S. colleges showed that only 15 percent offered a seminar on digital methods, dropping to only 9 percent in institutions classified as primarily undergraduate.[2] Given that those figures represented digital humanities more broadly, access to more specific history provision must have been considerably scarcer.

Representative of this need to self-teach was Zoe LeBlanc, then a Canadian PhD student studying African history in the United States, who took to Twitter on the day I finished the first draft of this chapter, seeking advice and reassurance from the digital crowd: "can a lowly grad student like me learn all the skills/methods/disciplines that are required for #dhist [digital history] research?" Over the course of the next hour, she tweeted passionately about the challenges she faced while trying to teach herself topics as diverse as computer vision, textual analysis, statistics, and data visualization, all while needing to demonstrate her prowess as a budding twentieth-century historian. The added pressure of recognizing that "my committee doesn't count this work until it's in a neat little narrative w/ bow on top" made her start "to feel like I'm doing more than 1 dissertation." Yet she was aware that there were scholars out there who had been able to bring together these disparate skill sets, which had apparently left her feeling inadequate: "what I really want to know is how all of you #DH/#dhist [digital humanities/digital history] ppl do it???"[3] LeBlanc was not alone in her struggles to self-teach digital skills. Many others who were facing similar challenges were also junior colleagues trying to navigate this interdisciplinary world while concurrently honing more traditional historical skills. Most stumbled along without clear support structures that could make the journey easier.[4] Shorter and LeBlanc represent two bookends in the search for a path into the world of computing and history, in a narrative that overlapped considerably with the needs of those seeking to teach themselves quantitative skills in the 1970s, '80s, and '90s.[5]

By looking in turn at the ways historians self-taught statistics, software, and programming skills, this chapter considers the options scholars faced when confronted with the two challenges of self-teaching: what to learn, and how to learn it. If technologically adept historians were to play a role as the vanguard of early adoption on behalf of the historical professions, they needed somewhere to hone their skills. As I outline in this chapter, there were many avenues for this self-teaching, which were available through what has been called by many the invisible college—an informal network of support that steps in where the university has fallen short.

While the advice available from the invisible college proliferated, the lack of a coherent sense of what technologically driven history sought to do and the lack of expertise within many history departments hindered decision making by would-be learners who were unable to build an understanding of the field through the piecemeal offering of skills. The problem was made worse by a lack of a coherent vocabulary for articulating what they really needed to learn for their own scholarly goals. Second, and related, as the skills on offer became increasingly ephemeral, so too did the learning resources, too often resulting in quick learning solutions rather than deep understanding, to the detriment of the field and its potential for impact on the research landscape in particular.

Teaching One Another Mathematics

While economic historian Allan Bogue estimated that 40 percent of history graduate programs in the early 1980s offered quantitative training—the "digital" skills of the day—he highlighted the fact that a majority of would-be learners were on their own or facing inadequate or superficial teaching.[6] U.S. historian of race politics J. Kousser, who was entirely dissatisfied with the provision of statistical training on offer, claimed that a majority of historians in the Social Science History Association in 1987 had "learned their statistics largely or wholly through self-study," with only a fifth having had formal training at university.[7] While some were able to turn to teaching provision in other departments, many had to look for self-taught opportunities. According to research by political historian John Reynolds, the peak of quantitative publishing among historians came in 1985.[8] To be publishing at that level, one might infer that they had learned their skills at least five years earlier, if not more, suggesting that the mechanisms for self-teaching must have been in place by the late 1970s.

They were. A number of statistical textbooks by historians for historians began to appear in the late twentieth century to meet this rising demand (table 5).[9] It was perhaps the first time that a substantial new interdisciplinary skill—in this case, mathematics—was being translated at scale specifically

Table 5. Select textbooks published to teach statistics to historians.

Author(s)	Title	Date	Editions to Date
C. M. Dollar & R. J. Jensen	*Historian's Guide to Statistics*	1971	2
Roderick Floud	*An Introduction to Quantitative Methods for Historians*	1973	14
Lauren Haskins & Kirk Jeffrey	*Understanding Quantitative History*	1990	4
Konrad Jarausch & Kenneth Hardy	*Quantitative Methods for Historians*	1991	1
Robert Darcy & Richard C. Rohrs	*A Guide to Quantitative History*	1995	1
Pat Hudson	*History by Numbers*	2000	3
Charles Feinstein & Mark Thomas	*Making History Count*	2002	3

for historians. While the later "digital" history may not have been the direct descendent of the quantitative historians, they do owe the group a substantial debt when it comes to laying the foundation for self-learning resources through the models established in statistical textbooks aimed at historians.

Despite all aiming to instill their readers with a foundation in statistics, not all of these books took the same pedagogical approach. The table of contents in Feinstein and Thomas's 2002 *Making History Count* resembles a pure statistics textbook. Despite many historical examples throughout, on the surface there was almost nothing to suggest a historian was the target market, apart from the case study titles in chapters 14 and 15. Even the sheer heft of the 547-page tome made it clear that this was a reference work, and not one meant to be read cover to cover.

> Table of contents for C. Feinstein and M. Thomas, *Making History Count* (2002)
> 1. Introduction
> 2. Descriptive statistics
> 3. Correlation
> 4. Simple linear regression
> 5. Standard errors and confidence intervals
> 6. Hypothesis testing
> 7. Non-parametric tests
> 8. Multiple relationships
> 9. The classical linear regression model
> 10. Dummy variables and lagged values
> 11. Violating the assumptions of the classical linear regression model
> 12. Non-linear models and functional forms
> 13. Logit, probit, and tobit models
> 14. Case Studies 1 and 2: unemployment in Britain and emigration from Ireland
> 15. Case Studies 3 and 4: the Old Poor Law in England and leaving home in the United States, 1850–1860.[10]

Three decades earlier, economic historian Roderick Floud took a different approach, structuring his book as a journey from historian to quantitative historian. Instead of beginning with mathematics, he began where historians were already familiar, helping them to consider their sources as data. To this, subsequent chapters carefully added quantitative layers, focusing on the types of statistical tests most commonly relevant to historians, thinking about distributions, change over time, and relationships between historical entities.

Table of contents for R. Floud, *An Introduction to Quantitative Methods for Historians* (1973)

1. Classifying historical data
2. Arranging historical data
3. Some simple mathematics
4. The preliminary analysis of data, I: frequency distribution and charts
5. The preliminary analysis of data, II: summary measures
6. The analysis of time series
7. Relationships between variables
8. The problem of imperfect data
9. Calculators, computers and historical data.[11]

New volumes continued to appear aimed at historians and humanists. These books did not seek to make statisticians of historians; instead, most sought to provide a structured learning experience for historians looking for an accessible way into statistical principles. What made them distinct from generic texts on statistical learning was the history-specific content, allowing the reader and the author to communicate in the shared language of the historian, acknowledging some of the unique pitfalls of working with historical records which may not have warranted mention in a generic statistics book. For example, economic historian Pat Hudson warned that historians needed to be aware of applying mathematical economic models to times and places in which they were inappropriate. A model that was built to describe the way a free-market economy functioned would not be appropriate to gauge the economy of a society based on serfdom.[12] For a non-historian, this type of advice would seem superfluous, but it was a vital warning for scholars of the past.

By adopting the printed book as the mechanism for transmitting this self-learning, these statistics textbooks took advantage of a thousand years of technology that encouraged a clearly considered structure to the learning experience. The act of turning the page imposed a linear method of learning that was controlled by the author, and could be quality controlled by editors and peer reviewers during the production phase. Many of the resources that would become fundamental to the self-learning ecosystem had been designed as supplementary textbooks to be used to support in-class learning. The tendency of the academic book market to pair these types of texts with in-class teaching provided an incentive for authors to apply pedagogical principles of learning. The distinction between what was meant for self-learning and what was a part of the curriculum was thus always blurred. Floud's book read like a work meant to accompany a series of weekly in-class activities, and its fourteen editions suggest it may well have been used thus in many classrooms around the world.

Some historians did manage to learn through these types of resource. Edward Ayers claimed to have taught himself multiple regression in order to conduct his quantitative history of crime in the U.S. South.[13] However, not everyone found it so easy to learn statistics in depth. While a great strength, the printed nature of the stats textbook was also its greatest pedagogical weakness. While these texts offered a valuable starting point for historians, it was unclear where authors thought their readers should next turn in order to progress to intermediate levels. As introductory texts, readers could only scratch the surface, and the statistical sciences were fraught with many dangers and wrong turns for the ill-informed. While tests would return a result when presented with data, the wrong test used in subtly wrong ways would not return a meaningful or defensible one. If qualified statistically trained peer reviewers did not review this poor research, it also risked making its way into the published literature and wrongly influencing historical debates. Statistics was procedural but also required deep understanding to be done responsibly.

This problem only became exacerbated in the twenty-first century, when digital "tools" became more common, leading software developer Rebecca Sutton Koeser to accuse historians of uncritically "trusting others to do the math," and leading the British Academy in 2012 to fund mathematical training for humanities scholars they felt were being held back by a lack of skills.[14] In light of this, medievalist Robert Sinkewicz warned in 1989 that scholars would be wise to seek out "local experts" in "Economics and Social Sciences departments" if seeking to do anything beyond basic calculations.[15] This was wise advice, but it complicated the notion of self-teaching. Unless such a colleague or local expert was on hand, there was no obvious way for students to ask if their data met the criteria for a regression analysis, for example, or which test would be most appropriate for their needs. The problem was that these books lacked a dynamic feedback loop that was prohibitive for learners beyond what could be offered through examples and solution sets. The environment was thus one in which self-learning could only take a typical historian so far before collaboration, mentorship, or structured learning became key.

Keeping a Critical Eye on New Opportunities

Statistical textbooks aimed at historians could not fulfill all of the field's needs, because quantitative skills were not the only ones relevant to computing and history that suffered from under-provision in the formal curriculum. In the

1970s and '80s, the microcomputer revolution transformed the digital world when off-the-shelf software rose to prominence.[16] As these new desktop machines for a mass-market slowly replaced the punch-card-eating mainframe computers, new opportunities arose. With the advent of computer monitors, the mouse, and keyboard, programmers began designing software for new types of uses, and historians took notice. A range of products began to appear that were potentially of use to historians: spreadsheets, databases, and statistical programs, to name a few. While statistical principles generally proved enduring, this new software was supremely ephemeral. The approach needed to create self-teaching resources about software was unique, and thus the didactic textbook style used in statistical learning was rarely applied, in part because it was unnecessary. Software was traditionally disseminated with a user manual that gave details on where to click or what to type. The instructions were not designed for historians but for users more generally, and perhaps they sufficed to fill that market in most cases. Instead, energy went into helping historians decide if a piece of software was right for their needs, either by demonstrating how software had been used in a particular project, or through a critical review of one's options.

As early as the 1970s, historians were already writing about how they used software with their work, and what they thought of various packages that were available. In 1973, Roderick Floud evaluated a number of packages, singling out SPSS (Statistical Package for the Social Sciences—a popular statistics program), TSP for time series calculations, and COCOA for concordance and text processing, as worthy of the historian's attention.[17] Software was so vital in the fifty-six essays of the 1987 *History and Computing* edited by British historians Peter Denley and Deian Hopkin that the book included a dedicated index, allowing readers to quickly jump to chapters that focused on their favorite program, to learn of examples of how a historian had used it in their work. From the long list of options, I only recognize a handful of programs as I read in 2020 (the programming languages FORTRAN and C, the statistical package SPSS, the operating system Unix, the design modeling principles of computer-aided design, or CAD, as well as a method of finding homonyms, known as Soundex). The remaining have proved more ephemeral, including Clare's Betabase (a database package), Modok (for documentation) and Palestine 1947 (a simulation of the Israeli-Palestine conflict), all of which have been relegated to obscurity.[18] This only highlights the unique nature of the challenge facing historians using technology, as the shelf life of a digital skill was far shorter than those at the core of the discipline, including statistics, paleography, and close reading. Denley and Hopkin's volume may not have withstood the test of time, but its publication showed that there was a need for printed means of sharing advice about software use, as well as showing examples of how it had been employed.

These contributions acted as vital bridges between the new software and the needs of scholars. This was important as historians attempted to shoehorn generic programs to their specific needs. With few exceptions, software developers did not write for historians in the 1970s through the '90s. More often, if developers paid attention to historians at all, it was to point out how the software they already produced could be useful for scholarly work. This was the case for Superfile, a database program that appeared as a full-page magazine-style advertisement in Denley and Hopkin's 1987 *History and Computing*.[19] With the historical market as yet so tiny, historians found ways to fit their work into the software that was available, relying on colleagues writing about best practices to teach them what was out there and what it could be used for.

Leading by example as in the chapters of Denley and Hopkin's volume, was one way of helping scholars facing a bewildering array of software options from competing companies operating in the same market. However, as software required an investment of both time and money, it was important to get it right, and others took a more structured approach to giving scholars the tools with which to navigate the choices and make good decisions. Frameworks for evaluating the merits of a given program appeared. Among these was educational technologist Derek Blease's 1986 *Evaluating Educational Software*, which encouraged his readers to ask themselves whether adopting a particular program for a task would in fact make the process more efficient.[20] By asking readers to consider the role software played in their scholarly practice, he encouraged them to seek solutions to problems they actually faced. This was important because most packages simply provided a new option for performing an old process, and one needed to make sure the excitement of a digital alternative did not preempt level-headed decision making.

The introduction of "word processors" was a good example of the open but critical approach many took to software as well as the ways they sought to share this new technology with colleagues. As interest in word processors rose throughout the 1980s they became more difficult to ignore. They had both their early adopters and their critics. Tim Hitchcock was in the former category, claiming to have written the first "born digital" history DPhil thesis at Oxford in 1984.[21] In 1987 archaeologist and linguist Sebastian Rahtz published a chapter on word processing, which he believed was poised to revolutionize the study of texts, and which he implored educators to include as a vital part of the formal curriculum.[22] In 1989, lexicographer Ian Lancashire and information scientist Susan Hockey offered a workshop on it for humanities computing scholars attending a conference in Toronto, so that the experts in the field could gain exposure to the tool everyone was talking about.[23] And in 1991, historian of business Janice Reiff wrote of the excitement buzzing between scholars looking forward to the first graphical user interface for the word-processing software WordPerfect.[24] However, not everyone was enamored by what would become one of the staples of the historian's toolkit. In 1989, typographer Allison Black delivered a paper warning that while "desktop publishing has a lot to offer . . . we should not be so dazzled by its superficial merits as to forget its limitations and to abandon more traditional methods of document design."[25]

Thirty years later, what those "traditional methods" were, I suspect few people remember, and certainly fewer historians would question the merits of word processors for document design. They changed the way historians practiced their craft, leading to the gradual dismissal of typists who converted senior scholars' notes into manuscripts.[26] They would alter the way historians wrote, allowing for endless tinkering, cutting and pasting, and as science and technology specialist Sherry Turkle noted, gave writers "the ability to quickly fill the page, to see it before you think it."[27] Despite her enthusiasm for word processing, Reiff noted that it had quite quickly changed peer review, allowing for more demands for revision than in the recent past.[28] It then promptly faded into ubiquity, becoming so pervasive that we no longer noticed its hold. Before this ubiquity, critical reflections and hesitation by scholars such as Black provided the context for proceeding with caution toward the digital option. Many of the self-teaching guides that appeared helped readers make sense of the ways that word processing differed from typewriters, which were the presumed system that everyone already knew at the time. For example, in 1993 international historian Evan Mawdsley and early modern Danish historian Thomas Munck warned readers that the "CARRIAGE RETURN key should never be used except where a new line is indispensable (as for a paragraph): the computer will determine its own line-breaks."[29] An automated process had replaced the ding of the typewriter's bell at the line end, and scholars needed the means for learning about that change.

The critical conversations about digital technologies also found their way into the subject specific history journals of the 1980s and '90s, some of which devoted considerable space to the new skills and software packages they felt were relevant to their readers. One of the early adopters was the journal *Social History*, which ran an intermittent "noticeboard" in the 1980s to share ideas

Table 6. Technologies reviewed by *Economic History Review*, by year.

Year of Review	Technology	Reviewer(s)
1990	Spreadsheets	Roger Middleton, Peter Wardley
1991	Database management systems	Jean Colson, Roger Middleton, Peter Wardley
1992	Computer assisted learning (CAL) packages	David Dunn, Roger Middleton, Peter Wardley
1993	Statistical packages	Roger Middleton, Peter Wardley
1994	Textual retrieval and analysis software	Roger Middleton
1995	None reviewed (shortened entry)	James E. Everett
1996	Internet	James E. Everett
1997	Digitization	James E. Everett

Sources: Middleton and Wardley, "Annual Review of Information Technology Developments for Economic and Social Historians, 1990"; Colson, Middleton, and Wardley, "Annual Review of Information Technology Developments for Economic and Social Historians, 1991"; Dunn, Middleton, and Wardley, "Annual Review of Information Technology Developments for Economic and Social Historians, 1992"; Middleton and Wardley, "Annual Review of Information Technology Developments for Economic and Social Historians, 1993"; Middleton, "Annual Review of Information Technology Developments for Economic and Social Historians, 1994"; Everett, "Annual Review of Information Technology Developments for Economic and Social Historians, 1995"; Everett, "Annual Review of Information Technology Developments for Economic and Social Historians, 1996"; Everett, "Annual Review of Information Technology Developments for Economic and Social Historians, 1997."

and information related to the use of computerized analysis of data.[30] The noticeboard inspired colleagues at the *Economic History Review* to conduct an extended annual review of information technology deemed important to the field, which ran from 1990 to 1997. Each year focused on what the reviewers felt was the technology of the year from the perspective of economic historians. The reviews provided an effective glimpse into the progression of relevant software over time, covering spread sheets, databases, and statistical software packages, before moving into more conceptual categories, including the Internet and digitization. The topics give insight into the type of work these scholars engaged in with their computers over time (table 6).

The treatment of each review was impressively extensive, particularly during the years that economic historian Roger Middleton was involved when they ran at article length. Each typically included a discussion of competing software related to the annual theme, a tabular product feature comparison, and a critical analysis of the role the technology could play in the workflow of the historian. For economic historians, these reviews provided a worthwhile annual glance at what was important, allowing them to decide if it was worth investing in the skills needed to adopt the technology as part of their practice.

A Procedural Shift

While quite obviously distinct from the didactic statistics textbooks, perhaps most ironic about the self-learning resources available to historians seeking to become users of software was the degree to which they very rarely actually taught historians how to use software. Instead, they offered inspiration for what might be done and encouraged historians to be critical consumers. The fast pace of change was undoubtedly partly to blame for that, though it did not stop some people from trying. The newly established *Journal of the Association of History and Computing* (1998–2010) toyed with a more practical approach just as the *Economic History Review* phased out its annual critical roundup, and was an important review space for various pieces of software, techniques, and methods. As historian of the twentieth century Scott Merriman noted, at early editorial board meetings, the journal considered making it a space for "hands-on" articles such as discussions of "how to do history and computing."[31]

The digital skills of the new millennium were appearing in the age of the Internet, of blogging, and of social media, all of which brought fundamental changes to the publishing industry, and by virtue of association, to the self-teaching resources. The barrier to entry for publishing had been lowered, and no longer was a full-length textbook the only form a self-learning resource could reasonably take. The blogosphere thus quickly became a space full of advice for the novice, sidestepping the official historical journals and supplementing what had been printed on paper in earlier decades. The challenge for self-learners became navigating it and finding answers that were appropriate to one's needs. Advice was often contradictory, and rarely presented with enough context for a newcomer to understand if it was guidance appropriate for them.

A long-running debate about the value of computer programming for historians was a good example of the labyrinth of advice scholars had to navigate. The question of *to code or not to code* for historians had been brewing since the 1970s, with scholars falling on all conceivable sides of the argument. The debate would culminate in 2014 in the "hack versus yack" conversations, given a chronology and context by literature and libraries scholar Bethany Nowviskie, who dismissed it as a tongue-in-cheek catchphrase that went viral, but which drove a wedge between those who hacked (built things with their computers) and those who yacked (wrote scholarship, presented at conferences).[32]

While the debate was usually framed as whether or not to code, behind it was a more important question: did historians need to learn how to make their own tools, or was off-the-shelf software sufficient? In 1971, Edward Shorter was convinced that only a handful of historians would be able to learn programming.[33] Roderick Floud did not question the historians' ability, but in the 1970s he felt that coding was unnecessary in most cases, highlighting only the need to write "special purpose programs" to clean and structure textual data as a pre-processing stage of the workflow.[34] By 2001, computer scientist Nancy Ide suggested that programming was "no longer necessary to provide the kind of methodological and conceptual framework in which to conceive and carry out computer-assisted work."[35] Despite her belief, a few years later there were seemingly more historians writing code than ever before. In 2008, William J. Turkel offered a retort to Ide, suggesting that "if you don't program, your research process will always be at the mercy of those who do."[36] Three years later, medievalist Fred Gibbs admitted he "remained on the fence for some time" over the issue, revising his digital history syllabus repeatedly as he wrestled with the importance of coding for historians.[37] Others suggested that, while programming was useful, it should not be taught at the expense of more important things. For example, in 2012 information scientist Simon Mahony and Italian studies scholar Elena Pierazzo asserted that it was less vital than research methodology training.[38] Meanwhile, in the same volume, philosopher Geoffrey Rockwell and French literature scholar Stéfan Sinclair noted that as "job ads are often articulated in terms of competencies," tangible skills should not be overlooked.[39] Finally, information specialist Miriam Posner suggested that learning to code was gendered in Western culture, and that men were both more likely to do it and also to have access to the learning opportunities that allowed it.[40]

These views were an excellent window into the value of programming for the type of work these scholars did, in the place and time that they operated, but with a few exceptions are probably best understood as advice intended for immediate consumption. Shorter was writing in an era in which most historians "thought a computer was somebody who kept score at baseball games."[41] Ide was working at a time when commercially available software was on the rise, which gave historians many new tools not yet fully exploited. Turkel was responding to the post-digitization era in which historians were newly presented with billions of words of (often messy) machine-readable text and few tools at the ready with which to clean it up. Mahony and Pierazzo both worked in research-intensive English universities where PhD students were expected to do nothing but produce original research under a tight timeframe typically lasting no more than four years. Anything done in addition to research thus risked the quality of the thesis, and their view of what was important reflected that system.

This debate highlights the difficulty facing those seeking to learn. The arguments these scholars made for or against programming were rarely put into the context of the conditions under which they operated—both in terms of the time they were writing, and the type of work they did. This was the proverbial eternal present rearing its head in which scholars were only concerned about what was most useful *right now,* assuming it would also be relevant tomorrow and into the future. Advice was plentiful in the invisible college, but context was thin for those without institutional support. The debate also failed to address the underlying aptitudes behind coding: algorithmic thinking, or the ability to break a task down into discrete steps that could be followed by either a computer or a human. One might even call it project planning. Concern about this practical emphasis had been around since the 1980s. In 1987 Ewa Swenson feared this overly procedural approach overlooked the more pedagogically sound option, which was to ensure that people knew "how to recognize problems, identify and characterize them, understand their nature. And then to determine which tool may be appropriate for the problem."[42] Such language was unusual in the new millennium, but to be fair, one had to recognize the bombardment of practical coding guides that were undoubtedly influencing the way historians approached the self-teaching market.

Self-teaching in technology is a major industry, becoming increasingly important in the late 1990s and early 2000s. Major technical publishers ranging from the "For Dummies" series to O'Reilly Media filled bookstores, publishing hundreds of programming and Web development introductions targeted at would-be technology professionals.[43] These mass-market solutions were not invisible to those writing for a historical audience. Nor did they long remain restricted by the limits of the physical page. The rise of the Internet in the 1990s meant that learning resources increasingly shifted online, many offered for free. One of the key changes as a result of this online shift was the introduction of a dynamic feedback loop, which made it possible to test comprehension dynamically. The W3Schools website had been offering tutorials on the technologies of the Web since 1998. By 2002, the site also offered an interactive option under the banner of a "Try it Yourself" window in which code could be tried and the results visualized immediately, changing the experience into one of tutorial-based learning.[44] This added a feedback loop that was not as readily available for the statistical self-learners of the 1970s and '80s, and it offered a trial-and-error alternative or addition to written instructions alone.[45]

The W3Schools interactive learning platform was taken to new levels in 2011 by Codecademy, a website that similarly taught computer programming skills openly and for free.[46] Codecademy's setup allowed the learner to try a new concept in a virtual environment that would both let them see the outputs of their coding efforts, and also prevent them from moving on to new concepts until they had completed the task correctly. KhanAcademy offered a similar learning experience for those seeking to learn mathematics. Both Codecademy and KhanAcademy used virtual badges, scores, and point systems to gamify the learning experience and encourage progression for those who found such rewards enticing. These and other online open learning environments taught countless people the syntax of various programming and encoding languages, as well as basic statistics, if not a deep understanding of core principles. Despite its weaknesses the dynamism of these sites had corrected one of the core weaknesses of the static statistical textbooks of earlier decades.

However, the improvements had their limits. The skills on offer were only those for which there was a mass market, cutting out historian-specific skills, or even those developed within adjacent fields such as humanities computing and linguistics. Yet, they were an improvement in the sense that they expanded the proverbial bookshelf open to self-learners, and in many cases were a pedagogical improvement on the textbooks of yore for the reasons outlined above. Nevertheless, those textbooks maintained one significant advantage over new digital skills: the stability of vocabulary. The book format worked for statistical learning because, while the software a historian used to conduct a statistical regression analysis may have evolved somewhat, the need to understand what a regression analysis was and when to employ it had not. Perhaps most importantly, the language of mathematics remained relatively stable. A scholar of 1980 could discuss statistics with a scholar of 2010, because though the field had evolved it had not adopted a new language to discuss old concepts. The same was not necessarily true of other computational skills. Both software and programming languages made longitudinal conversations problematic. The half-life of software was substantially shorter than that of core statistical principles, and the same was true of programming languages. The new digital skills were endlessly evolving, as was the vocabulary used to describe it. New major programming and coding languages appeared at least once a decade, from FORTRAN in the 1950s, to BASIC in the 1960s, C in the 1970s, C++ in the 1980s, Python and R in the 1990s, as well as the languages of the Web: HTML, CSS, JavaScript, and PHP. Unlike the universal language of mathematics, computing had a rapidly evolving vocabulary. JavaScript's "arrays" functioned in much the same way as Python's "lists," and it was up to the scholar to learn and understand that. The shifting vocabularies across languages and programs made it difficult for a learner to achieve and retain long-term mastery without constantly engaging in new learning. A historian who learned Python in the 1990s may have had substantially similar skills to a historian who learned FORTRAN in the 1950s, but they may not have had the vocabulary to converse meaningfully with one another. This common language, and the traditional publishing format taken by those seeking to teach statistics made it unique among the self-taught skills of the digital era.

This kept digital historical work under constant threat of obsolescence. This was not a new problem, but was instead one being rediscovered in the 1990s. As noted in the opening of this chapter, Edward Shorter's 1971 *The Historian and the Computer* was eminently practical, almost to the point of hand-holding. Nearly fifty years later it is amusingly outdated, and yet the publisher included it in its "Books That Live" series, which meant "in the publisher's estimation it is a book not for a single season but for the years."[47] Step-by-step instructions proved troubling wherever they appeared. One of the key examples was economic historians M. J. Lewis and Roger Lloyd-Jones's *Using Computers in History: A Practical Guide*, published in 1996, which offered procedural instructions for using Microsoft Excel spreadsheets, making graphs and constructing databases.[48] The book made liberal use of screenshots, shifting the work into a much more ephemeral category than the statistical textbooks that preceded it. This was increasingly about where to click, rather than a means to developing high-level skills, leaving the learner at the mercy of the software's developers who might update the user interface at any moment, rendering the screenshots obsolete. This sustainability problem was one that would continue to haunt digital history self-learning resources well into the 2010s. Some projects managed to sidestep the sustainability problem by pretending to offer nothing more than an immediate solution. The private-public collaborative MarcoPolo Internet Content for Your Classroom website provided practical advice for busy U.S. primary and high school teachers looking for tangible ways to help their students take advantage of the Internet in the early new millennium. President Bill Clinton lauded the project for providing "unprecedented access to the kind of world-class educational materials that in the past only the wealthiest school districts could afford."[49] Advertised via an ephemeral magazine distributed to teachers, its defunct search engine and website are now forgotten, but its approach was perhaps the right one in such a fast-changing environment. The practical approach only grew in popularity in the new millennium as scholars began to talk about "new methods" and "new tools" with which they could analyze the mountain of newly digitized sources.

One of the most influential self-learning guides aimed at historians too suffered from sustainability issues despite being the most commonly used textbook on digital history syllabi more than ten years after it had begun to show its age. In 2005, Dan Cohen and Roy Rosenzweig published *Digital History: A Guide to Gathering, Preserving, and Presenting the Past on the Web*. Unlike the "For Dummies" books, it was clearly aimed at historians seeking to understand the Web's potential for their work, rather than industry professionals who needed to learn minimum standards. The book took a procedural bent, without explicitly being a tutorial or manual. While practical, *Digital History* was more in the vein of the advice venues described above than the *how-to* offerings available for technical learners. It was published in a print edition but also made available openly online. Despite being online, it has never been updated, and has become rather dated, providing a snapshot of what putting material on the Web required in the early 2000s. It was not the first book to appear online, but it did help pave the way for other digital history works to adopt a similar open model. In the next decade, almost no digital history learning resources would be printed on paper, opting instead for the flexibility of the Web. *Digital History* proved hugely influential and was perhaps most significant for its role inspiring others to adopt the genre of technical writing for historians in the post-digitization era of the early new millennium.

One of the most significant of those to take up the torch was computational historian William J. Turkel, who started a blog called *Digital History Hacks* (2005–8) a few months after Cohen and Rosenzweig had published their book. In his opening post, Turkel noted that while *Digital History* had provided an excellent resource for those looking to learn how to present history online, there "seem to be far fewer resources for historians who want to create tools for doing historical research."[50] Turkel devoted his blog to this pursuit, citing the influence of the O'Reilly Publishing introductory "hacks" intro textbooks as his model.[51] His posts focused on the research needs of historians, and in particular addressed some of the challenges faced by scholars working in the early years of the new millennium who were working with digital collections (in many cases for the first time).

Turkel was one of the first historians to really take on the challenge of the new mass-digitized archives of the early twenty-first century. As discussed in chapter 2, these digital archives would revolutionize access to primary sources, but the most common user interface was a search box that would lead readers to a single-page image that could be close read but not easily computationally analyzed. For those just looking to find a few interesting and relevant sources with a simple keyword search, the new digital archives were a blessing. However, with a background in language analysis, Turkel was more interested in analyzing than in reading texts. He was thus motivated to find a way to reverse engineer the digital archives, to help scholars bring the sources to their own machine, where they could be close read, remixed, changed, marked up, or analyzed in any way they desired.

He and a growing number of textual scholars began looking for ways to access those texts that had been trapped in databases. Turkel wrote posts about "scraping" and "spidering" the Web (the process of using code to download targeted Web pages automatically), which sought to empower scholars to create methods to address aspects of the research workflow that were not already facilitated by ready-made software. This gap was caused by the fact that those needs were too niche for commercial developers to take notice; for example, the need to sidestep the limits imposed either directly or accidentally by publishers who had built digital archives in the mass-digitization era. Though it managed to fly largely under the radar, this "scraping" of the Web was controversial because it challenged the business model of commercial publishers, who had invested heavily in transcribing these sources so that they could be keyword searched. The publishers relied on continued library subscriptions to their collections to pay the bills. If scholars could download and share the texts among themselves, the business model could come under threat.

Turkel's posts also included lessons on humanistic fabrication (prototyping, building, making), as well as a series he called "Easy Pieces in Python."[52] Two years later, the "Easy Pieces" series had evolved into the *Programming Historian*, focusing heavily on the Python programming language.[53] Not surprisingly, the *Programming Historian* diverged from Cohen's *Digital History* in its emphasis on programming and working to extract content from the Web, rather than putting it up online. In only four years between the publications of these two works, these substantial shifts in constructing and deconstructing the Web highlighted the extent to which digital history learning was always reacting to the very immediate technical hurdles of the day.

Though much of the *Programming Historian* published by Turkel was about learning to code, it was different from projects such as Codecademy and W3Schools, because it considered how technology could be useful to historians, rather than how to use technology for its own sake. Digital archaeologist Shawn Graham noted that it was "not a computer science course: it is instead a series of hands-on examples, focused on the what and how" that made it uniquely useful for historians seeking self-learning initiatives.[54] Turkel described it using a cooking metaphor:

> Think of it like learning how to cook. . . . Learning how to program is like learning to cook . . . it can be a very gradual process. One day you're sitting there eating your macaroni and cheese and you decide to liven it up with a bit of Tabasco, Dijon mustard or Worcestershire sauce. Bingo! Soon you're putting grated cheddar in, too. You discover that the ingredients that you bought for one dish can be remixed to make another. You begin to linger in the spice aisle at the grocery store. People start buying you cookware. You get to the point where you're willing and able to experiment with recipes. Although few people become master chefs, many learn to cook well enough to meet their own needs.[55]

Despite being disseminated online, originally the *Programming Historian* was a fairly traditional self-published volume with a clear linear learning progression not unlike the statistical textbooks that came before it. Its tutorial case studies relied on the pages of the Canadiana.org website, which were unfortunately updated shortly after the release of the project, breaking many of the examples. In an effort to increase the sustainability, a team was brought in to grow the *Programming Historian*, which was opened to contributions by others in 2012 and the examples in the existing lessons refocused on the Old Bailey Online.[56] The team hoped the Old Bailey Online would prove more stable than Canadiana, in part because its funding had run out and thus they had no impetus to make further updates. While the efforts to improve sustainability have continued to prove more difficult for the *Programming Historian* team than the authors of the statistics textbooks, the project did manage to bring some innovations to the self-learning market for historians.

The new version of the project adopted the peer review systems of traditional academic publishing, initiating a new genre of digital history pedagogic writing that kept cultures of quality control in mind. Between its launch in 2012 and the end of 2017, the project published sixty-seven English-language tutorials from contributors across the digital scholarly world, making it a platform for sharing method. The original idea for the new version was to encourage contributors to branch off from existing lessons, maintaining a treelike structure if not a perfectly linear model.[57] However, the idea was quickly dropped when new proposals arrived that did not fit clearly with existing lessons but which were judged to be obviously valuable to historians. While a large proportion of early lessons focused on data manipulation and Web scraping, as the project progressed, these new ideas resulted in lessons on linked data, network analysis, and augmented reality. This represented an evolution that was not entirely divorced from the vein in which Turkel created the project, focusing on the process of acquiring and structuring rather than analyzing information. Notably absent in the Programming Historian tutorials were skills that could obviously and directly lead to research findings through computational analysis. Of the sixty-seven English-language tutorials published to the end of 2017, only seven met this criterion:

- Shawn Graham, Scott Weingart, and Ian Milligan, "Getting Started with Topic Modeling and MALLET" (2012)
- Vilja Hulden, "Supervised Classification: The Naive Bayesian Returns to the Old Bailey" (2014)
- Heather Froehlich, "Corpus Analysis with Antconc" (2015)
- Peter Organisciak and Boris Capitanu, "Text Mining in Python through the HTRC Feature Reader" (2016)
- Taylor Arnold and Lauren Tilton, "Basic Text Processing in R" (2017)
- John Ladd, Jessica Otis, Christopher N. Warren, and Scott Weingart, "Exploring and Analyzing Network Data with Python" (2017)
- Ryan Deschamps, "Correspondence Analysis for Historical Research with R" (2017)

This was in sharp contrast to the rhetoric of digital history's potential as a source of new methods and new questions. Despite these lofty promises, research methods in digital history would take much longer to appear in the self-learning resources, despite no shortage of historians using advanced data analysis for research (cultural historian Ben Schmidt's *Sapping Attention* blog is a key example). Few people were willing to explain those methods in this subject-neutral space, in part because in many national contexts there was a lack of scholarly credit for such work, and in part because these analyses were not inherently computational skills but interdisciplinary and often social-science-based approaches that drew on the analysis of well-structured machine-readable data. Schmidt's methods could best be described as a combination of linguistics and statistics. Turkel's more recent "Digital Research Methods with Mathematica" (2015) took a similar approach, with sections

Table 7. Lesson categories and number of entries in the *Programming Historian* as of 16 February 2017.

Topic	Lesson Count
Introduction to Python (based on the original lessons)	17
Data manipulation	13
Data management	5
Distant reading	5
Mapping and geographic information systems	5
Web scraping	5
Digital exhibits and augmented reality	4
Application programming interfaces	3
Linked open data	1
Network analysis	1

Source: Afanador-Llach et al., "Lessons," programminghistorian.org/lessons (IA: 16/02/2017).

on word frequencies, pattern matching, concordance, and TF-IDF (term frequency-inverse document frequency).[58] These were all concepts in linguistics, which were increasingly being used by historians to answer historical questions with the mass-digitized archives that had become available. That raised questions as to where one might need to turn to learn the relevant skills: historical pedagogy sources, or linguistic ones. It also harked back to Zoe LeBlanc's plea on Twitter, asking when exactly she was meant to fit that extra learning into her already busy schedule.

While the proliferation of topics that moved beyond Turkel's original vision had opened up new skills to historians, the linear progression was lost. The "Getting Started" lesson from the original tutorials was dropped, and from 2012 to 2017 the lessons were organized alphabetically (table 7).[59]

The alphabetical categories were a helpful way of breaking down the lessons, but they provided no obvious path in for the learner who did not know where to start. The listing assumed that someone was coming to learn something specific and that they could identify which skills they needed to acquire. In July 2017 the lesson directory became even more dynamic, when the team adopted a faceted browsing system that kept the above classifications but added another set of filters that attempted to help users understand where each skill fit within the traditional research workflow (fig. 5). This post-linear model increased usability and brought the project in line with the expectations of dynamic websites, but it did not address the issue of where to start or where to go next.

In the longer narrative arc of digital pedagogy learning resources, the *Programming Historian* and the earlier statistical learning books aimed at historians shared a history-first focus. The examples, data, and asides were

| ACQUIRE (10) | TRANSFORM (29) | ANALYZE (8) | PRESENT (17) | SUSTAIN (3) |

APIS (2)   PYTHON (19)   DATA MANAGEMENT (6)   DATA MANIPULATION (16)   DISTANT READING (7)

SET UP (7)   LINKED OPEN DATA (2)   MAPPING (9)   NETWORK ANALYSIS (3)   WEB SCRAPING (6)

DIGITAL PUBLISHING (8)

RESET TO SEE ALL LESSONS (67)

SORT BY PUBLICATION DATE ▲   SORT BY DIFFICULTY ▼

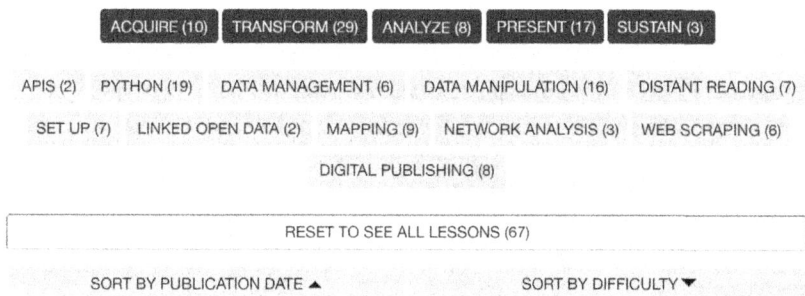

Figure 5. Screenshot of the new lesson categories in the *Programming Historian* as of January 2018, including the new high-level workflow categories at the top. (This work was done by Fred Gibbs and Amanda Visconti: programminghistorian.org/lessons.)

all focused on the needs of the historian rather than the generic learner. The skills on offer were representative of the digital history era of the post-digitization wave, focusing primarily on working with digital data and largely ignoring the earlier quantitative skills advocated by the cliometricians. It also tended to adopt the procedural rather than the conceptual model (though not exclusively). Screenshots were common, as were explicit directions on how to do something rather than necessarily how to abstract the skills or tasks behind the activity. This included lessons I wrote, as the project team struggled to find a balance between telling the reader enough to get through the material on their own, and giving so much procedural instruction that they followed it blindly without thinking and learning. The project was also different from the statistical textbooks in other important ways. It provided a platform for anyone to submit a lesson for peer review, making it able to respond to new technologies and ideas without the need for a new printed edition. It gave readers many options and paths for learning, without defining those paths. Though the original set of Python lessons was written to be followed in order, the broader offering had no "start here," in contrast to the statistical guides by scholars such as Floud, or the traditional linear nature of historical arguments in academic books and articles. The nonlinear nature of the tutorials made it flexible for educators who may have only wanted to introduce one or two topics, but it meant that readers without any source of support or guidance were necessarily disadvantaged.

Just as *Digital History* had inspired the *Programming Historian*, it too inspired a number of similarly self-published pedagogical endeavors aimed at historians. In 2009 I published "How to Write a Zotero Translator," which provided a practical introduction to JavaScript as well as a practical means of contributing to open source citation management software Zotero.[60] Inspired by the *Programming Historian*, twentieth-century U.S. historian Jason Heppler released the *Rubyist Historian* in 2010, with a focus on the Ruby language rather than Python.[61] In 2013 Geospatial Historian was launched by Canadian environmental historians Jim Clifford, Josh MacFadyen, and Daniel Macfarlane, introducing digital mapping skills to historians.[62] The same year, Miriam Posner helped would-be digital scholars reverse engineer a number of projects via a blog post, "How Did They Make That?," which highlighted the key concepts behind some popular projects so that they could identify the best starting point for their own endeavors.[63] Meanwhile, in 2018 historian of religion Lincoln Mullen's *Computational Historical Thinking with Applications in R* was still being written openly on the Web.[64] This growth of historian-focused pedagogical material was a boon for historians seeking to upskill but who lacked access to traditional learning structures. However, the printed lesson and interactive tutorial could never serve the full needs of learners. There was still an important role for face time, which was a crucial supplement to these resources throughout the whole computational and digital eras.

Workshops, Short Courses, and Summer Schools

Facilitated sessions often came from those who provided technologically themed teaching at their own institutions, and who also provided for those elsewhere through workshops, short courses, and summer schools. Quite possibly the earliest workshops aimed at teaching computational skills to historians on any degree of scale were offered between 1974 and 1982 in Chicago by Richard Jensen of the Newberry Library. Jensen raised funding to host a series of summer institutes, each of which brought together between thirty and fifty historians from around the world to learn new skills. Students ranged from graduate students to established scholars. Morning lectures were followed by afternoons in the computer lab.[65] Quite a revolutionary idea at the time, Jensen's institutes inspired a wide range of events in the coming decades that brought people together to learn intensively, for a short period.

Many of them were advertised through discussion groups such as Humanist (1987–2020), whose logs include more than 11,000 mentions of "workshops," making them roughly half as prominent as "conferences" in the discussion threads.[66] The yearly mentions of workshops roughly doubled between 1990 and 2002, doubling again by 2009. Not every mention correlated to a unique event, but it is clear that getting together to learn was deeply embedded in the culture of digital scholarship. The British-based

Association for History and Computing, which was founded in 1987 (now defunct), prioritized training in its agenda, noting its "commitment to the dissemination of computing techniques among history teachers. Courses and summer schools are being organized at both international and branch level."[67] Ensuring would-be scholars had a place to learn and people to learn from was clearly high on the digital agenda.

Over the years, there have been a number of different strategies for offering this directed short-term learning. One of the key ways organizers made it easier for people to attend workshops was to pair events with an existing major conference. This was the approach taken in 1989 when Ian Lancashire (Toronto) and Susan Hockey (Oxford) held a "Summer School in Humanities Computing," scheduled to coincide with the 16th International Association for Literary and Linguistic Computing Conference in Toronto.[68] Interested participants could extend their stay to take advantage of two-hour seminars, with a person on hand to answer any questions, making it a more flexible learning approach than written tutorials alone.

The pre-conference digital workshop had deep roots in the field. By attaching the workshop to an already-scheduled activity that expected to draw scholars interested in new methods, the organizers were able to tap into a ready-made audience, and keep travel costs down for those attending from afar. However, attending a major international conference in humanities computing represented a substantial commitment to the field, and was unlikely a space someone looking to get their toes wet would consider attending. This raised questions about who might have benefitted from these in-person workshops, suggesting that one already had to have made inroads into the digital scholarly community before one would have access to the learning opportunities to get more involved. In that light, these workshops paired with conferences are perhaps better viewed as continuing professional development, rather than a place for newcomers.

This pre-conference workshop approach continued to be popular into the new millennium. The annual "Digital Humanities" conference, run by the Association of Digital Humanities Organisations, continued to offer pre-conference workshops in the 2010s. Sessions had to be proposed by organizers in response to a call, just as scholars submit paper, panel, and poster proposals.[69] Pre-conference workshops had also increasingly become associated with history-first events. This was particularly the case in the United States where great distances separated scholars from one another, and where getting together was a bigger commitment than it was in a small densely populated country like the United Kingdom or Germany. Thus, in America, digital history workshops were regularly connected either formally or informally to the annual American Historical Association (AHA) conference, which was the nation's largest yearly gathering of historians.[70] As the AHA conference was the chief venue for job-seeking early-career American scholars to set up interviews, this linking of the conference, the job search, and continued professional development all in one may have seemed like a leveling opportunity. Of course, it also conferred a degree of privilege, and many early career scholars have complained about having to choose between paying the bills and paying to attend these events in order to gamble on the chance of a career.[71]

Not all events were attached to conferences. Others too have tapped into the market for digital learning, opting instead for the "summer school" approach championed by Jensen in the 1970s. From 1994, *Syllabus* magazine hosted annual events for educators wanting to think about how "personal computing could improve teaching in the classroom," focusing on the importance of digital pedagogy skills as well as those needed for research.[72] A few years later in 1997 in New York, the American Social History Project hosted a weeklong workshop for historians and high school history teachers considering the ways the Web changed opportunities for teaching the past.[73] Examples in Europe were also plentiful. In 1996, the Netherlands Historical Data Archive offered a "New Media and Advanced Methods for Historical Research" summer school at Leiden, which introduced students to advanced topics such as optical character recognition for transcribing historical documents, advanced statistics using SPSS, and text analysis strategies.[74] Though many of the events and workshops in the late twentieth century privileged the needs of literary and linguistic scholars, the event at Leiden showed that there were opportunities specifically aimed at historians interested in learning how to use research software. The fact that history-themed summer schools continued to appear in the late 2010s revealed a continuing need for this professional development. In 2014, American studies scholar Sharon Leon and public historian Sheila Brennan at the Center for History and New Media launched a "two-week intensive summer institute for mid-career American historians."[75] The mid-career element was an important recognition that not everyone had been given the opportunity to learn during their own study, but that leaving them without the opportunity to upskill was not in the interests of the profession.

Despite the short-term value that these events provided to those lucky enough to attend, the history-focused Leiden summer school never became a permanent fixture, and the event put on by Leon and Brennan was a one-off.

This was an inherent pedagogical weakness in many of these offerings. As noted by medievalist Malte Rehbein and textual scholar Christiane Fritze's self-reflection on their digital editing summer school in 2010, the fact that the event only ran once left them few opportunities to tweak the learning experience. Participants at the Europäische Sommeruniversität "Kulturen & Technologien" held at Leipzig University commented that there had been "too much" theory. The organizers concluded that an intensive course cannot provide both depth and breadth, and thus must be satisfied offering a "starting-point for further self-directed studies or learning-by-doing."[76] Without a follow-up event, there was not an opportunity for the educators to refine their teaching, and the quality of instruction may not have been at its peak in these one-off events.

By 2000, the University of Oxford had taken steps toward addressing this problem by establishing the first stable home for a digital humanities (not digital history) summer school when the Humanities Computing Unit launched a weeklong seminar series.[77] They pitched it as a way to "see how new technologies can help you in your work."[78] The summer school in Oxford would continue annually, eventually adopting the moniker DHOxSS for Digital Humanities at Oxford Summer School. On the other side of the planet, in 2001, early modernist Ray Siemens established the Digital Humanities Summer Institute on Canada's west coast, which too was still running in 2019.[79] Unlike the Leiden event, neither of these events were designed for the explicit needs of historians, and both have strong links to the Text Encoding Initiative and thus textual scholars (literature, linguistics, scholarly editing). Nevertheless, their geographically stable and annually updated program was part of the wider offering to historians seeking facilitated training in digital skills. The number of similar summer school offerings has grown, with the University of Lancaster in the north of England offering short residential courses in their areas of specialty, dating back at least to 2011.[80] Their offering has since expanded from its original emphasis on corpus linguistics, and by 2017 included courses on spatial analysis and natural language processing.[81] Meanwhile, similar initiatives post-2015 have been held around the world, including in Switzerland, Spain, Germany, and South Africa.[82]

Some universities opted for even more formal training options for those in need of professional development. In 2002, the Institute of Historical Research (IHR) in London began offering Databases for Historians and Internet Data short courses.[83] As of this writing the databases course is still offered, but the program now also includes courses on data preservation, online academic profiles, and digital tools.[84] The IHR is known in the London area as a chief supporter of the field of historical research, and its mission is to "promote the study of history," making it a natural home for research training for historians. Its extensive free seminar series also included a "digital history" seminar during term time (2012–present), where scholars could come to learn the latest digital research.[85] Paired with these paid short courses, it provided considerable professional development opportunities for those lucky enough to live or work nearby.

In 2014, Texas A&M University launched a more substantial for-credit semester-long course, Programming for Humanists, which introduced a range of mark-up languages (as opposed to procedural programming).[86] The remote-learning course was free for Texas A&M staff and students but charged between $400 and $2,500 for outside applicants.[87] For those seeking the comfort of a clear university structure for their learning, it was but another opportunity. These large, structured, well-funded events provided access to continued professional development for scholars and students alike. They were, however, unusual. Much more common was the one-time workshop or short event that offered to explore a specific skill or tool with participants.

Between 2005 and 2008, scholars looking to host workshops in the United Kingdom found support through the ICT Methods Network, a scheme funded by the Arts and Humanities Research Council (AHRC) to promote the sharing of digital methods in the humanities.[88] The thirty-eight events sponsored by the network crossed many disciplinary boundaries but included a number that were structured for the benefit of those studying the past or working in cultural heritage. They included:

- Web Portals and the Historic Environment
- Skills in Advanced Text Encoding with TEI P5
- Digital Restoration for Damaged Documents
- Text Mining for Historians
- Large-Scale Manuscript Digitization
- Methods in Geospatial Computing for Mapping the Past
- Audio and Acoustics in Heritage Applications.[89]

Many of the events are well documented, providing a clear insight into the aims and teaching methods employed. The Text Mining for Historians two-day event hosted by corpus linguist Zoe Bliss at the University of Glasgow in 2007 devoted one day to a series of presentations by experts and demonstrations of tools and concepts; the second day offered practical tutorials and a chance for participants to test out the new methods.[90] In many respects, it offered a similar form of support for those seeking continued professional development, as had the event offered by Lancashire and Hockey nearly twenty years earlier, but without the connection to a major conference or longer summer school.

The very structured approach led by experts was both very British, and in rather stark contrast to an American unconference, THATCamp, which was first held at the Center for History and New Media in 2008. The "unconference" eschewed the pre-planned workshop agenda for an agenda set on day one of the event by the participants themselves.[91] It was inspired by the format of BarCamp, a Silicon Valley unconference that proved popular with the tech community, and which the team at the Center for History and New Media decided to try for digital historians. As was so often the case with digital historians, rather than invent the format, they adopted and tested it on behalf of the historical professions. Typical of many North American digital projects in the early years of the millennium, THATCamp was framed as *cool*, and described as an experience that was meant to be "fun" and "democratic."[92] THATCamp and the unconference model of course came with its own risks. By implying that one has invented a new type of event that was *fun* or *better* or *friendly*, one might have attracted a great audience and even had a great time. One also implied that "traditional" events were *not fun*, or *not good*, or *mean-spirited*, raising the ire of colleagues who might otherwise have been won over with more carefully chosen rhetoric.

In a 2012 talk, founder Tom Scheinfeldt described THATCamp as a part of the "invisible college" of support for scholars, and as a reaction to the excessive overheads, effort, and anxiety that seemed to go into so many major scholarly conferences. As conferences were merely a mode of getting people together, Scheinfeldt challenged the need for so much stress and planning. THATCamp also sought to eschew the model of public speaking in which "I as the speaker prove how smart I am, and you as the audience member in the Q&A try to prove how stupid I am." Historian of Eastern Europe Mills Kelly suggested it was more lively than "the standard scholarly conference where three or four presenters sit in the front of the room and read papers at the audience."[93] Scheinfeldt and Amanda French were able to roll out the THATCamp model more widely thanks to a substantial grant from the Andrew W. Mellon Foundation, which provided guidance and a Web-based infrastructure to support other THATCamps.[94] In the decade since the first event at the Center for History and New Media in 2008, it exploded, with nearly three hundred camps held around the world. French estimated that more than six thousand people had participated in one of these camps in the first five years that they had been running.[95] The traveling teching-up event made headway with other organizations as well. Software Carpentry, established in 1998, hosted more than five hundred workshops to help groups of scientists improve their software development skills. Digital curator James Baker, then of the British Library, put together a team that launched Library Carpentry in 2015 as a means of offering similar skills development opportunities for library and collections management professionals.[96]

Conclusion

THATCamp and related events provided a good service for those who participated. Attendance was generally inexpensive, with one of the tenets to keep costs low. The distributed nature of the events meant that people were encouraged to wait until one came to their area or host one themselves rather than travel great distances to attend. These learning events were part of the wider ecosystem that was the invisible college, which was evolving to meet the needs of historians. That ecosystem included published books with strong linear progressions, pick-and-mix tutorials, advice about software or tool selection, and in-person short courses and workshops. There was a blend of solitary reflection time and face time, giving different means of learning and reinforcing new skills.

Yet for many, there was something missing. As historian of religion Alan Jacobs noted, "the first purpose of THATCamp is to get people who *want* to know stuff in the same room with people who *do* know stuff and give them the opportunity."[97] While the event could usually be relied on for socializing and the passionate exchange of ideas, there was no guarantee for the time-pressed historian that an agenda-free event would bring them together with the skills or ideas they sought to learn. It was akin to the blind date of the continued professional development world.

Many self-learners likely underwent an element of feeling around in the dark as they tried to navigate this unsupervised pedagogical space that included a wide range of skills and activities, all described as "digital." As the self-learning resources proliferated, the number of paths people could take through them multiplied. Without a firm chronological grasp of historian's experiments with technology, and without a vocabulary to articulate what they needed to know, those new to the game could feel thrown into the middle of an ever-expanding soup without any way of knowing where to start. Many of these resources made the problem even more difficult by too often presenting themselves as an enduring solution to a problem that may have only existed at the time of writing. Whatever was technologically difficult *today* was "digital history." The problems of 2000 were anachronistic by 2004 when the *real* problems had emerged, only to see the cycle repeat itself in 2008, when again the *real* problems were before us. Much confusion could have been avoided with a clearer means of describing those challenges in the wider context of the evolving activities of interest to historians.

From the Newberry's social science summer schools of the 1970s, to the workshops of the 1980s that focused on word-processing skills, to the IHR's "databases for historians" short-course, to the DHOxSS's focus on mark-up and TEI, to Cohen and Rosenzweig's emphasis on learning what the Web could teach us, to the Programming Historian's stress on reverse-engineering the Web, and finally to Turkel's linguistic-based "Digital Research Methods with Mathematica," they all took a *problem-of-today* approach. Each was a product of a single struggle faced by historians working in an ever-changing environment. This emphasis on the problems of today was of course very natural. Unless those various problems were put into historical context, learners would continue to struggle to find their own path through a growing number of books, tutorials, and events that offered conflicting advice. Because of the quickly changing nature of technology and the fact that it was so interdisciplinary, each scholar needed help formulating his or her own journey into digital skills development.

When Zoe LeBlanc turned to Twitter in 2017 to vent her frustrations, it was not for a lack of self-learning resources, but a lack of bespoke advice. LeBlanc wanted to understand which skills were needed and where to turn next after reaching a novice level of aptitude. She wanted to know if she was doing it *right*. In her case, and in the case of many others, it was social media—first blogs and then platforms such as Twitter—that provided semblances of answers to those questions. Within moments, her Twitter monologue turned into a series of dialogues with other digital scholars who chimed in offering advice or words of support. In the end, while responding to digital literary scholar Ted Underwood, LeBlanc expressed what she really wanted: "Mostly just wish I had an access to a lab full of brilliant ppl like you so I could test ideas before going to [*sic*] far down a rabbit hole."[98] In other words, she wanted supervision. The fact that LeBlanc went looking for support on social media could be seen as a failure of the traditional academy. As a PhD student, the support she needed about historical skills development should have been coming from her PhD committee, or at least from her university. No academic department would out-source historiography training to Twitter, yet LeBlanc and many like her were forced to go thus looking for technical support because it was still assumed that a history supervisor needed to be an expert in the time and place that the student was studying, rather than in the research methods needed to generate new knowledge about it. Changes to the profession brought about as a result of evolving technology were beginning to challenge that assumption, but the universities had been slow to react and the supervision required for "digital" work was too often not available within the existing structures of the history department. If for no other reason, that meant that the invisible college that had developed to support learning had been a vital lifeline for historians wanting to learn new skills, and it was evidence of a failure of higher education to adapt quickly enough to the ways that changes in technology were affecting the discipline. With that failure, it was perhaps not surprising that historian of the U.S. South Edward Ayers suggested that the biggest impact of computers on historical studies was a "deepening and broadening of professional conversations," which used technology and social media to support the development of new virtual communities.[99]

5

The Rise and Fall of the Scholarly Blog

Long before social media, there was the scholarly journal, which developed in 1665, when the *Journal des Sçavans* was first published in Paris, followed shortly thereafter by the *Philosophical Transactions of the Royal Society* in London.[1] More than three centuries later, these journals are still publishing—though both had to be revived at various points. The model for scholarly communication that they helped to pioneer remained remarkably stable over the centuries. Hundreds of years later, historians still submitted articles to journals. Peer reviewers and editors still performed their roles as gatekeepers of quality. Tenure and promotion decisions were still based on historians' success with these systems. The journal has never been the proper venue for all types of scholarly conversations, however.

As journals continued to publish, a number of historians took part in a quieter revolution in scholarly communication, which was far more experimental and far less formal than the academic journal or monograph. First through newsletters distributed via the postal system, and then through Listserv discussion groups, blogs, and finally social media, new virtual communities of historians developed, enabled by the transformation of communication in the digital era. These new communities, best characterized by the rise of blogging in the new millennium, helped to make historical studies a more self-reflective space. It presented new opportunities for hierarchies to be inverted and injustices to be outed, but it also presented new platforms for learning about interdisciplinary research opportunities that could complement traditional approaches to historical studies.

This is not an untold story; a number of bloggers have offered their versions of it. Civil rights historian Ralph Luker, who features prominently in the pages that follow, wrote a chronology of blogging in 2005, just as the practice was beginning to take off. Aviation historian Brett Holman built briefly on this in a 2015 post that celebrated the tenth year of his history blog, *Airminded*. The same year, historian of religion Rebecca Goetz recounted some of the blogging-related moral panics that surfaced as historians expressed their concerns about this new fangled (and presumably dangerous) toy.[2] This chapter draws together those brief blog posts but also connects to more scholarly analyses of blogging, including information scientist Sara Kjellberg's probing into the motives of bloggers, historian of the Web Matt Burton's PhD dissertation on scholarly communication, and digital humanist Melissa Terras's conclusions that her blogging had a positive impact on the exposure of her research.[3]

It does so by putting blogging into a longer chronology of informal scholarly communication, and tracing it through distinct phases that included anonymous ranting, confident scholarly expression, and shameless self-promotion. This chapter highlights the rise and fall of the activity that, above all others, came to characterize a self-aware community of "digital" scholars in the early twenty-first century. For a few years, blogging helped establish a shared identity, which expanded into an imagined community of "digital humanists" that included scholars from a range of disciplinary backgrounds. This new community challenged the disciplinary boundaries and customs of the historian as never before, while amplifying a set of voices that were often on the margins of the traditional hierarchy. For many active in this space, the draw of being part of digital *humanities* was stronger than the need to be known for one's historical work. This was indicative of the ways that the terminology adopted by these practitioners to describe themselves reflected the building of a community rather than a description of their work.

Technological developments thus provided opportunities for historians to communicate in new ways and with new aims. It gave them opportunities to be heard and to use their voice to challenge the status quo as never before. This chapter asks: What did historians do with these new opportunities? What purpose did blogging play in the lives and careers of historians in the late twentieth and early twenty-first centuries? And how was the scholarly landscape different than it had been before the rise of the Internet?

Conversing at a Distance

While journals are important, they cannot serve effectively as the sole venue for scholarly conversation. The scholarly newsletter evolved around 1920 to meet an added need, offering, as social theorist Christopher M. Kelty described, a "tool of coordination and collaboration that emerge whenever a scientific or technical problem overruns the bounds of a single laboratory or office."[4] Scholarly societies were keen to facilitate these additional conversations, and in the process maintain control over publication and dissemination. The American Historical Association launched *Perspectives on History* in 1964; the Canadian Historical Association followed with the *CHA Bulletin* in 1975.[5] An unknown number of similar scholarly newsletters circulated in the twentieth century, paid for by nominal fees and disseminated through the mail.

One newsletter in particular helped lay the foundation for a shift to an unmediated space. Not run by historians at all, the *Old English Newsletter*, founded in 1967 by members of the Old English Group of the Modern Language Association of America, proved an effective stepping-stone into digital scholarly communication.[6] Two decades after it launched, the newsletter inspired the creation of the Listserv discussion group ANSAXNET in 1987 (derived from "Anglo-Saxon Net"), which was initially an attempt by Patrick W. Conner to identify and connect every Old English scholar with access to the BITNET system. BITNET was a relatively new initiative, established in 1981, which allowed scholars of participating universities to send messages of up to a thousand lines across the telecommunications network.[7] Any member of the Old English Group could join ANSAXNET and receive or send messages to the whole group, making it open to subscribers but invisible to the rest of the world. Conner's role was crucial to reducing the barrier to entry for scholars looking to make virtual connections. As a form of communication, discussion groups like ANSAXNET would continue to be one of the most important venues for sharing scholarly information for two decades.[8]

Technologist Willard McCarty played a similar role for humanities computing scholars when he sent the first message on the Humanist discussion group on 17 May 1987. At the time of writing more than thirty years later, Humanist was still active as a result of McCarty's dedication to what he pegged a "seminar," which he believed invoked "the academic metaphor of a large table around which everyone sits for the purpose of argumentation, in the etymological sense of 'making bright and clear.'"[9] U.S. historian Edward Ayers described these new venues as "a perpetual annual conference, with everything from plenary speeches to intense private conversations."[10] Both ANSAXNET and Humanist included contributions from historians, without explicitly being spaces for them. Instead, the historically inclined mixed with like-minded humanists who found it advantageous to be part of (or at least able to listen in on) the increasingly inter- and multidisciplinary discussions. Other electronic discussion groups more relevant to historians also appeared, including HUMGRAD for postgraduates, HIST-NEWS and IHR-INFO for historians, and CTI-ECON for economic historians, as well as the H-Net system in 1992, with its proliferation of discussion groups broken down by area of research interest.[11]

Though these early discussion groups predated the World Wide Web, they helped establish some of the conventions of virtual scholarly communication. It is telling that both Conner and McCarty chose to highlight social rather than technical dynamics in their 1992 reflections to mark the fifth anniversary of the projects. They both drew on sociologist Marshall McLuhan's idea of the global village made possible through technology as a metaphor for what one might hope to achieve.[12] McCarty proudly reported that the first intentional joke appeared less than two months after Humanist first started publishing, while Conner beamed about the first "Gday mate" that connected him electronically to colleagues Down Under.[13] Both spoke of the culture of communication that developed in the discussions. On Humanist, McCarty noticed that the crowd was largely self-policing, able to exert "collegial pressure" when required "to bring an objectionable member to his or her senses." He recalled that the first editorial censorship was not needed until more than a year after launch. Conner wrote of flattening the academic hierarchy by enforcing a first-names-only policy because "a graduate student at an American land grant institution, for example, must be capable of exchanging information, without intimidation, with a professor at Oxford or Yale."[14]

Thus it was about more than mere communication. It was about challenging the status quo of a traditionally elitist and hierarchical academy. That said, however, those virtual spaces were not democratic. Sociologist Uwe Matzat suggested that special interest discussion groups provided an audience for those who maintained them and those with the social capital to dominate discussions, disadvantaging early career researchers and people further from the center of the network.[15] Conner certainly admitted that his place at the epicenter had brought him professional benefits, noting in particular his "direct access" to the editors of a number of substantial projects in Old English studies as a key perk. McCarty saw it slightly differently, highlighting the labor-intensive requirement of the seminar convenor to read and curate the submissions, suggesting "one hour each day is not unusual," which implied perhaps he and fellow editors or stewards of these communities had earned any benefits that came their way.[16] Whether the editor was the beneficiary of or servant to the community, these special interest discussion groups of the 1980s and '90s and many more like them helped establish the preconditions for the social media era that would follow.

A Rant in the Virtual Common Room

The leap into the social media era came from Rob MacDougall, then a Canadian PhD student studying the history of technology at Harvard. MacDougall published the earliest blog post about the historical craft written by a historian, on 25 January 2001.[17] In the post, he complained about citation management software Endnote. He claimed the software had been getting his citations wrong "in subtle ways" and that he "had to spend FIFTEEN HOURS (no lie) digging through [his] notes to recheck each one of 200+ footnotes." It was not exactly about history, but it was certainly a commentary on what it was like to be a historian. MacDougall signed off with a tongue-in-cheek curse of "a black death on the employees of Niles Software and all their progeny." It would be dishonest to call MacDougall's blog a "history" blog. Most of his posts were not about history; instead the history-themed entries were sparingly intermixed within wider musings on life, from Y2K to asking his fiancée to marry him.[18] The first dedicated history blogs would not appear for another year or so, with early examples, including games studies scholar Esther McCallum-Stewart's *Break of Day in the Trenches* (February 2002) and historian of religion Rebecca Goetz's *Historianess* (July 2002).[19]

The blog post is often touted as a dramatic new invention, but it was merely an evolution. Historian of slavery Caleb McDaniel reflected on the similarities between how he felt about his blogging and how diarist Henry Clarke Wright had described his own writing two centuries earlier.[20] Meanwhile, Andrew Sullivan suggested that group blogs had developed in very similar ways to the early magazines centuries ago, with "a few like-minded souls collaborating on a literary-political project."[21] More recent parallels could also be seen. The content of the conversations on Humanist and early blogs was remarkably similar. As noted by historian of Latin America Chad Black, for every example of someone like MacDougall venting on his blog about a piece of software, there was a post by a historian on Humanist that was similar and earlier.[22]

What was distinct about MacDougall's blog was its audience—or perhaps lack thereof. Humanist boasted a hundred members within four months of first publication, growing to 1,800 by 2011.[23] It was a virtual space where people who shared a common interest could spend time together, initiating conversations, listening, and responding to others. A new blog was different because it had no audience, and by default only the owner could initiate a conversation. It was akin to the self-published fanzines or zines associated with fandom in hobbyist domains such as sci-fi, punk rock, and comic books.

By the 1990s, zines had become closely linked to Riot Grrrl, a feminist punk music counterculture movement, and the zines became an important outlet for the feminism espoused by that movement. Zine publishing had a do-it-yourself attitude and self-consciously rejected many of the structures of control in the media industry, allowing anyone to create their own platform and seek an audience.[24] The blogger and the zine publisher thus had similar hurdles to overcome and a shared desire for a space of one's own.

This notion of a space of one's own was important for early bloggers. Commenting would rise in prominence over time, but the blog was the domain of the blogger. You could visit, but there could be no mistaking whose space it was. In MacDougall's case, his post about Endnote and those like it helped historians take some tentative steps into an unfiltered online space of their own, which invited anyone who wanted to come and read. It offered immediate access to a platform, unbounded by editorial gatekeepers and quality control of any kind. It was a little soapbox, in a sea of other people's soapboxes that one could visit if they liked, and free of the deluge of unwanted contributions from noisy or belligerent contributors to the virtual mailing lists.

The blog post was a subtle twist on the discussion group that brought with it the spirit of the zine. It represented a breaking off on one's own rather than the invention of a new mode of scholarly communication. Blogs also provided a space that the more traditional scholarly societies did not. Mac-Dougall's complaint about Endnote would not likely have been accepted for publication had he submitted it to the AHA's *Perspectives on History*. It was unpolished and whiney. It did not make a substantial contribution to the field; but it might have been worth saying as a warning to others putting their faith in software. With no trees at risk in the digital printing process, no need to steal time on the department photocopier to publish a zine, and no limits on column inches, this new form of expression provided a new form of soapbox. The hierarchy of controlling the dissemination of ideas had been sidestepped by a graduate student with a simple upload to a Web server.

What blogs sought to achieve is often misunderstood. The earliest history blogs are often remembered as a means of breaking down boundaries between disciplines. Because they were totally open, anyone could stop by and read or comment. Technologists might cross paths with historians, who might go seeking dialogue with sociologists, or artists, or private enterprise, and new ideas could be fertilized. This did happen, but despite this great potential, early blogging was predominantly an echo chamber of historians talking to each other.

As information scientist Sara Kjellberg highlighted, blogs played an important social role for scholars hoping to achieve a "feeling of being connected."[25] More than one blogger I interviewed spoke of their intellectual isolation during graduate research. Blogging was a way of reaching out beyond the people nearby, to create a cohort of like-minded people. Burton called this support network the "invisible college."[26] The vast distances between North American cities may help explain why historians there seemed most eager to reach out to this invisible college. Not everyone needed it, of course. Some scholars were able to get this feeling of connection without the Internet, but this came down largely to happenstance of geography. In certain elite universities, the common room was a physical space where scholars could meet and make connections, but these spaces were not ubiquitous. The Internet helped bridge those physical distances and made it easier to keep in touch with like-minded individuals. Historian and early blogger Josh Greenberg suggested that networks of "parlours" were a better metaphor. For him, reading someone's blog had a feeling of visiting a friend in their space, to share some time and some ideas. The parlour metaphor fits well with the seventeenth- and eighteenth-century equivalent of scholarly blogging: the pamphlet, or the Republic of Letters, in which people exchanged ideas via physical bits of paper shepherded across the Western world, or what historian of France David Garrioch referred to as a network of "epistolary friendships."[27] Edward Ayers too used a spatial metaphor, preferring to see "cyberspace" as a space that one entered, giving them the power to unite "by affinity and passion rather than by the mere accident of physical locale." He noted that the early language of "chat rooms," "dungeons," "bordellos," and "sanctuaries" all echoed a notion of entering a space with the help of a machine.[28]

The tone of early history blogging reinforced its role as a virtual common room or parlour visit. It was not the formal writing of an academic paper; quite often, it was something that someone needed to get off of his or her chest. Like MacDougall's early complaints about Endnote, the rant proved a popular format. Tim Hitchcock, the cofounder of the Old Bailey Online, London Lives, and several other digital archives, described his blog as "a space for me to rant in that most seventeenth-century sense of the word."[29] Hitchcock was different from many of the early bloggers in one very important way: he was an established professor of history when he launched *Historyonics* in 2007. That made him not only a latecomer to blogging, but he also wrote from a position of security. This was in sharp contrast to the number of ranters who counted themselves among the profession's most vulnerable members.

These early ranters wrote from the margins; many of the most celebrated digital history bloggers were graduate students or those on the job market. Ralph Luker would later call this an inversion of the hierarchy in which the "30-year-old graduate student is the elder statesman."[30] Luker himself became a prominent blogger and community builder among historians on the Internet. Despite being many years senior of most of these early bloggers, he wrote from the margins as a historian who had been very publicly denied tenure in 1994, which led him to pursue a hunger strike before resorting to work on hourly paid jobs outside of the academy.[31]

Marginalization was not exclusively a hurdle for those who turned to blogging. When Willard McCarty launched the Humanist discussion list in 1987, it was as a protest movement, which "rose out of anger and frustration at being excluded from the academic world by the stain of computing." When the group first launched, McCarty noted that he was determined not to add any "established figures." He had originally struggled to obtain a tenure track position, and worked in what would later be called an "alt-ac" (alternative academic) position in a humanities computing lab. He recalled that in the early 1980s, a connection to computing was a "death sentence for an academic career."[32] Two decades later, some suggested the same would be the case for blogging historians. In 2005, a pseudonymous "Ivan Tribble" penned "Bloggers Need Not Apply" in which they recounted the risks to job-searching historians who had allowed such a detailed and public record of their quirks and private beliefs to appear online: "If you stick your foot in your mouth during an interview, no one will interrupt to prevent you from doing further damage. So why risk doing it many times over by blabbing away in a blog?" Tribble's article highlighted a level of paranoia toward blogging: "Several committee members expressed concern that a blogger who joined our staff might air departmental dirty laundry (real or imagined) on the cyber clothesline for the world to see. Past good behavior is no guarantee against future lapses of professional decorum."[33] The article was intended to offer advice on public personae, but it drew criticism from bloggers who saw it as an attack on their community and their right to be humans with diverse interests and outlets of expression. Tenured (and thus secure) professor of media studies Kathleen Fitzpatrick blasted back within hours, highlighting in particular the logical fallacy in Tribble's conclusion. She noted that "the assumption of future guilt based on an absence of historical wrong-doing is simply insane," while also disparaging that "I find myself, not to put too fine a point on it, seriously pissed off by the infuriating combination of condescension and authoritarianism on absolutely unedited display in this article."[34] Historian of mathematics Dan Cohen took a softer approach, noting that he had tried to lead by example within historical blogging by adopting a style that "carefully avoided the use of extreme adjectives and hyperbole" hoping to "disarm those who believe that blogs can be nothing but trouble."[35] For Tribble, the problem may have seemed new to blogging, but the opportunities to stick one's foot in one's mouth were much older. Humanist discussion group included at least one request to two quarreling contributors: "If you two can't kiss and make up, then could you at least step outside?"[36]

However, not everyone disagreed with Tribble; someone writing under the name "CC Rider" commented that "if a blog is going to keep someone from getting a job, it seems to me it's the candidate's fault," and instead suggested that the problem could be avoided: "the best academic blogs that I know of are (like this forum) anonymous."[37] Anonymity fit both with the tendency to adopt a pseudonym in the early days of the social Web, but it also reflected the significant risk of bullying and sexual harassment that women in particular faced, highlighted extensively by communication scholar Susan Herring's research on social spaces in the early Internet, or on historian of slavery Jessica Marie Johnson's reflections on being a woman of color in the blogosphere.[38]

Shrouded in the veil of anonymity, these early rants were a new opening of Habermas's public sphere and specifically lent themselves to the language of protest written by those who sought change and new conversations.[39] One of the most influential early ranting spaces was established two years after MacDougall's post about Endnote. An anonymous historian of the Scottish enlightenment, writing under the pen name "Invisible Adjunct," launched her blog about her employment insecurity in higher education in February 2003, outlining the blog's purpose in her first post: "The purpose of this blog *is* largely therapeutic. Quite simply, the black dog of depression is snarling at my feet, and I am desperately trying to fend him off with whatever means I find at my disposal."[40] Most historians have probably never heard of the Invisible Adjunct, but over the course of the next year she poured her heart out, often several times per day, highlighting the injustices of the casualization of the academic workforce and the challenges of being a mother and a part-time scholar, and providing sufficient detail into her own life to firmly place a human behind the rants. Three hundred and ninety days and 180,742 words later, it was all over. The Invisible Adjunct signed off with an emotional good-bye: "A few months ago, I made a vow to myself that this would be my last semester as an invisible adjunct. Since I've failed to secure a full-time position in my final attempt at the academic job market, what this means, of course, is that I made a vow to leave the academy. Six more weeks of teaching, and I head for the nearest exit."[41] The response from the blogging community was one of mourning, drawing on the language and tone of a loving obituary. Within weeks of shutting the blog, 212 people had commented on her "Signing Off" post, expressing their appreciation for her contributions to the scholarly community. In tribute, Timothy Burke added the blog to his coedited "Hall of Fame" of history blogs, crediting the Invisible Adjunct as someone who "held up a mirror to higher education and asked whether it liked what it saw."[42] Ralph Luker posted a now lost series of links to blogs referencing the closing of Invisible Adjunct, while Ben Wolfson established a page where people writing about academic life could add their blog to a "webring" (an early means of helping people find relevant websites on a similar topic via links) in honor of the Invisible Adjunct because her leaving "doesn't mean the conversation has to stop."[43]

This outpouring arguably exceeds the impact of much of the scholarly history research published at the same time as the signing off of the Invisible Adjunct. Two hundred and twelve tearful good-byes rates favorably against the number of citations since gained by the articles published in *Past and Present* or the *American History Review* volumes that appeared the month Invisible Adjunct stopped publishing. None of those published articles managed to provide clear evidence of as much engagement as did the anonymous blogger.[44] Among those who noticed the closing of the Invisible Adjunct in 2004 was the author of the now-lost *Heart of Canada* blog, a snippet of which can still be read on Josh Greenberg's archived blog:

> Something's happening in the blogosphere, a shift, a reorientation, a great loss. . . . In the past two or three days, several pillars of academic blogging have posted notice that they're leaving not only the academic blogosphere, but academia, itself. This includes the stalwart Invisible Adjunct, the gentle Household Opera, the hilariously bitter Academic Game, and perhaps even the sharply pointed Critical Mass. Their leaving follows an earlier exit by the insightful Frogs and Ravens, although she still blogs (and knits). Does it mean anything that they're all women, given the already horrific shortage of women in tenured positions? I grieve.[45]

Perhaps these pseudonymous writers simply exhausted themselves with their pace of writing, often contributing at a frenzied pace on top of any paid employment, social commitments, and research they were conducting. The notion that bloggers burned themselves out is certainly supported by an analysis of the history blogosphere (2003 and 2015). As figure 6 shows, a

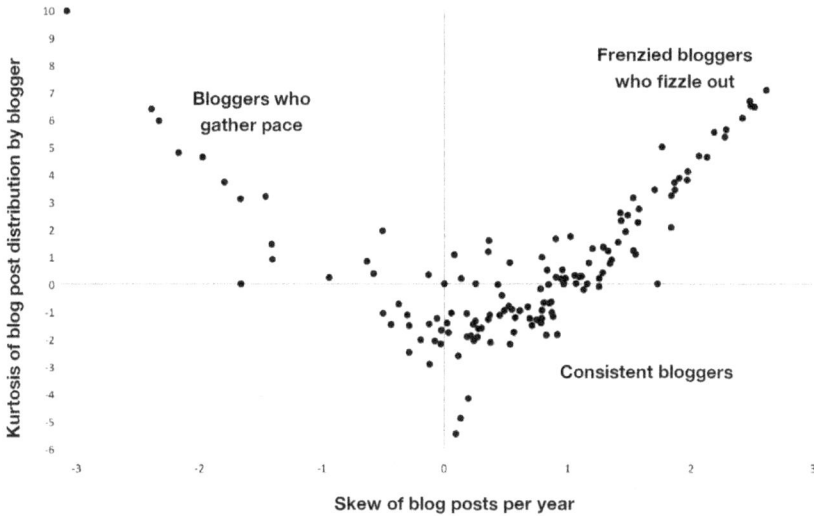

Figure 6. The skew and kurtosis of the posts per year in 144 history blogs that started writing between 2003 and 2015, taken from the *Cliopatria* Blogroll. (A positive skew means more posting early in the blog's life. A positive kurtosis means the peaks in the distribution are sharper, pointing to a greater enthusiasm at certain points in the blog's life-cycle that were not sustained.)

number of bloggers were prolific when they first established their blog, only to fizzle out after a few years.

Whatever their reasons for leaving, there was a clear sense of loss felt by readers at the time, compounded by the fact that these women, particularly the Invisible Adjunct, did not achieve their goals. The casualization of academic labor was bemoaned long after, from Australia to Canada, and beyond.[46] Public historian Larry Cebula, a historian at Eastern Washington University, wrote an open letter on his blog to his students warning them of the demise of the tenure track system in the United States, noting: "No, my esteemed student, you are not going to be a history professor. It isn't going to happen. The sooner you accept this the better."[47] In this light, we might say that the Invisible Adjunct had failed to enact change.

However, despite the immediate failure to solve the problems of the academic job market, this early group of blogging historians did achieve successes. They built a new online community of readers and writers interacting passionately with each other that had a new relevance and immediacy that could not be achieved in the traditional print avenues. Their scholarly discussions operated with a new speed. Instead of waiting months or years for a retort to their ideas, they often got it within hours. They mentioned one another, extended kudos, and challenged one another's ideas, just as historians did in the scholarly literature.

Writing Together toward Interdisciplinarity

Writing together became the important story of second-wave history blogging. In 2001, Rick Shenkman wrote a brief post on his newly founded History News Network (HNN) about U.S. president Bill Clinton's legacy. Shenkman was a journalist who had hosted a cable TV show that put the news into historical perspective.[48] He adapted the model for the Internet and started writing. The HNN project would grow to include ongoing contributions, primarily from U.S. historians, and managed to break down the barrier between academics and the general public in a way that the virtual common room had not. The collaborative public-facing blogging model would be copied by a group of Canadian graduate students (*Active History*, 2008–present), by the London School of Economics (*Impact Blog*, 2011–present) and by an Australian news group (the *Conversation*, 2011-present), all of which encouraged scholars to write about how research helped us understand society.[49]

HNN was different from other history blogs of its day because it was not really a blog, despite its blogging characteristics. It was entirely hosted online and had no print version; it consisted of reasonably short posts; each post had a date, an author, and a title; and posts were displayed in reverse chronological order. From a mechanical standpoint, it was a blog. But Shenkman quickly retreated into his journalistic comfort zone, and HNN was registered as a tax-exempt charity (more bureaucracy than any blogger would endure). It had an advisory board of senior scholars with impressive-sounding credentials, and it was hosted by George Mason University's servers. It had a staff of four, and a team of eight interns, who were eventually put in charge of different "departments," just like at a newspaper. Prospective authors could pitch ideas for stories as in the mainstream media.[50] Perhaps the most important distinction was the editorial workflow; these were carefully constructed essays that had to meet Shenkman's threshold of quality.

The HNN team did prove willing to adopt blogs as part of their package, hosting a number of them over the years, of which *Cliopatria* stands out as particularly important. *Cliopatria* (2003–12) was initiated by Ralph Luker, the aforementioned tenure-denied historian. Its creation involved bringing together a number of prolific history bloggers late in 2003. It survived for years in a largely ephemeral environment, incorporating the efforts of an evolving network of both prominent and early career scholars until 2012, when Luker bid farewell by thanking the fifty contributing historians to the project.[51]

The idea of writing together clearly had significant appeal. Josh Greenberg suggested that people came to join these conversations after a period of "lurking" and reading the work of others.[52] However, it was other people who brought blogging to friends and colleagues. Greenberg was one of those people. In May 2004 he announced on his blog that he was moving to the Center for History and New Media (CHNM) at George Mason University— the institutional host of HNN and *Cliopatria*.[53] In the months after his arrival, a significant proportion of the CHNM team started blogging, starting with Jeremy Boggs, one of the center's history PhD students, who started a blog at Clioweb.org almost immediately after Greenberg appeared. By Christmas of the following year, other Center members too had started blogs: U.S. studies scholar Sharon Leon (July 2005), historian of Eastern Europe Mills Kelly (October 2005), historian of mathematics Dan Cohen (November 2005), historian Tom Scheinfeldt (December 2005), and librarian and archivist Trevor Owens (July 2006).[54] While not everyone at CHNM blogged (founder and director Roy Rosenzweig never did), Greenberg's influence had a significant impact on local uptake. This created a new dynamic, with a critical mass of bloggers who shared a virtual space, and a physical one.

That made them distinct from the lonely graduate student using the blog to rant into the ether. Importantly, they were reasonably secure academics writing openly under their own names, in support of the work they did at CHNM, but not directly on behalf of it. Theirs was a personal voice rather than an institutional one. It meant that their water-cooler conversations made their way into print, extending the experience of working at CHNM to the wider world as never before. Cohen particularly established himself as a leader in blogging among historians, and he crafted an audience by promising to "set a higher mark for myself" writing posts that "will function more like well thought out mini-articles, and transfer to this blog's audience my understandings of the digital humanities in as great a depth as possible." In doing so, Cohen kept the passion, while eschewing the "half-baked and the half-written" approach that immediate and unfiltered publication all too often promoted.[55]

This planned approach to blogging helped to amplify the impact of CHNM blogging more broadly and across disciplines. Though never directly controlled, the team at CHNM projected a loud voice in the blogging world by linking to and promoting each other, and by (usually) staying on topic. In the case of Cohen in particular that meant building on CHNM's own mandate of exploring the role of new media for the field of history. This carried forward the successful book *Digital History: A Guide to Gathering, Preserving, and Presenting the Past on the Web* (2005), which he cowrote with Roy Rosenzweig. On the back of this book and the blog, Cohen built a significant international reputation, not for his historical research (on Victorian mathematics), but for his views on technology in the public humanities. The team at CHNM were instrumental in labeling these conversations on technology "digital humanities."[56] This interdisciplinary appeal to digital humanists rather than historians opened up a broader audience of scholars across the humanities and as more people did the same it helped create a community who felt that their identity as a humanist was as important, if not more important, than their discipline-specific background. Interestingly, these CHNM scholars made few attempts to engage with the official "digital humanities" organizations such as the Alliance of Digital Humanities Organization (ADHO) that operated as traditional scholarly societies. This small group of new self-proclaimed digital humanists opted instead to create an unofficial cluster of digitally minded scholars that communicated via social media and often showed open disdain for the scholarly hierarchy. This meant ignoring those who had entered the "digital humanities" field earlier and in other ways, leading to many groups claiming ownership of the term with different notions of what it meant. These interdisciplinary digital humanities bridges created by historians were further reinforced in 2007 when Cohen, Scheinfeldt, and Kelly launched a monthly podcast, *Digital Campus* (2007–15), on which they discussed the role of digital media and technology in the universities, libraries, and museums of the day.[57] For students learning about history and technology from these blogs and podcasts, this distinctly non-research and non-disciplinary focus undoubtedly influenced the way they perceived the field.

In the first decade of the new millennium, with HNN, *Cliopatria*, and the blogs of the CHNM team all saved on servers at George Mason University, a relatively small school in Virginia could certainly have laid claim as the epicenter of history and even digital humanities blogging. Together, these blogs would become some of the most influential in the academic world, without engaging directly with the historiography of traditional scholarship. Instead, they had new conversations on public history, technology, interdisciplinarity, and innovation in publishing. They had evolved from the rant, eschewed anonymity, and once they found their comfort zone, would also lead the way in exploring how that blogging could transform knowledge dissemination in the twenty-first century.

Curation and the Fight for the Center Ground

Hossein Derakhshan was not a historian, but a prominent Iranian Canadian political blogger who shared his views on Iranian politics via his blog,
Hodor.[58] At his peak, his blog attracted twenty thousand readers each day,
and he boasted of being able to "empower or embarrass anyone I wanted."
For embarrassing the Iranian government in 2008, he received a twenty-year
prison sentence. When he was unexpectedly released six years later, he returned to the Internet to find a space he no longer recognized and in which
he no longer carried clout, noting that "an entire era" had passed while he
had been behind bars. Not only had the Internet forgotten about him, but
the way people found content had changed dramatically.

Instead of an Internet powered by the ideas of bloggers, Derakhshan noted
that people scarcely visited websites directly. Instead they received information through filtered algorithms that he called "the stream," which "picked
everything for you. According to what you or your friends have read or seen
before, they predict what you might like to see."[59] These streams were particularly visible to Derakhshan because, while they slowly encroached into
the lives of people around the world at a rate that was almost imperceptible,
he opened a door one day to be confronted with this new way, all at once.
These streams were increasingly curated by companies; Facebook, Twitter,
Instagram, and other social media sites became the first port of call in many
people's daily Internet routine.[60] It raised important questions about structures of power on the Internet.

In many respects this was a reaction to the new "attention economy" in
which everyone was competing for eyeballs and clicks.[61] With too much to
read, new ideas began to emerge for how to curate the best content into an
easy-to-peruse list. Early bloggers tended to create these lists themselves,
subscribing to Really Simple Syndication (RSS) feeds, which could be checked
periodically via an RSS feed reader such as Google Reader. These readers
were websites similar to e-mail in-box, on which one could see at a glance
any new posts. It was a system that put the reader in control, and it was with
this approach that Derakhshan had been familiar. But times were changing.
By 2013 the algorithms had become so prominent that Google decided to
discontinue its Google Reader, citing declining usage.[62] While alternative
readers continued to offer this service, the decision by Google to exit the
marketplace suggested that the algorithms were winning.

Perhaps ironically, the blogging community had been party to the innovations that led to this algorithmic selection of material. Long before the

"stream," the blogroll was a staple of early blogs—a list of blog titles and links that acted as a recommendation to one's readers. It was human curated rather than algorithmically derived, but it served a similar function. Among *Cliopatria*'s most important initiatives was the *Cliopatria* Blogroll, a substantial list that grew to 1,947 history blogs, last updated in 2011.[63] The *Cliopatria* Blogroll was unique for its attempt to provide a complete list of the history blogosphere at the time. Importantly, the list *was* curated. Luker encouraged self-nominations by people with newly established blogs, but he checked them and in at least one case he turned down a request, noting that it "isn't yet clear to me that the bench there is as deep in history as we like to see."[64] A substantial number of these blogs are still available on the open Web, while a number of others can be read on the Internet Archive Wayback Machine.[65] Organized into one of thirty-two history-focused categories that included "Military History," "Digital History," and "Early Modern History," the blogroll became a tool for newcomers to use to find people writing on topics they might find interesting, and included 216 blogs in European languages ranging from Catalan to French.

Finding quality content could be challenging for newcomers, so *Cliopatria* contributor and early modern historian Sharon Howard adopted an idea known as a "blog carnival," which she dubbed a History Carnival and launched in January 2005, providing a brief synopsis of thirty worthwhile posts that had appeared on the blogs of historians in the past month.[66] Its function was akin to the calendars of primary sources, which are not transcriptions but synopses meant to give historians enough detail to understand what they might find in an original source.[67] The posts were nominated by the community who were invited to tell Howard what had been worth reading that month. In her first entry she included a "thanks to everyone who sent links, especially links to blogs I'd never seen before and to posts that I'd managed to miss first time around."[68] Howard's "Carnival" was designed to rotate between bloggers who would each volunteer to host it on their own blog. The project would continue without pause until September 2017, when it reached edition 168 before going on hiatus. There is something of an archivist in the idea, providing structure to a loose network of independent bloggers uploading their ideas to disparate servers around the world. The *Cliopatria* Blogroll listed eleven "Carnivals" that focused on particular themes, all of which had their roots in Howard's first post.[69]

The idea of identifying and celebrating the "best of the blogosphere" was extended by *Cliopatria*, which launched a series of annual awards (2005–11). The *Cliopatria* Awards acted as a filter, but also rewarded ingenuity. Early winners included Rob MacDougall for "best post," and *Cliopatria* contributor and historian of Africa Timothy Burke as "best writer" (raising questions of impartiality), and John Jordan, an MA public history student who put forth an impassioned case for a "Canadian Wikipedia" to counter the much louder voice of U.S. editors of the site.[70] Digital Humanities Awards (2012–19), initiated by textual editing scholar James Cummings, then at Oxford, took up the torch of awarding the best digital projects based on popular vote and community nominations, but without any pretense of representing an authority or professional body of scholars.[71]

Experiments at the CHNM, led by Dan Cohen in particular, sought to build on Howard's carnival idea to curate the whole of the digital humanities blogosphere. Digital Humanities Now (DH Now) was launched in 2009 as an attempt to bring the best of digital humanities blogging to a single portal, curated by members of the community. This digital humanities focus was distinct from the history focus of the *Cliopatria* Blogroll and reflected the broader ambitions of CHNM highlighted above, to reach beyond historians and into interdisciplinary audiences. The project's volunteer editors actively monitored hundreds of blogs, declaring the "best" posts of the week part of the "editor's choice," which was then promoted via the DH Now website and Twitter feed. The initiative was an experiment with a form of post-publication peer review that acknowledged the importance of the self-publishing blogosphere while also recognizing the value of peer review. The interdisciplinary list of blogs that they followed, originally known as the "Compendium of Digital Humanities," was available on the open Web and scholars could self-nominate their blog, without guaranteeing it would be accepted. DH Now was a human-powered algorithm for quality that was meant to offer a shortcut toward the best material.[72]

This idea was extended in 2011 with the *Journal of Digital Humanities* (*JDH*), which took the best of the best from DH Now and worked with authors to publish posts as journal articles. It was an attempt to legitimize blogging by dressing it up in the clothes of academic research and adding layers of editorial gatekeeping and quality control. Yet *JDH* proved controversial, raising questions of authority. It was most definitely a grant-funded CHNM project controlled by a group of unelected scholars and purporting to speak on behalf of a wider community. Unlike many journals, there was no scholarly society behind it, nor could one get onto the editorial board except by invitation. If this was to be a voice for the field, it was a challenge that they would have to overcome, and controversy did not take long to rear its head. Postcolonial literature scholars Adeline Koh and Roopika Risam had hosted a symposium focusing on postcolonial digital humanities over the summer of 2013 and approached *JDH* with an idea for a special issue.[73] *JDH* agreed, and the pair were given editorial guidelines, which did not include a round of peer review. Shortly before the scheduled publication, the journal changed the workflow and instead insisted that the material be sent for blind external review.

It is likely that the experimental publication was merely continuing to innovate on the fly, and that the change of policy had nothing to do with Koh and Risam, and everything to do with trial and error. However, communication quickly broke down, and the digital technologies that had enabled these new scholarly conversations escalated the issue very quickly and very publicly. After the conversation made its way into the public sphere, both sides sought to tell their story through blog posts and Twitter. The journal editors say that they "concluded that the special section was not ready for publication and proposed a period of further elaboration and review." Koh's view, posted on her blog, was that this was instead a "sudden about-turn" and that they had been singled out for "special treatment" that had not been imposed on other special-issue editors.[74]

Koh intended her post to challenge a moving target, but it highlighted an important issue of privilege in this new space that sought to legitimize blogging as scholarship. Was the new space fair? Was it substituting one hierarchy for another? New media scholar James O'Sullivan commented in support, insisting that "Digital humanities, as an emerging field, needs to avoid pockets forming within which groups of scholars, who are undoubtedly pioneers and highly respected, dominate proceedings."[75] *JDH* was certainly hierarchical. One could not even submit an article. Instead, a post had to be noticed and promoted by the "editors choice" system, before being again selected as worthy of *JDH* publication.[76] These human filters helped impose new hierarchies on the history blogosphere, and claimed authority for determining what constituted "the best" in a community that had been founded on a rejection of such hierarchies. Getting noticed by the DH Now editors involved a degree of chance that could be improved by sufficient celebrity. Whether intentionally or not, from Koh's perspective, this may also have appeared like a different treatment when acting as a guest editor. Koh and Risam withdrew the issue in protest, and Koh outlined her frustration on her blog.[77]

The fact that the special issue in question was about postcolonialism perhaps helped direct the ensuing discussion, pockets of which quickly became about race, gender, and privilege rather than the quality of the work under review or what constituted a good model of publication for the journal. Women's studies scholar Siobhan Senier commented that "the bar is suddenly raised for two guest editors who just 'happen to be' junior women of color," harking back to the blogger as a person writing from the margins in protest against the center that was the established academy.[78] Except this time the center was the blogging community itself, or at least a core group of historians who had claimed the center ground with good intentions. One of the authors of the articles in question, historian of gender Michelle Moravec, evoked similar language to that of Senier, noting that she was "well aware of the long history of submissions by women of color being lost, or edited without their consent, or solicited and then rejected as 'not good enough.'"[79]

Twitter exchanges were equally heated, rarely focusing on the issue itself, and often pointing out that Koh had posted screenshots of the e-mail exchanges with the *JDH* editor (a junior scholar) without permission and thus was acting in bad faith to criticism.[80] The fallout of this late-summer exchange in 2013 was long lasting. *JDH* failed to publish its next two scheduled issues. It resumed for two final issues in spring and summer 2014 but then ceased publishing altogether. The official line on the website was that the publication was "an experiment in scholarly communication" and that it "accomplished its mission."[81] However, the journal had never presented itself as a short-term experiment, and it would seem that the controversy of the ill-fated postcolonial issue had sapped the editorial team of their authority in the field. The journal never recovered.[82]

In the aftermath, Koh tweeted about an alternative: "The Digital Humanities needs to create a platform for open and non-hierarchical dialogues #DHThis."[83] It was the first glimpse into an attempt to address the inequality of DH Now and *JDH*. Koh, working with a small team, quickly launched DHThis, a website that removed the closed group of editors and instead let anyone up-vote (promote) worthy blog posts, drawing on the technology used in popular social sharing sites such as Slashdot (1997) or Reddit (2005).[84] The site included an attempt to re-flatten the editorial hierarchy that had developed in DH Now and *JDH*. The site did manage to promote a number of relevant stories. However, true to form for voting-led websites, DHThis voters quickly promoted a video of a cute kitten to the front page, perhaps reinforcing the importance of editorial controls.[85] DHThis disappeared from the open Web in September 2015, presumably when its owners decided not to renew the domain.

Mainstream Impact and New Voices

When Dan Cohen implored academics to "start your blogs" in 2006, I doubt even he could have predicted how many would do so. While historians blogging about history had preceded Cohen's call to action, the number of history blogs continued to grow into the new decade, with many gaining mainstream attention. Particularly in the United Kingdom, there was another motivation: the need to demonstrate "impact" of research as part of the periodical national initiative to measure and rank the research outputs of academics across the country (known as the Research Excellence Framework, or REF, which was a renaming of the earlier Research Assessment Exercise, RAE).[86] Because of the impressive audiences many historians gained through their blogs, the format was increasingly seen in the academy as a way to reach a different audience than one could expect to engage with through traditional scholarly publishing. From about 2010, major funded projects at U.K. universities were almost expected to have a blog as part of the outreach and impact strategy, from the Digital Miscellanies Index (2010–16), to the Intoxicants and Early Modernity Project (2013–16), to the Digital Panopticon (2013–17) project. They all had blogs, usually run by funded PhD students or postdoctoral fellows who it was assumed would "get it" because of their age and presumed digital nativism.[87]

While these project blogs were an interesting insight into the process of running a major funded research project, they often lacked the passion and edge that made blogs popular in the previous decade. They could have a corporate feel to them as employees carefully tried to fulfill their mandate without crossing a line. The rant had been sanitized from these spaces and replaced with the project update. This self-promotional institutional use of blogs and social media was well entrenched even by 2009. My study of social media use by archives and archivists showed that archives (institutional) had adopted a common practice of broadcasting their own blogs and websites, whereas archivists (people) were much more likely to share content they felt was interesting or useful.[88] The project update was thus a continuation of that institutional use of social media.

Despite these vanilla project blogs, the history blogosphere continued to thrive in pockets where passionate bloggers poured out their ideas and experiences of the archives, and as before, much of the passion came from early-career historians. In the autumn of 2009, Lucy Inglis began blogging about Georgian London in her blog of the same name. Her accessible prose and pithy articles about life and history in London quickly gained a

Table 8. Four types of digital humanities blog posts as defined by Matt Burton, *Blogs as Infrastructure for Scholarly Communication* (141).

Extra-Academic	Para-Academic	Meta-Academic	Quasi-Academic
Off-topic, navel gazing	Important but no space in traditional publications	Infrastructure of social academic life	Ideas in progress or seeking a different audience than journals afford
"Reminders that the people writing these blogs are human"	Technical discussions, technique, methodology	Calls for paper, job postings, new publications	Research or substantial editorial (keynote addresses), shared in progress or in part.
less traditionally "academic"	⟶		*more traditionally "academic"*

substantial audience, leading to a popular book, *Georgian London: Into the Streets* (2013).[89] The book was featured in London's bookstore windows for years after its publication. Inglis was one of a number of historians who started turning to blogs not just to share but also to *do* historical research. In 2014 Tim Hitchcock highlighted Ben Schmidt's *Sapping Attention* blog as instrumental to crafting "one of the most successful academic careers of his generation," while he credited Jennifer Evans with "writing her next book via her blog, *Early Modern Medicine*."[90] The same passions continue to flow from historians across and beyond the English-speaking world who use blogging or other forms of social media as part of their research activity. Burton classified this form of research-focused blogging as "quasi-academic" in his four-part categorization of blogging in the humanities, which included navel gazing, technical or methodological discussions, news about the field, and serious discussions of work in progress (table 8).[91] The quasi-academic post was on its way to the type of published outputs that were familiar to scholars, and thus the blog was playing a role in traditional scholarly activities in a way it previously had not.

By about 2012, many senior historians began to use their blogs as a space to share the text of keynote addresses. Andrew Prescott, historian and former head of the Department of Digital Humanities at King's College London, published seventeen keynote addresses to his blog between 2012 and 2015. Tim Hitchcock routinely did the same on his blog, *Historyonics*. Students too posted talks they had delivered, including PhD history student Robert Rock, who shared a talk he gave on the history of counterfeiting.[92] This practice of electronically sharing the text of a talk was perhaps more common in the United Kingdom than elsewhere, in part because British historians were more likely to write a talk word-for-word than their North American counterparts—though Larry Cebula's 2012 forum post "In which I sit through a conference session" ranted against a similar growing tendency at North American conferences. Interestingly, Cebula's message board rant appeared a few months later as a reworked version, published as part of the *Chronicle of Higher Education*'s official offering, standing as an example of the informal becoming formalized through a process of post-publication review.[93] Cebula may have had a point about the boring nature of papers read aloud; however, a written talk shared online did leave historians with a paper trail that might not otherwise be available for those who could not attend. The Institute of Historical Research in London had experimented with posting "electronic" seminar papers to the Web back in the 1990s, in a service that had become defunct by 1998. Efforts to digitally archive talks were boosted in 2007 by Apple, which launched iTunes U as a space for sharing lectures in audio format. Historians extended this idea to create their own conference archives. In Canada as early as 2008, the Network in Canadian History and Environment began audio-recording talks across the country and posting them online on the society's website.[94]

Publishing keynote addresses had connections to the establishment. In the United Kingdom, the Royal Historical Society annually published and distributed books of all keynotes in its *Transactions of the Royal Historical Society,* which "should be based closely on the paper actually read to the meeting or conference of the Society."[95] The blog therefore became another venue for what was already an acceptable and established practice within the historical profession. As a technology, it had served historians, while also forcing them to change in subtle ways. While you cannot yet order a printed copy of Andrew Prescott's collection of keynote addresses, the intellectual gulf in terms of publishing, between what he had posted to his blog and what the Royal Historical Society committed to paper, was slim. They were both doing their best to ensure that intellectual conversations of merit were preserved so that they could continue to influence the field. Blogging had become a substantial part of the way the historical profession expressed itself, rather than a ranting space on the sidelines, as it first emerged.

Conclusion

As a space for experimenting with scholarly communication, blogging led to a number of innovative new ideas. Many of these new experiments were adopted, co-opted (often begrudgingly), and adapted by the establishment. Some elements of the traditional academy became casualties of this new form of expression. As the number of historians with blogs exploded, the history and computing journals that had been founded in the twentieth century faltered. Among those that fell were *Computers and the Humanities* (1966–2004), *Computing in the Humanities Working Papers* (1996–2008), and the *Journal of the Association of History and Computing* (1998–2010). However, peer-reviewed conversations did not stop among digital scholars, but they occurred in new journals: *Digital Humanities Quarterly* (2007–present), *Digital Studies/Le champ numérique* (2007–present), and the *Journal of Digital Humanities* (2011–14). These publications were led by different groups of people, reinforcing the watershed between the research of the 1980s and '90s and those operating in the new millennium, as well as the tendency for "digital" work to ignore the past while looking instead to the future. Without wanting to suggest a strong causal connection between the fall of these journals and the rise of scholarly blogging, it is certainly difficult to ignore the correlation.

Despite their earlier impact, the influence of blogs declined substantially in the second decade of the new millennium. They were eclipsed first by microblogging sites such as *Twitter*, allowing the conversations to shift into something more like the real-time chat rooms of the early Web, but with nicer graphics and mobile integration. Twitter too found competition in YouTube and Instagram, which by the late 2010s were the key platforms for "influencers" in the new social economy and increasingly visual social media world. Thus, the blog was not what it had once been. However, what the blog did was to provide a new energy for communicating with new types of people, crossing disciplinary lines with greater ease than ever before. As Tara McPherson noted, it had been a rejection of traditional academic hierarchies, and a branching out to find new spaces to build connections with geographically disparate colleagues.[96] But it was more than that. It was also one of the clearest ways that historians' practices were influenced by technology.

Its story is crucial to the understanding of historical studies in the age of the Internet. As mentioned, in 2007 Tim Hitchcock had called his blog a "space for me to rant in that most seventeenth-century sense of the word." By 2014 he had a different way of describing his activities on the blog: "If I give a talk, I turn it into a blog. Not everything is blogged, but the vast majority of the public presentations I make as part of my job, will be. And while many of these texts will never contribute to an academic article, about half of them do. As a result blogging has become part of my own contribution to what I think of as an academic public sphere. It becomes a way of thinking in public and revising one's work, to make it better, in public."[97] Hitchcock was a latecomer to blogging (2007), but his own evolution as a blogger mirrors that which we saw in the historical blogosphere more broadly. As anonymity and ranting gave way to confident bloggers writing openly and level-headedly under their own names, forming communities of like-minded interdisciplinary or format-adventurous scholars, blogging increasingly became part of the historian's mainstream toolkit. Even if one did not read blogs, for a time they became difficult to ignore when they became a prominent part of the funding and impact economy for major projects. Early adopting historians were fundamental in bringing these new forms of communication to the scholarly professions. Many of the technical difficulties, and many of the tears and frustrations of the early ranters, had worked themselves out by the time of blogging's second decade. However, without that experimenting, ranting, and passion, less technologically adventurous historians may never have adopted blogging for their funded project updates, or used them as a venue for learning about interdisciplinary options for their research. Even if its heyday was fleeting, blogging is thus an ideal example of one of the ways that the trial and error of historians working with new technologies had a gradual and substantial impact on established practices.

6

The Digital Past and the Digital Future

As I wrote in the introduction, digital history does not need definitions. It needs histories. This book makes three contributions to the state of scholarship. First, we must revise our memory of technology's relationship with historical studies. It was not a tangential fanatical movement but a central force in a profession constantly evolving over the past fifty years. Second, we must choose our words more carefully. The word "digital" has come to mean too many things. Clear conversations between scholars across historical studies demand a more nuanced vocabulary, which this book provides in the glossary. Third, this history has shown how important it is to understand regional differences in experience. The story is not the same in Canada as in the United States, or in Britain, nor is it the same elsewhere in the world. Understanding the nuance between each local story is key to a strong profession able to communicate effectively across boundaries. All historians must therefore prepare for a more global future that technology will enable but that must be coupled with a culturally sensitive approach to international collaboration and new partnerships. In other words, the humanities will remain vital as the world continues to move in a digital direction and, as culturally aware interdisciplinary scholars, historians should seize the opportunity to take on a leadership role.

A History that Reclaims Technology

Until now, the scholarship on the history and philosophy of the field has largely left technology out of the story. From Novick's *That Noble Dream* and its emphasis on structuralism, to Jordanova's public-history-facing *History in Practice*, to Ankersmith's "Historiography and Postmodernism," and many others besides, technology is not key to the story of a field that preferred to believe its influences were intellectual rather than material. As the history I have presented shows, technology can no longer be left on the sidelines. Neither can historians continue to pretend that their field has been left untouched by the biggest change our civilization has ever seen. Technology has been central to many of the changes that the profession has faced since the coming of personal computers. Yet, a failure or unwillingness to remember pervades.

As I show in this book, by the second decade of the twenty-first century, technology had helped to change the historiography, though not always as historians expected it to (chapter 1). Many of the new research contributions were not building on the same historical conversations as those asked by the previous generation, but were instead focused on problems such as data quality and working with machine-readable texts.[1] It would take another generation for books such as Anthony McEnery and Helen Baker's *Corpus Linguistics and 17th-Century Prostitution* (2017) to turn back to the historiography with a full understanding of how machine-readable texts could be understood by historians at scale. Concurrently but separately, historians (chapter 2) experimented with new technologies that revised our understanding of the archive—from CD-ROMs, to the Internet, to mobile devices, and objects left out in the world, each presenting an opportunity for intrepid explorers. These new media gave historians new tools that transformed the experiences of a generation of historical consumers, from museum-goers, to school-aged children, to besotted lovers.

The rapidly evolving history classrooms of the twenty-first century too had changed (chapter 3). Not only did multimedia help bring primary sources into the room as never before, but "projects" became a dominant feature of a student-centered approach to teaching that often emphasized group work, practical skills, and a flipped classroom over the traditional lecture/seminar format.[2] These changes occurred most frequently in "digital" courses but were influenced by the "digital age" more than anything inherently technological. Meanwhile, for self-learners seeking to find out more about how to make the most of technology, a series of improvements to digital pedagogy provided dynamic websites designed to let them practice new skills in the absence of direct mentorship, and a network of workshops and summer schools provided opportunities to learn informally in the company of others (chapter 4). Finally, without the early experiments of scholar bloggers ranting into the ether (chapter 5), new opportunities to engage through social media may

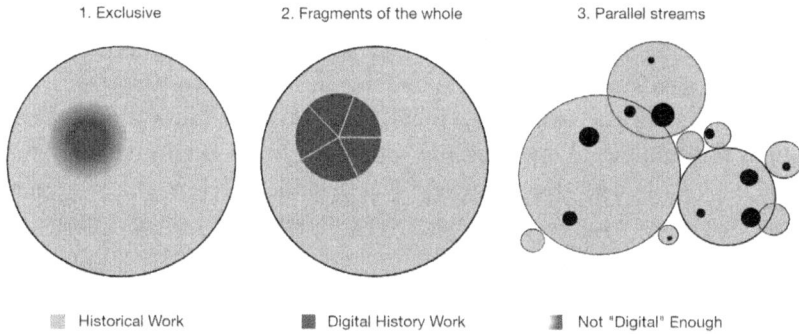

Figure 7. Models of understanding digital history activity.

never have been discovered. Remembering these ways that technologies and historians have come together provides the field with new stories that can be used to grow history's appeal with new audiences, and opportunities to think more broadly and with more context about how the whole field should continue to evolve.

Writing history back into story also means that the way that we perceive "digital history" relative to historical studies must be revised. Traditionally, we have understood digital work through either (1) an exclusive model, or (2) a "fragments of the whole" model, whereas the (3) parallel streams model is more appropriate—see figure 7.

The exclusive model explains digital history as a relatively narrow category of activity, usually encompassing the type of work most of interest to the scholar doing the explaining. In this model, the scholar stands at or near the center of the digital world, and the further one got from *what they did*, the less *digital* that work was, until eventually it was just *traditional* history. Dan Cohen and Roy Rosenzweig's *Digital History* (2005) was an example of this model, effectively defining digital history as a form of outreach involving uploading historical content to the Web. That made sense in 2005 but quickly became dated as attention shifted to new possibilities. Along the same lines, the "hack versus yack" debates of circa 2010 were centered on the idea that digital history was what *I* do, not what *you* do. This approach failed to capture the broad scope of activity, leaving the digital field with very fuzzy edges and with many people feeling the need to argue hopelessly about the true definition when competing visions left them on the outside.

The second approach is the "fragments of the whole" model. It is inclusive and, like the digital humanities "big tent," makes space for many different forms of activity. This was the approach Jane Winters (2018) took when she wrote about the "diversity of digital history," which included everything from communicating history, to historical data analysis, to digitization, to digital tools, and "new kinds of questions."[3] Winters used the term "fragmented" to describe these distinct activities, which is problematic because it implied that the pieces could be put together into something intellectually coherent that could be described as "digital history" (fig. 7, model 2). However, by looking at historians' evolving relationships with technology, it becomes clear that no coherent area of scholarly activity ever existed. If it had been intellectually coherent, we would never have been faced with the polyglot syllabus of the 2010s that tried to teach "digital history" by introducing topics as intellectually diverse as public history and big data analysis in the same course, and often without any historical content to speak of (mea culpa).

Instead, the model put forth in this book is the parallel streams model (fig. 7, model 3). It builds on earlier work by scholars such as Serge Noiret who was one of the few to have carved off "digital public history" as a subcategory of digital history work.[4] This book not only pushes us past the models of Cohen and Rosenzweig, of Graham, Milligan, and Weingart, and of Winters, but it pushes Noiret's digital subfields even further by insisting on many more categories, each with its own history. In other words: history is itself a bulbous field of different activities, and technology has touched that field in lots of different ways. Often those impacts had more to do with adjacent "traditional" work than with any of the other areas considered "digital." Technology had an impact *here*, and *there*, and *over there too*, rather than in any pattern that suggests an intellectual coherence to a "digital" movement.

The End of "Digital History" and the Beginning of a New Vocabulary

Second, if technology is to be central to the way historical studies remembers its evolution, then it cannot be centralized but must instead be diffuse. We must bring to an end our notion of a coherent "digital history" subfield. The best way to do that is to revise how we use the term "digital history." As a collective noun it still has relevance, but not to describe activity. Since the early new millennium it has been used effectively to describe an imagined community of historians whose members had drunk deeply of the philosophies and culture of the digital era and who had designs on making adjustments to the status quo in the profession and the wider world.[5] In other words, it described a group of people, and not what they did. Used in this way, "digital history" describes something closer to an adopted philosophy or the ethos of a political party. This community-focused function is one that "digital history" can continue to serve, even as we adopt new language to describe the work done by digital historians.

Like most imagined communities, members within often have more in common with outsiders than with each other. Despite their occasional differences of opinion with "nondigital" colleagues, a digital historian working on outreach projects probably has far more in common with other public historians than he or she does with a research scholar or classroom educator. The same is true for the other types of digital historian. The continued choice to describe one's work as "digital history" (as opposed to one's philosophy or cultural identity) thus masks the nature of relationships in unhelpful ways.

The term "digital history" perhaps first appeared in the 1990s, when Steven Mintz and Sara McNeil used it as the title of a new digital archive of U.S. history materials.[6] It gained in popularity after 2005, when Dan Cohen and Roy Rosenzweig published a book by the same name, advocating for a need for historians to engage with the Internet, which they imply would be to *do* digital history. Yet, digital historians don't *do* digital history. As I show throughout this book, "digital" work in history refers to so many different areas of intrigue that it is a meaningless descriptor, signifying little more than "new."

Instead, I suggest an unpicking of the term as it relates to the activities of historians. Each of the chapters in this book does exactly that, focusing in particular on one of five key areas well known to historians: research, collection management, teaching, learning, and communicating, to show how historians working with technology engaged with, influenced, and were influenced by parts of each. The treatment I provide here is not exhaustive, and I could have included many other chapters on issues as diverse as gender, editing, software development, heritage, open access, race, or postmodernism, to name a few. My examples were also necessarily selective, providing local case studies that may not have been representative of everyone's experience, as is natural in any history such a this. Nevertheless, I hope to provide a clear sense of how each activity was internally coherent as an attempt to push a certain branch of historical studies forward, without representing coherent effort across the "digital" domain.

Only by separating those various contributions into different histories, each with their own vocabulary that clearly draws lines between types of work, will future conversations be easier to have and digital contributions to history easier to understand in context. By framing future contributions under more descriptive categories, technology and digital culture can continue to contribute to the historical professions, but without implying that digital history is a cohesive effort leading toward a common endpoint.

What this means is that language is important and historians need to take care to say or write what they mean. Environmental historian Finn Arne Jørgensen is apparently already on board with this idea. In 2018 he tweeted in frustration that too many of the grant applications he read still relied on imprecise language designed to dazzle rather than explain: "digital humanities tools and methods are not magical tricks that can translate (vague) data into results and insights. Be very specific and realistic about what is to be done."[7] If one's work involves interdisciplinary quantitative historical research, call it that. If a historian is pushing the boundaries of user engagement studies, say so. If the goal is to discover new means of encouraging effective collaboration in the history classroom, then frame the conversation so that it contributes to wider discussions on that issue. Historians need to keep pushing the boundaries with technology, but they must stop calling it "digital history" when something more specific better reflects what they are doing. In most cases this vocabulary already exists; historians just need to use it. To help bring that vocabulary to the surface, I include in this book a glossary that outlines some key terms and phrases that will help facilitate conversations into the future. It does not seek to offer an exhaustive ontology, but it is a starting point aimed specifically at empowering historians to choose their words more carefully.[8]

Preparing for New Partnerships

Finally, historians interested in technology and digital culture still undoubtedly have much to offer the historical professions. The way to do that is increasingly likely to involve getting back in step with traditional practices, particularly where doing so helps ease the channels of communication. The 2017 push for more "digital argumentation," which saw the Programming Historian ask for more tutorials that helped historians analyze rather than manipulate data, and a white paper out of the Roy Rosenzweig Center for New Media on engaging with historians in the published literature rather than on social media, is evidence of that shift.[9] Doing so means carefully chosen rhetoric and continued attempts to build bridges whenever possible.

This book shows that working with technology has been a negotiation between cultures. The digital and the analog historian negotiate professional spaces. The future will also involve negotiation. With the continued push toward a global scholarly ecosystem, historians with technical expertise are well positioned to be leaders in international collaboration. This is a space in which historians will have to tread carefully and with respect, particularly when partnerships are forged with postcolonial societies where historic power dynamics could still be sensitive issues.

As I hope is evident throughout this book, history's relationship with computers was different in different parts of the world. The evolving digital syllabi (chapter 3) was just one illustration of that. The U.S. version of digitally inflected teaching was heavily influenced by new media and the Internet (chapter 2), whereas in England, local pressures and understandings of what historians do meant that courses tended to adopt a history-first approach, with a little digital analysis sprinkled in. Similar regional types of differences occur everywhere. It can be tempting to try to transplant local solutions into new environments, but more proactive solutions take into account regional variations. Despite the fact that understanding cultural differences is not inherently "digital," I suspect that "becoming more culturally aware" will become the "digital" skill of tomorrow, falling in with other ideas championed by digital historians that were not technological.

I hope this book provides the groundwork for some historians to become more aware of those cultural differences. The need for this awareness is growing because global interest in technology among historians is on the rise. The Digital Humanities Association of Southern Africa launched in 2017, and South Africa's North-West University advertised for the country's first digital scholar that same year.[10] These developments came after inviting a number of academics to the country in 2016 to share on-going digital work. Working with countries like South Africa poses new challenges and possibilities for historians from regions such as Europe or North America. Doing so means adapting to cultural differences in the way history is viewed and used in that part of the world. Some South African historians see history as a path to evidence-supported activism. While this is not unheard of in Europe, Canada, and the United States, the degree to which activism and history are linked in Africa may make some consciously dispassionate historians in the West uncomfortable (though the high-impact evidence-driven digital activism of the #BlackLivesMatter protests taking place as I write in June 2020 show that these practices may have spread beyond Africa). Working with places such as Africa also means maintaining an awareness of the effects lingering from decolonization. Africa is home to many so-called endangered archives, which suffer from a lack of funding and support and which could benefit enormously from collaborations that are led by local needs and local expertise.

A successful collaboration also requires understanding the local ecosystem, including how decisions are coerced in certain directions by matters of policy. For example, South Africa's Department of Higher Education and Training has traditionally produced an annual list of "approved" journals in which it encouraged scholars to publish all research. Historically, future research funding was linked to articles appearing in those journals, and it was a means for a member of the Global South to encourage high-quality research by subjecting its scholars to publications with a known level of rigor.[11] While these journal ranking systems may have been a helpful way for the government to measure the country's relative scholarly standing, interdisciplinary scholarship (including much of the history research described in chapter 1) may be hampered because the approved lists were dominated by mono-disciplinary journals.[12] Working with South African scholars, or anyone outside of one's immediate geopolitical environment, means adapting to policy pressures.

Making sure digital initiatives are culturally relevant has been an important challenge that the team at the Programming Historian have had to wrestle with as we sought to expand into the 400-million-person Spanish-speaking world. In 2017 the new Spanish-language team on the project, Maria José Afanador-Llach (Colombia), Víctor Gayol (Mexico), and Antonio Rojas Castro (Spain), began translating the publication's tutorials into Spanish. Rather than merely translate the text, they drew on their depth of understanding of Spanish cultures and the ways people studied and engaged with history in Spanish-speaking countries. As such, they translated the text but also adapted lessons to ensure that they drew on culturally relevant examples. As the translation work was likely to take several years, the team also made decisions about which lessons to prioritize, knowing which were most likely to have a positive impact on Spanish-language work.

Their local experience helped make the project a booming success. In 2016, the project received only three thousand visitors with Web browsers set to Spanish. The following year it was forty-six thousand, and in 2018 it had grown to two hundred thousand, most of whom visited from one of seven countries. Spain and Mexico are now among the top five countries in the world with visitors to the site, and Spanish-language visitors make up just over 20 percent of total volume. Over the course of that first year those seven Spanish-speaking countries had the largest percentage traffic increases of anywhere (table 9). The growing interest has led the team to expand Spanish recruitment, bringing on four new members, and publishing its first-ever Spanish-first lessons in 2019, taking the project beyond translation and putting Spanish-speaking historians in control of their own learning resources.

Table 9. Growth in Programming Historian website traffic from 2016 to 2018.

Country	Visitor Increase 2017–18	Percentage Increase
Peru	2,426	1,193
Ecuador	1,821	1,090
Colombia	5,682	1,073
Chile	4,373	946
Mexico	9,868	714
Argentina	3,699	551
Spain	11,468	402
TOTAL	39,337	508
Top Five Countries by Website Traffic		Website Traffic Volume 2018
United States		224,665
India		123,334
United Kingdom		51,032
Spain		48,700
Mexico		38,937
Top Ten Cities by Website Traffic		Website Traffic Volume 2018
Bengaluru, India		33,618
London, UK		17,641
New York, USA		14,864
Chennai, India		12,703
Madrid, Spain		12,528
Mexico City, Mexico		11,680
Hyderabad, India		11,658
Santiago, Chile		10,907
Bogota, Colombia		9,989
Pune, India		8,091

India too shows great promise as its economy continues to expand. This growth in technical skills in India means increased opportunities to work together in more advanced ways. In the past, Indians were involved in the creation of a number of digitization projects, including the Old Bailey Online, where Indian workers, whose names have not been credited in the same way as the project leaders, transcribed the 127 million words of text, for a fee. Today, India's version of Silicon Valley is booming. Four of the top ten cities in the Programming Historian's traffic logs are Indian: Bengaluru, Chennai, Hyderabad, and Pune (table 9), with Bengaluru bringing in almost twice as many visitors as its nearest rival, London. India accounted for nearly 14 percent of all traffic to the site, second only to the United States. The potential for India as a base for technical development for historical projects is on the rise.

These international opportunities are exactly the sort of challenges that "digital" historians have historically taken on. However, as is the case with many of the examples in this book, the challenges are not technical, but social. They are characteristic of the ways that the digital age has helped bring Canadian sociologist Marshall McLuhan's "global village" to life. It is up to historians to rise to those challenges as they continue to seek sensitive ways to influence the historical professions through new partnerships. A clearer vocabulary is a first step in allowing historians to articulate the changing roles and opportunities facing the field, and to position themselves productively to contribute to the future. Knowing the field's past only helps to frame that future work, by letting scholars understand where they have come from in a way that continuing to use the term "digital" simply does not.

Appendix

Digital History Syllabus Corpus (2002–2017)

By the new millennium, the way computing for historians was being taught had changed substantially from the course John Styles and Roger Middleton had been planning at Bristol in 1987. To get an understanding of what technology-intensive history teaching was and how it was changing, I put together a corpus of 130 self-described "digital history" syllabi from Canada, the United States, and England that were offered between 2002 and 2017 (fig. 8).[1] Because of the movement in the late 1990s to "make teaching a public activity," it became more common in the new millennium to openly share one's syllabus online.[2] However, the practice was not ubiquitous. While it represents all relevant syllabi I was able to find, this corpus is not complete; survivability usually depended on whether or not an educator decided to post a syllabus openly on the Web. Copies are much more likely to be found on personal websites than university-administered pages. We have copies of twenty-four syllabi from William J. Turkel at Western University in Ontario, who self-archived each instance of each course on his research website. By contrast, courses taught through password-protected course management systems were not discoverable. This was particularly common in England, where, apart from my own syllabi, all examples in the sample had to be collected by requesting them from colleagues of whom I was aware.

The corpus includes eighty-five unique courses, and an additional forty-five revised syllabi (fig. 9), often but not always by the same instructor. In some cases the revisions to syllabi were minor, often changing dates to reflect the new calendar year, however there were cases of substantial reworkings.

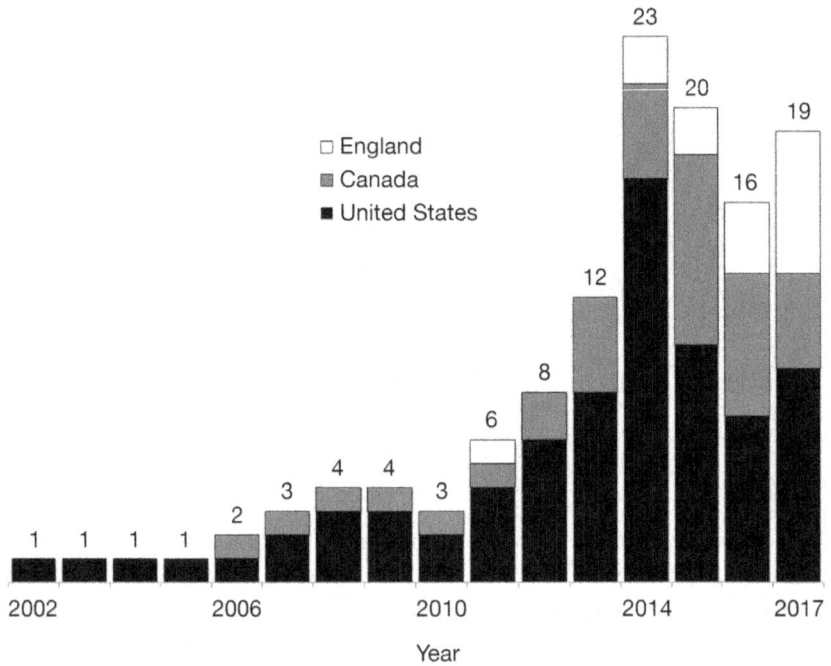

Figure 8. The number of syllabi in the corpus per country per year.

The distribution of courses on offer was uneven across the three countries and universities, as can be seen in table 10 and figure 8. A summary glance at the collection highlights a number of important characteristics in digital history teaching provision, which makes it possible to build up a profile of what a "digital history" course was (and perhaps what it should have been called instead): firstly by considering, by whom and where digital history was being taught, before looking at what and how digital skills were imparted on students and how that differed from traditional ways of teaching history.

It was not often easy to tell at what level a course was offered. Deciphering this often required local knowledge of the meaning of course codes. Some U.S. and Canadian universities teach undergraduate and graduate students together, sometimes with different assignments or learning requirements, blurring the line between syllabus and level further. This practice is incredibly rare in England. Of the thirty-five syllabi for which the level of study was clear, two-thirds were offered to graduate students. My impression of the remainder is that these courses were most commonly taught at upper-level undergraduate or master's level (with a few exceptions), building on a foundation of historical skill learned earlier in one's degree. All U.K.-based

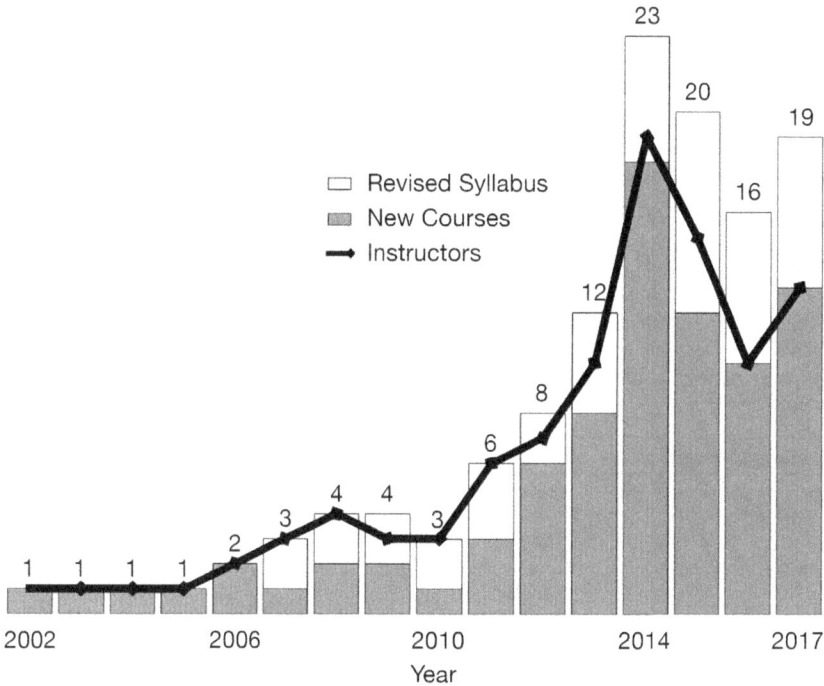

Figure 9. The number of syllabi and instructors per year in the corpus, separated by the first appearance of a course instance, and any revised syllabi that were also found.

Table 10. Characteristics of the digital history syllabi by country.

	United States	Canada	England	Total
Total courses	81	35	14	130
Unique courses	59	15	11	85
Universities	42	7	6	55
Unique instructors	51	8	8	67
Ratio male/female	37:13 (1 unknown)	8:0	6:2	
Earliest entry	2002	2006	2011	
Peak of activity	2014	2015	2017	
Most prolific university:	George Mason University (28 syllabi)	Western University (26 syllabi)	University of Hertfordshire (6 syllabi)	
Most prolific instructor:	Lincoln Mullen (9)	William J. Turkel (24)	Adam Crymble (5)	

courses in the set are undergraduate. Many of the more technically complex courses in the United States and Canada were at the master's level.

Table 11 gives a sense of what was offered on a digital history course. Each syllabus was classified into a number of categories to help build a picture of the modes of teaching employed.[3] Each classification fits within one of three broad areas:

- The balance between "history" and "digital"
- The type of "digital history" it sought to impart on students
- The use of or absence of specific resources and approaches commonly associated with digital history or traditional history courses (e.g., blogging)

Table 11. The classification system used for categorizing syllabi based on the style of delivery and specific content used in teaching. Includes number of matching syllabi— first instance of a course only.

	Number	Criteria
A. Historical emphasis (one category per course)		
High	11	Could reasonably be called a "history" class.
Moderate	21	Contained a historical theme as a starting point for exploring "digital" approaches.
Low	1	Contained historiographical readings, but no obvious historical theme.
None	40	Course was aimed at historians but contained no obvious historical content.
Unknown	12	Not enough detail to made a classification.
Total courses	85	
B. Approach (possible to be multi-classified)		
Cliometrics and quantitative	3	Course included explicit statistical training or introduction to quantitative skills.
Invented archive/engagement	53	Students required to upload material online (a narrative, an archive) for an audience (excluding blogging).
Programming, data cleaning, tool building	24	Students taught to program or about programming computers. Distinct from "encoding" in HTML, TEI, XML, or similar.
Data analysis and "big data"	42	Students taught how to use or about using "tools" or software that processed data in pursuit of building historical understanding.
Wide survey	41	Students exposed to a number of loosely related concepts, which do not necessarily coherently build on one another.
Total courses	85	
C. Specific content (possible to be multi-classified)		
Project-based	64	Students required to produce a final "project" that was not an essay.
Blogging	44	Students required to blog or keep a reflective practic journal or social media presence as part of their assessed work.
Cohen and Rosenzweig	31	The reading list included Dan Cohen and Roy Rosenzweig, *Digital History* (2005).
Historiography	20	Readings included articles and books that historians would regard as the outputs of historical research.
Total courses	85	

Glossary
A New Vocabulary

This glossary takes inspiration from Janice Reiff's 1991 extensive appendix of terminology in *Structuring the Past*. It encourages practitioners to use more precise language when discussing "digital" or "digital history" work.

algorithmic thinking   Associated with problem solving. The process of breaking a problem into a series of steps that can be followed by either a human or a computer. See chapters 3 and 4.

big data   Associated with **research** and analysis. To use big data is to use very large or very complex datasets as the source base for a study. The term was often used by historians to mean "more than you can close read"; few historical datasets are large enough to meet the accepted criteria of big data. See chapter 1.

blogging   Associated with scholarly communication. A blog or weblog is a website that includes diary-style entries written by the website owner (an individual or group of people). It is a form of self-publishing, and the term "blogging" simply means publishing to a blog. Often confused with **reflective practice**. Matt Burton has further broken down the concept of blogging based on the motives of the blogger (see chapter 5).

born-digital archive   Associated with collections. An archive of primary sources that was created in a computer and may not exist in a physical format. See chapter 2.

cliometrics   Associated with quantitative **historical research** of the late twentieth century. Sometimes also referred to as econometrics, new history, new economic history, or social science history. Still practiced as **quantitative history** in the twenty-first century. See chapter 1.

cocreation   Associated with collaborative projects. The process of working with stakeholders to produce a project that meets the needs of both the academic partner and the community who feels a sense of ownership over the history. Implies a sense of equality between both parties. Can be either an academic or public-facing initiative. See chapter 2.

collection management   Associated with collections. The professional administration of an archive or collection of primary sources. May include a combination of physical or digital objects. Closely associated with the GLAM industry—galleries, libraries, archives, and museums. Collection managers facilitate **historical research** without necessarily conducting it themselves. See chapters 1 and 2.

corpus linguistics   Associated with **research** and analysis. A form of research that involves the analysis of a body of texts using linguistic methodology (see **linguistics**). Sometimes associated with **big data** analysis and interdisciplinarity (see **interdisciplinary**). Requires an understanding of the field of linguistics. See chapter 1.

crowdsourcing   Associated with collaborative projects and collections. Drawing on the labor of publics to complete tasks that might otherwise be too laborious. Usually used for tasks that cannot easily be completed by a computer. Sometimes viewed as exploitative. See chapter 2.

cultural history   Associated with **research**. A branch of **historical research** that is concerned with the culture and traditions of past societies—no matter what **historical methodology** or so-called digital approaches are used (if any). Much "digital" work on textual sources is actually cultural history. See chapter 1.

curation   Associated with collections. The process of building or managing an archive or collection of primary sources. Involves selecting and contextualizing the contents of the collection. This may involve a great deal of researching but is generally not conducted with the explicit goal of answering **historical research** questions. See chapter 2.

data analysis   Associated with **research**. The process of putting a primary source or series of primary sources through an algorithmic test (see **algorithmic thinking**) that returns a result to be interpreted by the researcher. These tests are often mathematical, though that may not always be clear to a user who is not well-informed. See chapters 1, 3, and 4.

data cleaning   Associated with collections and **research**. The process of improving or standardizing the quality of data across a number of records in a collection. Often before a **data analysis** or as part of **collec-**

tion management. This can be done computationally or manually. See chapters 1 and 3.

data mining   Associated with **research**. The process of conducting **data analysis**, sometimes **big data** analysis, on a set of records with the hope of finding patterns or anomalies worth further investigation. See chapters 1 and 3.

demographic history   Associated with **research**. A branch of **historical research** concerned with populations and social structure in the past. Often associated with **cliometrics** and **quantitative history**. See chapter 1.

digital   A system or process rooted in finite mathematics and logic. For example, a system that uses 1s and 0s as the basis of its computational decision making. A digital representation of time uses a finite number of options—seconds, minutes, and hours. The opposite of analog, which can have infinite values (e.g., the sweeping shadow of a sundial). The term is routinely used imprecisely to describe anything to do with computers, the **digital age**, or **digital culture**.

digital age   Associated with **digital culture** and **algorithmic thinking**. The period associated with the era of personal computing. Sometimes also called the information age.

digital archive   Associated with collections. A collection of material that is either born digital (see **born-digital archive**) or contains digitized (see **digitization**) items and that is accessible via a computer—often on the Internet. See chapter 2.

digital culture   Associated with **algorithmic thinking** and the **digital age**. A phrase that captures the impacts of technology on the ways we think and act in both personal and professional spheres. Connected to the rise of the Internet and social media in particular.

digital humanities   Associated with **algorithmic thinking**. A highly contested term not unlike "digital history" but covering all humanities subjects. It evolved out of the humanities computing movement of the late twentieth century. See chapter 1.

digitization   Associated with collections. The process of converting a physical object into a format that can be stored in the memory of a computer. This involves selectively capturing certain attributes of the object at the expense of others. For example, taking a digital photograph of a letter and recording metadata about the letter's creator. Often associated with a **digital archive**. See chapters 1 and 2.

editorial   Associated with scholarly communication. A piece of writing expressing the opinion of the author. Often associated with **blogging** and **ranting**. Not generally accepted as the same as writing research findings for publication. See chapter 5.

encoding   Associated with scholarly editing and **Web development**. Not to be confused with procedural **programming**, this process involves embedding additional information within a digital object—for example marking up all mentions of people in a historical text. Commonly used in digitization to enable searching by types of information. See chapters 1 and 2.

flipped classroom   Associated with **pedagogy**. The practice of doing activities traditionally associated with homework during class time. The teacher becomes a guide for active learning rather than a "sage on the stage" delivering content. See chapters 3 and 4.

gamification   Associated with public history and collections. The act of adopting principles that make otherwise mundane activities fun in order to encourage further participation. Often associated with **crowdsourcing**. See chapter 2.

historical geography   Associated with **research**. The interdisciplinary study of history using the methods, approaches, or intellectual foundations of geographers. See chapters 1 and 3.

historical methodology   Associated with **research** and analysis. The approaches—often algorithmic (see **algorithmic thinking**)—to conducting **historical research** on primary sources. Historical methods may have been developed through research and a process of peer review but are generally not **historical research** in their own right. See chapter 1.

historical research   Associated with **research**. An argument-driven, evidence-based answer to a question about the past. Must be connected to a time, place, or historical theme. Generally speaking it must be peer reviewed before it is accepted as a part of the **historiography**. See chapter 1.

historiography   Associated with **research**. The body of peer reviewed scholarly literature that represents our combined intellectual understanding of the past. Linked specifically to **historical research** rather than other forms of research conducted by historians. See chapters 1 through 5.

human interaction space   Associated with **pedagogy**. A classroom or lab that is designed to encourage people to work productively and collaboratively. Often it contains a lot of new technology, but underlying it is a desire to get people to work together. See chapter 3.

image analysis   Associated with **research**. Like textual analysis, but with methodologies designed for analyzing and understanding images, either on their own or at scale.

information science   An academic field associated with the management and manipulation of data and information. Fundamental to many "digital" activities, including **collection management**, **data cleaning**, and **data analysis**.

interactive media   Associated with public history and **pedagogy**. Also associated with Web 2.0 and the idea of the **participatory Web** where users expect to be able to engage with content rather than merely consume it. Interactive media could include a **virtual reality** game or a **crowdsourcing** initiative in which users were asked to classify documents. See chapter 2.

interdisciplinary   Associated with **research**. Research that brings together different disciplines to create new approaches that could not be achieved separately. For example, applying linguistic approaches to historical problems in scholarly rigorous ways. Not to be confused with **multidisciplinary.** See chapter 1.

invented archive   Associated with collections. Sometimes referred to as an intentional archive. The use of computers to bring together primary sources into a collection that does not exist in a single archive or repository but that can be brought together virtually as a **digital archive**. See chapter 2.

invisible college   Associated with digital culture. A virtual community and a support network that is associated with the types of activities one might hope to find in a university but which are not always available. For example, someone to help you understand a new technology that might be relevant to your work. The invisible college is not a place but a means of obtaining that support informally from colleagues around the world. See chapters 4 and 5.

linguistics   An academic field associated with **research**. Much of the **textual analysis** that has been referred to as "digital" is the **interdisciplinary** application of methods developed by linguists to understand language. Often associated with a branch of humanities computing in the late twentieth century and with **corpus linguistics** approaches to large volumes of text. See chapters 1, 3, and 4.

machine learning   Associated with **research** and collections. A branch of computer science that uses statistics and **algorithmic thinking** to identify patterns in records. The term "learning" implies a level of artificial intelligence. See chapters 1 and 2.

macroscope   Associated with **research**. Sometimes associated with **big data** and "distant reading." This approach to history is the opposite of the microscope, standing back to see patterns in the big picture. See chapter 1.

meta research   Associated with **research**. The study of scholarly practices of historians or audiences of history. Though it may be very rigorous and peer reviewed, it is not to be confused with **historical research** because it does not seek to form conclusions about the past; rather, it seeks to form conclusions about the past's interpreters and audiences. See chapter 2.

mobile computing   Technology that can be taken away from the desk, including smartphones and wearable technologies. Often associated with place-based computing or **virtual reality**. See chapter 2.

multidisciplinary   Associated with **research**. Research that brings together scholars from different disciplines to collaborate and look at a research challenge together. The scholars then go back and report their findings to their distinct disciplines. Not to be confused with **interdisciplinary**. See chapter 1.

participatory Web   Based on the principle of Web 2.0 that users should be able to contribute to the Web, not just consume content on it. Led to the rise of social media; often associated with **crowdsourcing** and invented archives. See chapter 2.

pedagogy   Associated with teaching and learning. The theory and practice of teaching. See chapters 3 and 4.

programming   Not to be confused with **encoding**, this process involves writing commands or software that give a computer a series of instructions to complete a task. Based on **algorithmic thinking**. Commonly used in **data cleaning**, **Web development**, and **data analysis**. See chapters 1, 3, and 4.

project-based learning   Associated with collaborative work across the field. A challenge to the idea that historians and history students should express their knowledge only in essay format. Projects vary widely, from websites built by groups of students to academic CD-ROM projects of the 1980s. See chapters 2 and 3.

quantitative history   Associated with **research**. See **cliometrics**.

ranting   Associated with scholarly communication. Often confused with

blogging and the **editorial**. It is a passionate expression of an opinion, which may or may not be linked to reflective practice. Many historians used blogs as a space where they could rant, but the two are not intrinsically linked. See chapter 5.

reflective practice   Associated with **pedagogy** and scholarly communication. Often confused with **blogging**. It is the process of looking back on how an activity went and considering how improvements might be made in the process. Many historians used blogs as a space where they could reflect on their practice, but the two are not intrinsically linked. See chapters 3 and 5.

research   The systematic analysis of evidence with the aim of generating new knowledge. See chapter 1.

scholarly communication   The methods and means by which historians communicate their intellectual findings. These include **historical research** findings in peer-reviewed venues such as journals or scholarly monographs, and less formal information such as calls for papers, details of interest for professional development, and elements of community building. Also associated with **blogging**. See chapters 4 and 5.

self-learning   Associated with **pedagogy**. The process of teaching oneself new skills, or learning new skills outside of traditional classroom settings. May be through **written tutorials** or trial and error. See chapter 4.

social history   Associated with **research**. A branch of **historical research** concerned with experiences of non-elites. Often but not exclusively understood through **quantitative history** methods, and associated with **cliometrics** in the late twentieth century. See chapter 1.

software   Associated with all areas of "digital" work. Often mistakenly called a digital tool, software is a computer program that follows an algorithm to perform a predefined task or set of tasks. In many cases, that process could also be performed without the aid of a computer. See chapters 1 through 5.

software development   Associated with hacking and **historical methodology**. Often mistakenly called tool building. This is the process of writing a piece of **software**. See chapter 3.

software use   Associated with **research** and public history. Often mistakenly called tool use, this is the process of using **software** someone has already written. See chapter 3.

statistics   Associated with **research**. A branch of mathematics linked to the analysis and interpretation of data. Not to be confused with "digital" methods. Often linked with **cliometrics**. See chapters 1, 3, and 4.

student centered learning   Associated with **pedagogy**. A branch of teaching that puts students at the focus of classroom activity, rather than the teacher. See chapter 3.

textual analysis   Associated with **research**. A form of **data analysis** that uses text as the unit of study. Sometimes associated with **corpus linguistics, linguistics,** or **data mining**.

user studies   Associated with **research**. A branch of **meta research** that focuses on understanding the needs, preferences, or reactions of audiences interested in or engaged with history. Often aimed at improving audience or user experience or engagement. Not to be confused with **historical research**. See chapter 2.

virtual reality   The creation of a virtual or fictional immersive experience that lets users feel like they have been transported to the past. Often linked to mobile computing. See chapter 2.

Web 2.0   See **participatory Web**.

Web design   Associated with communication. The application of principles of design to the building of a website, with the intention of producing a clear and enticing user experience. See chapters 2 and 3.

Web development   Associated with communication. The technical development of a website, sometimes referred to as building the back end. See chapter 3.

written tutorial   Associated with **pedagogy**. A series of step-by-step instructions designed to allow **self-learning** or instructor-led-learning related to a technical task. The tutorial may introduce concepts related to **historical methodology, Web development,** or other technical matters. It may facilitate **historical research** or engagement skills, and may communicate the methods developed through research but is not to be confused with **research** itself. See chapters 3 and 4.

Notes

Abbreviations

GMUSC   George Mason University Special Collections
IA   Internet Archive Wayback Machine
PP Styles   Private Papers of John Styles, 1987–88
PP Hitchcock   Private Papers of Tim Hitchcock, 1991–1996
PP Short   Private Papers of Harold Short, 1993

A note on archived website URLs. The Internet is a constantly changing space and is difficult to meaningfully cite. Wherever possible, cited websites were either already captured by the Internet Archive Wayback Machine (IA) or were added to it.

To keep notes both accurate and terse, references are given to the shortest possible version of the website address, along with the date of the archived page as it was cited and as available in the IA, using the format "(IA: dd/mm/yyyy)." Where no URL is present, it is available in the bibliography. Should the live version change or be removed, the page can still be found. This approach acknowledges that it is a version of the site that is important to you as the reader, not the date that I accessed it.

Introduction

1. "NMC, Monday Morning, New Voices, New Stories" (1997), 37, GMUSC C0038/89/4, Roy Rosenzweig Papers.

2. Townsend, "How Is New Media Reshaping the Work of Historians?" historians .org/publications-and-directories/perspectives-on-history/november-2010/how-is -new-media-reshaping-the-work-of-historians (IA: 16/04/2016).

3. For example, see Becker, "Everyman His Own Historian"; Bloch, *Historian's Craft*; Carr, *What Is History?*; Elton, *Practice of History*; Kracauer and Kristeller, *History*; Hackett Fisher, *Historians' Fallacies*; Braudel, *On History*; Lowenthal, *Past Is a Foreign Country*; Novick, *That Noble Dream*; Wallach Scott, *Gender and the Politics of History*; Ankersmit, "Historiography and Postmodernism"; Appleby, Hunt, and Jacob, *Telling the Truth*; Nora, *Realms of Memory*; Jordanova, *History in Practice*; Wineburg, "Historical Thinking"; Booth and Hyland, *Practice of University History Teaching*; Gaddis, *Landscape of History*; Booth, *Teaching History*; Wineburg, "Crazy for History"; Thompson, *Postmodernism and History*; Tyrrell, *Historians in Public*; Bain, "They Thought the World Was Flat?"; de Groot, *Consuming History*; Banner, *Being a Historian*; Munslow, *History of History*; Townsend, *History's Babel*.

4. Novick, *That Noble Dream*; Ankersmit, "Historiography and Postmodernism"; Wineburg, "Historical Thinking."

5. Jordanova, "Historical Vision," 343.

6. Jordanova, *History in Practice*; Tyrrell, *Historians in Public*; de Groot, *Consuming History*; Banner, *Being a Historian*.

7. Gulldi and Armitage, *History Manifesto*.

8. Shorter, *Historian and the Computer*; Rahtz, *Information Technology in the Humanities*; Denley and Hopkin, *History and Computing*; Reiff, *Structuring the Past*; Mawdsley and Munck, *Computing for Historians*; Lewis and Lloyd-Jones, *Using Computers in History*; Andersen, "Defining Digital History"; Cohen and Rosenzweig, *Digital History*; Hirsch, *Digital Humanities Pedagogy*; Mills T. Kelly, *Teaching History*; Weller, *History in the Digital Age;* Graham, Milligan, and Weingart, *Exploring Big Historical Data*.

9. Black, "How Far Have We Come in the Digital Humanities?" parezcoydigo. wordpress.com/2010/10/14/how-far-have-we-come-in-the-digital-humanities (IA: 15/10/2010).

10. Ibid.; Nowviskie, "Eternal September of the Digital Humanities," nowviskie. org/2010/eternal-september-of-the-digital-humanities (IA: 06/11/2010).

11. For example, see Turkel, "Interactive Exhibit Design" (IA: 10/11/2012).

12. Blevins, "Digital History's Perpetual Future Tense."

13. Ayers, *What Caused the Civil War?* 79.

14. *Computers and the Humanities* (1966–2004); *Computing in the Humanities Working Papers* (1996–2008); *Journal of the Association of History and Computing* (1998–2010); *Journal of Digital Humanities* (2011–14).

15. Andersen, "Defining Digital History."

16. Rockwell et al., "Design."

17. Tonra, "How Do You Define DH?" dayofdh2014.matrix.msu.edu/members/ jtonra (IA: 18/09/2015).

18. Weingart, "A Working Definition of Digital Humanities," scottbot.net/ HIAL/?p=39749 (IA: 09/12/2013).

19. Gaffield interview, 2018.

20. McCarty interview, 2017.

21. Terras, "Peering Inside the Big Tent: Digital Humanities and the Crisis of Inclusion," melissaterras.blogspot.co.uk/2011/07/peering-inside-big-tent-digital.html (IA: 19/05/2012).

22. Nowviskie, "On the Origin" (IA: 12/01/2014).

23. American Historical Association. "Guidelines."

24. Ayers, "A Historian in Cyberspace," *American Heritage*; Ayers, "Pasts and Futures"; Ayers, "Does Digital Scholarship Have a Future?"; William G. Thomas, "Computing and the Historical Imagination"; Hitchcock, "Digitising British history since 1980," history.ac.uk/makinghistory/resources/articles/digitisation_of_history.html (IA: 02/09/2014); Putnam, "Transnational"; Gaffield, "Words, Words, Words"; Winters, "Digital History."

25. Hockey, "History of Humanities Computing"; Jockers, *Macroanalysis*; Nyhan and Flinn, *Computation and the Humanities*; Earhart, *Traces of the Old*; Murray, *Hamlet on the Holodeck*; Aarseth, *Cybertext*.

26. Fiormonte, "Digital Humanities"; Risam, "Navigating the Global Digital Humanities."

27. Sichani et al., "Diversity and Inclusion."

Chapter 1. The Origin Myths of Computing in Historical Research

1. Thomas, "Computing and the Historical Imagination," 59; Graham, Milligan, and Weingart, *Exploring Big Historical Data*, 19–26; Winters, "Digital History"; Gaffield, "Words, Words, Words."

2. Thomas, "Computing and the Historical Imagination," 59.

3. Quoted in Novick, *That Noble Dream*, 384.

4. Busa, *Index Thomisticus*; see Graham, Milligan, and Weingart, *Exploring Big Historical Data*, 19–26.

5. Julianne Nyhan's ongoing work looks at the hidden labor of Busa's female staff.

6. Winters, "Digital History"; Gaffield, "Words, Words, Words."

7. Utopian stories include *The Jetsons* (1963) or Disney's Tomorrowland (1955), or today's tech giants, including Google, Facebook, and Instagram. Dystopians count George Orwell's *1984* (1949) and H. G. Well's *The Time Machine* (1895) among their ranks.

8. Crane, "What Do You Do with a Million Books?"

9. For example, see Scheinfeldt, "Where's the Beef?" foundhistory.org/2010/05/wheres-the-beef-does-digital-humanities-have-to-answer-questions (IA: 23/12/2014).

10. *Domesday Book* (1086), E 31/2/2, National Archives.

11. Brewer, *Sinews of Power*.

12. Bryer, "Double-Entry Bookkeeping"; Landau, "Laws of Settlement."

13. For example, see Hitchcock and Shoemaker, *London Lives*.

14. Gordon, *History and Philosophy*.

15. Arkell, "Illuminations and Distortions."

16. Ravenstein, "Laws of Migration."

17. Novick, *That Noble Dream*, 1–33.

18. Margo Anderson, "Quantitative History," 247.

19. Eaton, "Review."

20. E. P. Thompson, *Making of the English Working Class*.

21. Thomas, "Computing and the Historical Imagination," 59.

22. Ibid.

23. Novick, *That Noble Dream*, 224–28.

24. Fogel, "New Economic History."

25. Conrad and Meyer, "Economies of Slavery," 95.

26. Fogel and Engerman, *Time on the Cross*; Banks, "Review."

27. Tomlinson, *Introduction*.

28. Richard White, "What Is Spatial History?" web.stanford.edu/group/spatial history/cgi-bin/site/pub.php?id=29 (IA 22/04/2016).

29. Zephyr, "Layers, Flows and Intersections."

30. Charlesworth, *Atlas of Rural Protest*; Mitschele, "Identity and Opportunity."

31. Beattie, "Pattern of Crime," 59.

32. Hay, "War, Dearth and Theft."

33. Gaffield interview, 2018.

34. Hay, "War, Dearth and Theft," 118; Sharpe, *Crime in Early Modern England*, 61.

35. Cockburn, "Early Modern Assize Records," 215; Samaha, *Law and Order*.

36. Whaples, "Quantitative History," 295–97.

37. Daunton, "Professor Martin Daunton" (IA: 14/09/2013).

38. North, "Cliometrics," 414.

39. Floud, "Professor Sir Roderick Floud" (IA: 10/05/2013).

40. Margo Anderson, "Quantitative History," 248.

41. Grief, "Cliometrics," 400.

42. Graham, Milligan, and Weingart, *Exploring Big Historical Data*.

43. Crane, "What Do You Do with a Million Books?"

44. Turnbull, "Historians, Computing," 134.

45. Morton, "Once."

46. Marche, "Literature Is Not Data: Against Digital Humanities," lareviewofbooks .org/essay/literature-is-not-data-against-digital-humanities (IA: 01/10/2013); Kirsch, "Technology Is Taking Over English Departments," newrepublic.com/article/117428/ limits-digital-humanities-adam-kirsch (IA: 02/05/2014).

47. Zampolli, "Introduction"; Turovsky, "Ten Years of Google Translate," blog. google/products/translate/ten-years-of-google-translate (IA: 30/09/2016).

48. Härtel, "To Treat or Not to Treat."

49. Terras and Robertson, "Downs and Acrosses"; Schmidt, "A TEI-based Approach to Standardising Spoken Language Transcription"; Sperberg-McQueen, "Text in the Electronic Age"; Driscoll, "Encoding Old Norse."

50. "TEI: History," *TEI Text Encoding Initiative*, 19 Nov. 2014, tei-c.org/About/histor y.xml (IA: 13/12//2014); "TEI P1 Guidelines for the Encoding and Interchange of Machine Readable Texts First draft 16 July 1990; Draft Version 1.1," *TEI Text Encoding Initiative*, 1 Nov. 1990, tei-c.org/Vault/Vault-GL.html (IA: 26/04/2001).

51. Hockey, "History of Humanities Computing," 16.

52. For an example of historians engaging intellectually with TEI for research, see Armaselu, Martins, and Jones, "Materiality of TEI Encoding."

53. Tomasek and Bauman, "Encoding Financial Records."

54. Allington, Brouillette, and Golumbia, "Neoliberal Tools (and Archives): A Political History of Digital Humanities," lareviewofbooks.org/article/neoliberal-tools -archives-political-history-digital-humanities (IA: 05/05/2016).

55. Hockey, "History of Humanities Computing."

56. Kirsch, "Technology Is Taking Over English Departments," newrepublic.com/ article/117428/limits-digital-humanities-adam-kirsch (IA: 02/05/2014); Marche, "Literature Is Not Data."

57. Fish, "What Is Stylistics?"

58. Robertson, "The Differences between Digital History and Digital Humanities," drstephenrobertson.com/blog-post/the-differences-between-digital-history-and -digital-humanities (IA: 19/08/2014).

59. Weingart, "Submissions to Digital Humanities 2014," scottbot.net/HIAL/ ?p=39588 (IA: 20/04/2014); Weingart, "Submissions to Digital Humanities 2015 (pt. 2)," scottbot.net/HIAL/?p=41053 (IA: 25/04/2015); Weingart, "Submissions to DH2016 (pt. 1)," scottbot.net/HIAL/?p=41533 (IA: 27/09/2016).

60. Busa, *Index Thomisticus*. See Graham, Milligan, and Weingart, *Exploring Big Historical Data*, 19–26.

61. Lieberman, "Text on Tap."

62. Robertson, "Differences between Digital History."

63. Crane, "What Do You Do with a Million Books?"; Moretti, "Conjectures."

64. Graham, Milligan, and Weingart, *Exploring Big Historical Data*; Börner, "Plug-and-Play Macroscopes."

65. Nicholson, "Digital Turn."

66. Crymble, "Digital History."

67. Blaney, "Problem of Citation."

68. Badke, "Treachery of Keywords"; Ramsay, "Hermeneutics."

69. Putnam, "Transnational," 390; Solberg, "Googling the Archive."

70. Moravec, "How Digitized Changed Historical Research," medium.com/on -archivy/how-digitized-changed-historical-research-d77c78540878 (IA 16/09/2018).

71. Beals, "Record How You Search," blogs.lse.ac.uk/impactofsocialsciences/2013/ 06/10/record-how-you-search-not-just-what-you-find (IA: 11/09/2013).

72. Putnam, "Transnational."

73. Magdy and Darwish, "Arabic OCR Error Correction"; Leydier, Lebourgeois, and Emptoz, "Text Search"; Torabi, Durgan, and Tarpley, "Early Modern OCR Project."

74. Holley, "How Good Can It Get?"; Binder, "Google's Word Engine Isn't Ready for Prime Time," hebinderblog.com/2010/12/17/googles-word-engine-isnt-ready-for -prime-time (IA: 21/02/2011).

75. Mühlberger et al., *Transkribus*, transkribus.eu (IA: 28/04/2015).

76. Sullivan, "When OCR Goes Bad," searchengineland.com/when-ocr-goes-bad -googles-ngram-viewer-the-f-word-59181 (IA: 20/12/2010).

77. Hitchcock et al., *Connected Histories.*

78. *17th and 18th Century Burney Collection Newspapers; House of Commons Parliamentary Papers.* Tate et al., "Technical Methods—About British History Online," british-history.ac.uk/about#technical (IA: 17/12/2014).

79. Hitchcock et al., "About This Project," oldbaileyonline.org/static/Project.jsp (IA: 13/05/2008); Crymble, "Identifying and Fixing Transcription Errors in Large Corpuses," adamcrymble.blogspot.ca/2013/02/identifying-and-fixing-transcription .html (IA: 21/01/2018).

80. Cayley, "Digitization for the Masses."

81. Hitchcock, "Privatising the Digital Past," historyonics.blogspot.co.uk/2016/06/ privatising-digital-past.html (IA: 05/05/2017).

82. Hitchcock et al., *Old Bailey Proceedings*, oldbaileynline.org:80 (IA: 13/02/2003); Tate et al., *British History Online* (IA: 02/08/2003).

83. Kreibich, "How to Ask for Datasets," medium.com/@ckreibich/how-to-ask -for-datasets-d5ef791cb38c (IA: 05/09/2015).

84. Hitchcock et al., *Connected Histories* (IA: 14/05/2011).

85. Hawtin, "Welcome to Our Newest CASS PhD Student!" cass.lancs.ac.uk/?p=1781 (IA: 03/10/2015).

86. Farquhar et al., *British Library Labs.*

87. Navickas and Crymble, "From Chartist Newspaper."

88. Nicholson, "Victorian Meme Machine"; Beals, "Stuck in the Middle."

89. Hargreaves, "Digital Opportunity"; *Copyright and Rights; Exceptions to Copyright*; John Kelly, "Text and Data Mining" (IA: 05/08/2016).

90. Hersh, "How Does Elsevier's Text Mining Policy Work with New UK TDM Law?" elsevier.com/connect/how-does-elseviers-text-mining-policy-work-with -new-uk-tdm-law (IA: 19/07/2014); "Gale Leads to Advance Academic Research" (IA: 05/09/2015); Cayley, "Digitization for the Masses."

91. Clifford et al., "Geoparsing History."

92. For example, see Goislard De Monsabert, "Importance of Consistent Datasets."

93. Aiden et al., "Quantitative Analysis"; *Google N-gram Viewer*, books/google. com/ngrams (IA: 28/09/2011).

94. Grafton, "Loneliness and Freedom," historians.org/publications-and-directories/ perspectives-on-history/march-2011/loneliness-and-freedom (IA: 08/01/2014); Aiden and Michel, "Thoughts/Clarifications on Grafton's 'Loneliness and Freedom,'" culturomics .org/Resources/faq/thoughts-clarifications-on-grafton-s-loneliness-and-freedom (IA: 16/07/2015).

95. Hitchcock, "Culturomics, Big Data, Code Breakers and the Casaubon Delusion," historyonics.blogspot.co.uk/2011/06/culturomics-big-data-code-breakers-and .html (IA: 31/03/2017).

96. Hitchcock and Shoemaker, "Making History Online."

97. Cockburn, "Early Modern Assize Records," 215; Samaha, *Law and Order*.

98. Huber, "*Old Bailey Proceedings*"; Blaxill, "Quantifying the Language"; Anthony McEnery and Baker, *Corpus Linguistics*.

99. Anthony, "AntConc"; Sinclair and Rockwell, *Voyant Tools*, voyeurtools.org (IA: 07/09/2011) and voyant-tools.org (IA: 31/03/2012).

100. For the exception, see Hitchcock and Turkel, "*Old Bailey Proceedings*."

101. Cohen et al., *Data Mining*.

102. Turkel, "A Naïve Bayesian in the Old Bailey, Part 1," digitalhistoryhacks .blogspot.ca/2008/05/naive-bayesian-in-old-bailey-part-1.html (IA: 21/01/2018).

103. Penny Johnston, "How Do You Define DH?" dayofdh2014.matrix.msu.edu/ members/pennyjohnston (IA: 12/04/2014).

104. Endres, "More than Meets the Eye"; Giacometti, "Evaluating Multispectral Imaging."

105. Wall et al., *Virtual St. Paul's Cross Project* (IA: 16/05/2013); Winters, "Virtual St Paul's Cathedral and Paul's Cross," ihrdighist.blogs.sas.ac.uk/2014/01/13/virtual-st -pauls-cathedral-and-pauls-cross (IA: 09/09/2014).

106. Marsh, "Sacred Space."

107. Wall et al., *Virtual St. Paul's Cross Project* (IA: 16/05/2013).

108. Milligan, "Mining the Internet Graveyard"; Milligan, "Lost in the Infinite Archive"; Milligan, "Automated Downloading" (IA: 18/06/2013).

109. Winters, "Digital History"; Gaffield, "Words, Words, Words."

110. Horbinski, "How Do You Define DH?" dayofdh2014.matrix.msu.edu/members/ ahorbinski (IA: 18/09/2015).

111. Scheinfeldt, "Where's the Beef?" foundhistory.org/2010/05/wheres-the-beef -does-digital-humanities-have-to-answer-questions (IA: 23/12/2014); Robertson, "Arguing with Digital History" (IA: 09/05/2017); Crymble, "The Five Lessons No One's Yet Written (But Need Writing)," programminghistorian.org/posts/call-to -action (IA: 10/05/2017).

112. Weingart, "'Digital History' Can Never be New," scottbot.net/digital-history -can-never-be-new (IA: 10/05/2016).

Chapter 2. The Archival Revisionism of Mass Digitization

1. Morse, *Improvements*.

2. *American Standard Code* (IA: 26/05/2016).

3. A. M. McEnery and Xiao, "Character Encoding."

4. Hitchcock, "Digitising British History," history.ac.uk/makinghistory/resources/ articles/digitisation_of_history.html (IA: 02/09/2014).

5. Hart, *Project Gutenberg*; Hart, "The History and Philosophy of Project Gutenberg" (1992), gutenberg.org/wiki/Gutenberg:The_History_and_Philosophy_of_Project _Gutenberg_by_Michael_Hart (IA: 02/09/2006).

6. Both Leslie Johnston and Tim Hitchcock provide useful timelines of major early digitization projects: Leslie Johnston, "Before You were Born," blogs.loc.gov/ thesignal/2012/12/before-you-were-born-we-were-digitizing-texts (IA: 07/12/2016); Hitchcock, "Digitising British History."

7. Noiret, "Digital History 2.0," 133; Ayers interview, 2018.

8. Schmidt, "Digital History and the Copyright Black Hole," sappingattention .blogspot.co.uk/2011/01/digital-history-and-copyright-black.html (IA: 14/05/2012).

9. Smith Rumsey, "Strategies," 12–14.

10. Fraistat, Jones, and Stahmer, "Canon"; Price, "Digital Scholarship"; Earhart, "Can Information Be Unfettered?"

11. Caswell, Punalan, Sangwand, "Critical Archival Studies," 2–5.

12. Stoler, "Pulse of the Archive," 237–56.

13. Winters, "Digital History."

14. Noiret, "Digital History 2.0"; Brier, "Confessions."

15. Brier interview, 2017; Ayers interview; Mintz interview, 2018; Reiff interview, 2018.

16. Brier interview; Roediger, "Review," 259.

17. Brier interview.

18. The first in this series was Brier, Levine, and Freeman, *Who Built America?* (1989).

19. Bruno, "Review."

20. Burns, *Civil War*; Cates, Fontana, and White, "Designing an Interactive Multimedia Instructional Environment," 5; Toplin, *Ken Burns's The Civil War*; Kenneth Williams, "Review," 95.

21. Lancioni, "Rhetoric."

22. Hazen, "Multimedia and Other Resources," h-net.msu.edu/cgi-bin/logbrowse .pl?trx=vx&list=edtech&month=9101&week=&msg=pdAcpEorQxVkK8liAoA1NQ &user=&pw= (IA: 26/05/2013); Ward, Burns, and Burns, *Civil War*.

23. Cates, Fontana, and White, "Designing an Interactive Multimedia Instructional Environment."

24. Aarseth, *Cybertext*, 81.

25. Ayers, *What Caused the Civil War?* 78; Ayers, "Doing Scholarship on the Web," *Chronicle of Higher Education*; Murray, *Hamlet on the Holodeck*, 126.

26. Fontana, "Lynn Fontana, Ph.D," *LinkedIn* (2017), linkedin.com/in/lynnfontana (cannot be archived).

27. Wayne Thomas, "Wayne P. Thomas, Ph.D," thomasandcollier.com/wayne-p. -thomas.html (IA: 21/04/2018).

28. Rosenzweig, "Who Built America? (Grant Application), 1995," 6, 44, in *RRCHNM20*, 20.rrchnm.org/items/show/349 (IA: 05/08/2015).

29. Dubnick, "CD-ROM REVIEW: Discovering American History," *H-Survey*, h-net.msu.edu/cgi-bin/logbrowse.pl?trx=vx&list=apsa-cived&month=9902&week =c&msg=IM9gvY1n8Yashf33arAdBg&user=&pw= (IA: 24/05/2013).

30. Goodman and White, "Who Built America?" 121.

31. Rosenzweig and Brier, "Why Read a History Book."

32. Brier, "Confessions."

33. "The American Social History Project, High School Collaboration" (1995), 3–6, GMUSC/6/8, Roy Rosenzweig Papers.

34. "The Center for History and New Media" (1994), GMUSC/C0038/6/8, Roy Rosenzweig Papers.

35. Rosenzweig, "So, What's Next for Clio?"

36. "CD-ROMs: American History and Literature Titles" (1997), 77–82, GMUSC/C0038/38/4, Roy Rosenzweig Papers.

37. Not to say there were none. See, for example, Corcoran and Marks, *Canada's Visual History CD-ROM*; Graham Reynolds, "Making Canadian History."

38. Mueller, "Re: Computers in the Class Room," h-net.msu.edu/cgi-bin/logbrowse .pl?trx=vx&list=h-latam&month=9406&week=d&msg=%2b1ygm%2bInun3O/3AP/ W2HMQ&user=&pw= (IA: 21/01/2018).

39. H-Amstdy Comoderator, "Future of Multimedia Research (3 responses)," h-net .msu.edu/cgi-bin/logbrowse.pl?trx=vx&list=h-amstdy&month=9408&week=a&ms g=MQJGfmlY8uziN8Wz6Br38Q&user=&pw= (IA: 21/06/2013).

40. Brodman, "Re: How Many Historians Have CD-ROM Drives?" h-net.msu .edu/cgi-bin/logbrowse.pl?trx=vx&list=h-teach&month=9412&week=a&msg=W4 T%2bGtKantfTXiwF6Er1gg&user=&pw= (IA: 21/01/2018).

41. Michalove, "H-Net Job Postings 1/2," h-net.msu.edu/cgi-bin/logbrowse .pl?trx=vx&list=h-albion&month=9309&week=&msg=CDe6RVscic4IYRBOsilicQ &user=&pw= (IA: 21/01/2018).

42. Fusco, "Re: Digital Video—MPEG," h-net.msu.edu/cgi-bin/logbrowse.pl?trx=vx &list=edtech&month=9401&week=c&msg=KqqRSmuGgg5OFUDLJ6kwCA&user =&pw= (IA: 04/09/2006).

43. Ayers, *Vengeance and Justice*.

44. Ayers interview.

45. Ayers et al., *Valley of the Shadow*: valley.lib.virginia.edu/VoS/usingvalley/valley story2.html (IA: 23/02/2016).

46. Ayers, *What Caused the Civil War?* 83.

47. Ayers, "Lincoln's America 2.0."

48. Ayers interview.

49. Ayers et al., *Valley of the Shadow*: valley.lib.virginia.edu/VoS/usingvalley/valley story2.html (IA: 23/02/2016).

50. Ayers et al., *Valley of the Shadow*: valley.lib.virginia.edu/VoS/usingvalley/valley story.html (IA: 23/02/2016).

51. Ayers interview.

52. Ayers et al., *Valley of the Shadow*: valley.lib.virginia.edu/VoS/usingvalley/valley story.html.

53. Horowitz, "Finding History on the Net" (1995), americanheritage.com/ finding-history-net (cannot be archived); Virshup, "Pixeling Dixie" (1998), wired. com/1998/05/pixeling-dixie (IA: 01/04/2019); Jeffrey Young, "A Historian Presents" (2000), nytimes.com/2000/06/29/technology/a-historian-presents-the-civil-war online-and-unfiltered-by.html (cannot be archived).

54. "American Memory," memory.loc.gov/ammem/index.html (IA: 04/05/1999).

55. Mintz and McNeil, *Digital History* (IA: 26/10/2003); Bender *History Matters* (IA: 08/02/1999).

56. Mintz interview; Schrum interview, 2018.

57. "Web Sites: A Work in Progress" (1997), 83–106, GMUSC/C0038/89/4, Roy Rosenzweig Papers.

58. Shenkman, *History News Network* (2009), historynewsnetwork.org/article/ 76806 (IA: 05/05/2017).

59. Bowen, "1997 President's Report."

60. Extracted from the *Andrew W. Mellon Foundation's Grant Database* (IA: 08/10/2014).

61. They consider a "record" to be a mention of an individual. A single primary source may contain many "records" by this measure. *Ancestry.com* (IA: 25/12/1996).

62. Kenney et al., "Collections," 6.

63. Putnam, "Transnational," 386.

64. Kenney et al., "Collections," 13.

65. Edmund King, "Digitisation of Newspapers."

66. Taycher, "Books of the World, Stand Up and Be Counted!" booksearch.blogspot .co.uk/2010/08/books-of-world-stand-up-and-be-counted.html (IA: 21/11/2012).

67. The schemes spent £42,859,797, £28,660,130, and £28,660,130, respectively. Dunning, *Digitising the Past*; Dunning, "List of Projects"; Dunning, "List of Digitisation Projects Funded Under UK's AHRC"; Dunning, "List of Digitisation Projects by UK's JISC."

68. Abby Smith, "New-Model Scholarship," 4.

69. "Business Plan 18 Dec.doc" (2001), PP Hitchcock.

70. "Impact Case Study REF3b—-The Old Bailey Online," *Research Excellence Framework* (2014).

71. "Application 12 Jan 2001.doc" (2001), PP Hitchcock.

72. Burns et al., *Clergy of the Church of England Database* (1999); Tate et al., *British History Online* (2002).

73. Spice and Watzman, "Nov 27: Online Library Gives Readers Access to 1.5 Million Books," cmu.edu/news/archive/2007/November/nov27_ulib.shtml (IA: 12/10/2008).

74. *Hathi Trust Digital Library*, hathitrust.org (IA: 19/09/2008); *Europeana*, europeana .eu/portal/en (IA: 22/07/2016); *Trove*, National Library of Australia, trove.nla.gov .au (IA: 11/11/2009).

75. Hitchcock, "Towards a New History Lab," sas-space.sas.ac.uk/2854 (IA: 02/12/2014).

76. "September 11 Digital Archive (2002)," 2, in *RRCHNM20*, 20.rrchnm.org/items/show/338 (IA: 05/08/2015).

77. Brennan and Kelly, "Why Collecting History Online Is Web 1.5," rrchnm.org/essay/why-collecting-history-online-is-web-1–5 (IA: 01/10/2016).

78. O'Reilly, "What Is Web 2.0," oreilly.com/pub/a/web2/archive/what-is-web-20.html (IA: 14/06/2009).

79. *Time* 168, no. 26 (25 Dec. 2006).

80. Andersen, "September 11."

81. Prelinger et al., *Understanding 9/11: A Television News Archive,* archive.org/details/911 (IA: 10/10/2017).

82. Scheinfeldt et al., *The September 11 Digital Archive*, 911digitalarchive.org (IA: 17/01/2002).

83. Cohen, "History"; Scheinfeldt et al., "Browse Items," *The September 11 Digital Archive*, 911digitalarchive.org/items/browse (IA: 22/11/2016).

84. Andersen, "September 11."

85. Frisch, *Shared Authority*, xx.

86. "Roy Rosenzweig to Jesse Ausubel (1 July 2004)," 3, in *RRCHNM20*, 20.rrchnm.org/items/show/338 (IA: 05/08/2015).

87. Lenstra and Alkalimat, "eBlack Studies," 171.

88. Rosenzweig et al., "About the Hurricane Digital Memory Bank," hurricanearchive.org/about (IA: 29/08/2006).

89. di Santis, *Portrait-Story Project*, portraitstoryproject.org (IA: 01/05/2008).

90. Smith Rumsey, "Creating Value and Impact," 2.

91. Howe, "The Rise of Crowdsourcing," wired.com/wired/archive/14.06/crowds_pr.html (IA: 13/01/2006).

92. Heppler and Wolfenstein, "Crowdsourcing Digital Public History," tah.oah.org/content/crowdsourcing-digital-public-history (IA: 18/04/2015).

93. Sridhar, "User Participation," 117.

94. Howe, "Rise of Crowdsourcing."

95. von Ahn et al., "reCAPTCHA"; von Ahn, "Curriculum Vitae," *Carnegie Mellon University* (2012?), cs.cmu.edu/~biglou/LuisvonAhn_CV.pdf (IA: 16/05/2017).

96. Ayres, "Singing for Their Supper," 3.

97. *British Library Georeferencer*, "About This Project," bl.uk/georeferencer/georefabout.html (IA: 14/01/2017).

98. Kowal, "Done! 2,700 Maps Georeferenced by Volunteers," blogs.bl.uk/magnificentmaps/2014/01/done-2700-maps-georeferenced-by-volunteers.html (IA: 21/01/2018).

99. At the time of this writing, John Warren had contributed corrections to 6,148,992 lines and was still averaging approximately 45,000 line edits per month in mid-2020: "Information about Trove User: JohnWarren" (accessed 11 June 2020): trove.nla.gov.au/userProfile?user=user:public:JohnWarren (cannot be archived).

100. Eveleigh et al., "I Want to Be a Captain!"; *Old Weather*, "Why Scientists Need You," classic.oldweather.org/why_scientists_need_you (IA: 19/02/2017).

101. Raddick et al., "Galaxy Zoo."

102. Seaward, "Transcription Update—14 October to 10 November 2017," blogs.ucl.ac .uk/transcribe-bentham/2017/11/14/transcription-update-14-october-to-10-november -2017 (IA: 21/01/2018).

103. Causer and Wallace, "Building a Volunteer Community."

104. Raddick et al., "Galaxy Zoo."

105. Danniau, "Public History," 131.

106. Causer, Tonra, and Wallace, "Transcription Maximized."

107. Navickas and Crymble, "From Chartist Newspaper," 239.

108. Pittman and Sheehan, "Amazon's Mechanical Turk."

109. Antón, Camarero, and Garrido, "Exploring the Experience Value."

110. Gaffield interview, 2018.

111. Mühlberger et al., *Transkribus,* transkribus.eu (IA: 28/04/2015).

112. Crymble, "Crowdsource Arcade."

113. Do, Zhao, and Wang, "SherlockNet," labs.bl.uk/British+Library+Labs+Com petition (IA: 03/08/2017).

114. "If Someone from the 1950s Suddenly Appeared Today," as.reddit.com/r/Ask Reddit/comments/15yaap/if_someone_from_the_1950s_suddenly_appeared_today/ c7qyp13 (IA: 07/02/2015).

115. Hardman, "Walkmanology," 44.

116. Crichton, *Westworld.*

117. Libin, *American Musical Instruments,* 7.

118. Sheldon, "Extended Museum," 8.

119. Hatfield_visitor, "Good Audio Tour," www.tripadvisor.co.uk/ShowUserReviews -g1135438-d531548-r475842601-Framlingham_Castle-Framlingham_Suffolk_East _Anglia_England.html#REVIEWS (cannot be archived).

120. Bederson, "Audio Augmented Reality."

121. Turkel, *Archive of Place.*

122. Turkel, "Geo-DJ, Part 1: The Idea," digitalhistoryhacks.blogspot.ca/2007/12/ geo-dj-part-1-idea.html (IA: 21/01/2018).

123. Banzi et al., *Arduino,* arduino.cc (IA: 18/01/2006); Saul Greenberg, *Phidgets,* phidgets.com (IA: 02/04/2002).

124. *Historypin,* historypin.org (IA: 07/07/2010).

125. *Street Museum.*

126. Tebeau, "Listening to the City"; Tebeau, Bell, and Souther, "Strategies."

127. "Smart Love Lock" (2014), smartlovelock.com (IA: 27/11/2015).

128. "Living Headstones," monuments.com/living-headstones (IA: 16/02/2012); "Qeepr," qeepr.com (IA: 26/12/2013).

129. Haahr, *Haunted Planet,* hauntedplanet.com (IA: 10/01/2012); Haahr, "Vampire in the Machine" (cannot be archived).

130. Bhattacharyya, "Toronto's Fort York National Site to get a Virtual Reality Retelling," hindustantimes.com/world/toronto-s-fort-york-national-site-to-get-a-virtual-reality-retelling/story-zLScLZr8iWAoeKAJ4Zw9GO.html (IA: 03/01/2016).

131. Hitchcock, "Digitising British History."

Chapter 3. Digitizing the History Classroom

1. Collinson, "Elizabethan Church."

2. Lawson and Silver, *Social History of Education*.

3. Boggs, "Three Roles."

4. Burnard and Proud, *Humanist*, 1989, dhhumanist.org/Archives/Converted_Text/humanist.1988–1989.txt.

5. Kolb, *Learning Style Inventory*.

6. Purvis, "Teacher as Moderator."

7. Alison King, "From Sage on the Stage."

8. Vincent and Ross, "Learning Style Awareness."

9. Wineburg, "Historical Thinking," 81; Wineburg, "Crazy for History"; Bain, "They Thought the World Was Flat?" 209.

10. "Application 12 Jan 2001.doc" (2001), PP Hitchcock.

11. "Committee on History in the Classroom" (1980), GMUSC/C0038/6/7, Roy Rosenzweig Papers.

12. Cutler interview, 2019; "History Teaching Alliance" (1995), GMUSC/C0038/6/8, Roy Rosenzweig Papers.

13. Cutler interview.

14. Reiff, *Structuring the Past*, 58.

15. Hirsch, "</Parentheses>," 7; Siemens, "The Humanities Computing Curriculum," web.viu.ca/siemensr/HCCurriculum (IA: 29/03/2009).

16. Mills Kelly, *Teaching History*; Booth and Hyland, *Practice of University History Teaching*; Booth, *Teaching History*; Hirsch, *Digital Humanities Pedagogy*.

17. Shorter, *Historian and the Computer*, 59.

18. Jonathan Gershuny and Alan Lewis, "Course Outline, University of Bath" (October 1987), PP Styles; Michael Young and Willmott, *Symmetrical Family*.

19. "Computer Techniques and Economic Theory in Historical Analysis" (1987), PP Styles.

20. "Partial Syllabus" (1987), PP Styles.

21. John Styles, "Lecture Notes—Information in History" and "Lecture Notes—Dealing with Data" (1987), PP Styles.

22. John Styles, "Lectures: Computer Techniques and Economic Theory in Historical Analysis" (1987), PP Styles.

23. Cockburn, "Early Modern Assize Records."

24. Roger Middleton to Professor Bernard Alford, "Memo 8701," 15 Oct. 1987, PP Styles; "New Earnings Survey, 1974–1996" (2010), reference no. 006810, Office of National Statistics.

25. This was in addition to $20,000 tuition: Burnard and Proud, "Computers and Teaching in the Humanities."

26. Roger Middleton, "Course Description" (1987), PP Styles.

27. Roger Middleton, "Course Description: Computer Teachniques and Economic Theory in Historical Analysis" (1987), PP Styles.

28. Short interview, 2019.

29. Harold Short, "Humanities Computing Courses at King's College London 1993" (1993), PP Short.

30. "Database" (1992?), PP Hitchcock.

31. "Exam" (1993), PP Hitchcock.

32. Tim Hitchcock, "Partnership Award" (1991), PP Hitchcock.

33. Ibid.

34. McGillivray, "Research-Centred Humanities Computing at Calgary," web.viu .ca/siemensr/HCCurriculum/abstracts.htm#McGillivray (IA: 29/03/2009).

35. Gorman, "Wired Historian" (IA: 10/10/2004).

36. "The New Media Classroom" (1997), 45, GMUSC/C0038/89/4, Roy Rosenzweig Papers

37. Davidson, "Collaborative Learning for the Digital Age," chronicle.com/article/ Collaborative-Learning-for-the/128789 (IA: 29/08/2011).

38. Reiff, *Structuring the Past*, 56.

39. McDaniel, "Why Study Digital History?" wcm1.web.rice.edu/why-study-digital -history.html.

40. McClurken, "Teaching and Learning with Omeka."

41. McClurken, "Digital Literacy"; Tebeau, "Pursuing e-Opportunities."

42. Josh Greenberg, "Blogging and Other Literary Forms," blog.epistemographer. com (IA: 07/07/2003); on Turkel quietly dropping it from his Interactive Exhibit Design class in 2016 after a decade of student blogging at Western University, see Turkel, "History 9832B" (IA: 23/06/2016).

43. Turkel, "History 513F Digital History" (IA: 30/12/2007); Schön, *Reflective Practitioner*.

44. Mills Kelly, "Teaching and Learning" (IA: 06/09/2012).

45. Graham, "hist3907b-winter2015 . . ." (IA: 22/01/2018).

46. Torget, "Course Syllabus" (IA: 17/10/2014); McDaniel, "Syllabus" (IA: 08/12/2014).

47. Mhobbs, "Class T-shirt," chnm.gmu.edu:80/history/faculty/kelly/blogs/ h696f05/archives/2005/11/class_tshirt.html#comments (IA: 23/12/2011).

48. Tebeau, "Pursuing e-Opportunities."

49. Gaffield interview, 2018.

50. McClurken and Slezak, "Research-Based Web Sites."

51. Seefeldt, "Hist 470" (IA: 11/10/2012); McClurken, "Hist 471C3" (IA: 06/04/2013); Whisnant, "History 671" (IA: 22/02/2016).

52. Madsen-Brooks, "Hist 381–001" (IA: 20/12/2014); Langer, "Hist 8885 Syllabus" (IA: 13/10/2016); Gibbs, "Digital Mapping" (IA: 24/12/2014).

53. Kelly, "Lying About the Past" (IA: 02/03/2009).

54. Jane, "The Real Story of Edward Owens," lastamericanpirate.net (IA: 29/01/2009); Appelbaum, "How the Professor Who Fooled Wikipedia Got Caught by Reddit," theatlantic.com/technology/archive/2012/05/how-the-professor-who -fooled-wikipedia-got-caught-by-reddit/257134 (IA: 18/01/2012).

55. Fitzgerald, "Here There Be Monsters," themorningnews.org/article/here-there -be-monsters (IA: 16/09/2012).

56. Petrik, "Clio II" (IA: 24/07/2014).

57. Turkel, "Interactive Exhibit Design" (IA: 10/11/2012).

58. Turkel, "Digital Humanities 1011B" (IA: 09/08/2013).

59. Turkel, "The History Department with a Fab Lab," williamjturkel.net/2013/02/02/ the-history-department-with-a-fab-lab (IA: 27/02/2013); Richard Lane, *Big Humanities*, chapter 1.

60. Kedgley, "Development."

61. Elliott, MacDougall, and Turkel, "New Old Things."

62. Turkel, "The History Department with a Fab Lab."

63. Hitchcock and Turkel, *"Old Bailey Proceedings."*

64. Beichner et al., "Introduction to SCALE-UP"; Beichner et al., "Student-Centred Activities."

65. Lage, Platt, and Treglia, "Inverting the Classroom."

66. Brown and Campione, "Guided Discovery."

67. Cosgrave (@mikecosgrave), *Twitter*, 13 March 2017, 3:10pm, twitter.com/mike-cosgrave/status/841305479192158208 (IA: 22/01/2018).

68. Harford, "What Makes the Perfect Office?" timharford.com/2017/02/what _makes_the_perfect_office (IA: 21/02/2017); "Inside Google's New York City Office: Why Your Workplace Stinks," time.com/3024615/inside-googles-new-york-city-office (cannot be archived); Wakefield, "Google Your Way to a Wacky Office," news.bbc .co.uk/1/hi/7290322.stm (IA: 16/10/2013).

69. Hedge, "Open-Plan Office."

70. Irving, "Collaboration."

71. Davies, "Groupwork"; G. G. Smith et al, "Overcoming Student Resistance."

72. For the first instance of a "contract" between collaborating students, see McClurken, "Syllabus" (IA: 28/03/2016).

73. Düring, "Assignments" (IA: 26/03/2016).

74. Moretti, "Conjectures."

75. Cohen, "Clio Wired," (2009) (IA: 24/12/2009); Cohen, "Clio Wired" (2010) (IA: 07/11/2016).

76. Ide, "What Humanists Need to Know about Computers (and Computer Science)," web.viu.ca/siemensr/HCCurriculum (IA: 29/03/2009).

77. Turkel, "Max Programming" (cannot be archived).

78. Turkel, "Digital Humanities 1011B" (IA: 05/09/2014).

79. "Digital History" (IA: 11/02/2017).

80. Mullen, "Clio 3," 4, 3 (IA: 20/09/2014).

81. Thirty-two of the sixty-one courses offered data analysis, compared to twenty-two offering programming.

82. Baker, "Digital Skills" (cannot be archived); Beals, "Digital History."

83. Friedman, "New Viewpoints" (IA: 04/02/2017).

84. Koeser, "Trusting Others."

85. Milligan, "HIST 303" (IA: 12/04/2014).

86. Embarrassingly, see Crymble, "Intro" (IA: 11/08/2015).

87. Goldstone, "Teaching Literary Data; What Makes It Hard," andrewgoldstone.com/blog/ddh2018preprint (IA: 30/01/2017).

88. Parry, "How the Humanities Compute in the Classroom," chronicle.com/article/How-the-Humanities-Compute-in/143809 (IA: 01/04/2014).

89. Cordell, "How Not to Teach Digital Humanities," ryancordell.org/teaching/how-not-to-teach-digital-humanities (IA: 02/02/2015).

90. Blevins, "Digital Historian's Toolkit" (IA: 26/11/2014).

91. Caesar, "Digital History" (IA: 04/02/2017).

92. Molesworth, Nixon, and Scullion, "Having"; Morgan, "Poorer Students 'Less Likely to Graduate with a Good Degree,'" timeshighereducation.com/news/poorer-students-less-likely-to-graduate-with-a-good-degree/2016762.article (IA: 04/06/2016).

93. Abigail Lane, "Young People Are Having to Take Career Decisions Too Early," theguardian.com/careers/young-people-take-career-decisions-too-early (IA: 29/09/2015).

94. "Advice for Speakers," at Winters, *Digital History Seminar*, ihrdighist.blogs.sas.ac.uk/advice-for-speakers (IA: 10/11/2016).

95. Booth, *Teaching History*; Booth and Hyland, *Practice of University History Teaching*.

Chapter 4. Building the Invisible College

1. Shorter, *Historian and the Computer*, 1, 59, dust jacket.

2. Susan White, Chu, and Czujko, *2012–13 Survey*, 4, 27; *Teachers of History in the UK*.

3. LeBlanc, (@Zoe_LeBlanc), *Twitter* (25 July 2017, 10:15pm), twitter.com/Zoe_LeBlanc/status/889670373675065347 (IA: 22/01/2018); (10:25pm), twitter.com/Zoe_LeBlanc/status/889672882074386434 (IA: 22/01/2018); (10:26pm), twitter.com/Zoe_LeBlanc/status/889673121925656576 (IA: 22/01/2018); (10:28pm), twitter.com/Zoe_LeBlanc/status/889673633400074240 (IA: 22/01/2018).

4. Martin, "How to Gain DH Experience without Institutional Support," digital-humanities.org/answers/topic/how-to-gain-dh-experience-without-institutional-support#post-2145 (IA: 09/06/2014).

5. Kousser, "State of Social Science History," 17.

6. Bogue, *Clio and the Bitch Goddess*, 220; Kousser, "State of Social Science History," 16.

7. Kousser, "State of Social Science History," 17.

8. John Reynolds, "Do Historians Count Anymore?"

9. Margo Anderson, "Quantitative History," 248.

10. Feinstein and Thomas, *Making History Count*, v–xii.

11. Floud, *Introduction*, table of contents.

12. Hudson, *History by Numbers*, 20.

13. Ayers, *What Caused the Civil War?* 68–69.

14. Koeser, "Trusting Others"; Gaffield, "Words, Words, Words."

15. Sinkewicz, "Database Advice," *Humanist*, 1989, dhhumanist.org/Archives/Converted_Text/humanist.1988–1989.txt.

16. Floud, *Introduction*.

17. Ibid., 211.

18. Denley and Hopkin, "Index of Software," in *History and Computing*, 342.

19. Denley and Hopkin, *History and Computing*, 345.

20. Blease, *Evaluating Educational Software*.

21. Hitchcock, "Digitising British History since 1980," history.ac.uk/makinghistory/resources/articles/digitisation_of_history.html (IA: 02/09/2014).

22. Rahtz, "Processing of Words."

23. Lancashire, "ALLC/ICCH Conference, Summary Announcement," *Humanist*, 1989, dhhumanist.org/Archives/Converted_Text/humanist.1988–1989.txt.

24. Reiff, "Structuring the Past," 69.

25. Burnard and Proud, "Computers and Teaching in the Humanities, 1988 Conference Report," *Humanist*, 1989, dhhumanist.org/Archives/Converted_Text/humanist.1988–1989.txt.

26. Sweet, *Analysis*.

27. Turkle, "How Computers Change the Way We Think," chronicle.com/article/How-Computers-Change-the-Way/10192 (2004, subscription only).

28. Reiff, "Structuring the Past," 46–47.

29. Mawdsley and Munck, *Computing for Historians*, 29.

30. Speck, "Introduction"; "Historical Computation Noticeboard."

31. Merriman, "View from Here."

32. Nowviskie, "On the Origin."

33. Shorter, *Historian and the Computer*, 72–73.

34. Floud, *Introduction*, 212–13.

35. Ide, "What Humanists Need to Know about Computers (and Computer Science)," web.viu.ca/siemensr/HCCurriculum (IA: 29/03/2009).

36. Turkel and MacEachern, *Programming Historian* (IA: 17/07/2014).

37. Gibbs, "Coding in the Humanities," fredgibbs.net/blog/teaching/coding-in-the-humanities (IA: 25/10/2012).

38. Mahony and Pierazzo, "Teaching Skills or Teaching Methodology?"

39. Rockwell and Sinclair, "Acculturation."

40. Posner, "Think Talk Make Do."

41. Shorter, *Historian and the Computer*, 17.

42. Swenson, "The Following Is from Ewa Swenson (ESWENSON at UTORONTO),"
Humanist, 1987, dhhumanist.org/Archives/Converted_Text/humanist.1987–1988.txt.

43. For example, see Margaret Young, *Internet for Windows*; Flanagan, *JavaScript*.

44. "Try It Editor" (IA: 24/01/2002).

45. Fouh et al., "Exploring Students Learning Behavior."

46. *Codecademy* (IA: 20/08/2011).

47. Shorter, *Historian and the Computer*, iv.

48. Lewis and Lloyd-Jones, *Using Computers in History*.

49. "MarcoPolo" (2000?), 34, GMUSC/C0038/88/9, Roy Rosenzweig Papers.

50. Turkel, "Digital History Hacks," digitalhistoryhacks.blogspot.ca/2005/12/
digital-history-hacks.html (IA: 22/01/2018).

51. "Hacks" (IA: 13/09/2011).

52. Turkel, "Teaching Young Historians to Search, Spider and Scrape," digital
historyhacks.blogspot.ca/2005/12/teaching-young-historians-to-search.html (IA:
22/01/2018); Turkel, "A Few Arguments for Humanistic Fabrication," digitalhistory
hacks.blogspot.ca/2008/11/few-arguments-for-humanistic.html (IA: 07/04/2014);
Turkel, "Easy Pieces in Python: Word Frequencies," digitalhistoryhacks.blogspot
.ca/2006/08/easy-pieces-in-python-word-frequencies.html (IA: 22/01/2018).

53. Turkel, "The Programming Historian," digitalhistoryhacks.blogspot.ca/2008/01/
programming-historian.html (IA: 22/01/2018); Turkel, "The Programming Historian
Is Now Available," digitalhistoryhacks.blogspot.ca/2008/05/programming-historian-is
-now-available.html (IA: 22/01/2018); Turkel and MacEachern, *Programming Historian*.

54. Graham, Milligan, and Weingart, *Exploring Big Historical Data*, 58.

55. Turkel and MacEachern, *Programming Historian*.

56. Crymble et al., *Programming Historian*, 8–10.

57. Ibid.

58. Turkel, "Digital Research Methods with Mathematica," williamjturkel.net/
digital-research-methods-with-mathematica (IA: 25/08/2015).

59. Turkel and MacEachern, "Getting Started," in *Programming Historian*, 5–14.

60. Crymble, "How to Write a Zotero Translator," niche-canada.org/member
-projects/zotero-guide/chapter1.html (IA: 26/09/2009).

61. Heppler, "The Rubyist Historian: The Series," jasonheppler.org/2010/12/10/
the-rubyist-historian-the-series (IA: 07/02/2011).

62. Clifford, MacFadyen, and Macfarlane, *Geospatial Historian*, geospatialhistorian
.wordpress.com (IA: 09/05/2017).

63. Posner, "How Did They Make That?" miriamposner.com/blog/how-did-they
-make-that (IA: 10/10/2013).

64. Mullen, *Computational Historical Thinking* (IA: 09/01/2015).

65. Reiff interview, 2018.

66. There were 11,297 mentions of the term "workshop" and 24,133 of the term "conference" in the *Humanist* corpus between 12 May 1987 and 3 February 2017.

67. Hopkin, "Association for History and Computing," *Humanist*, 1990, dhhumanist .org/Archives/Virginia/v04/subject.html.

68. Lancashire, "ALLC/ICCH Conference."

69. For example, see "CfP" (IA: 01/08/2017); "DH2017 Call for Papers" (IA: 06/02/2017).

70. Shevlin, "Digital Humanities at AHA," earlymodernonlinebib.wordpress. com/2010/01/12/digital-humanities-at-aha (IA: 24/01/2010); "Getting Started" (IA: 30/06/2017).

71. Peters, "The Cost of Applying for Academic Jobs," chronicle.com/article/the -cost-of-applying-for/46220 (IA: 16/09/2011).

72. "Syllabus" (2002), 3, GMUSC/C0038/91/7, Roy Rosenzweig Papers.

73. "New Media Classroom II" (1997), GMUSC/C0038/89/4, Roy Rosenzweig Papers.

74. "Leiden Summer School," *Humanist*, 1996, dhhumanist.org/Archives/Converted _Text/humanist.1995–1996.txt.

75. Leon and Brennan, "Scholars as Students."

76. Rehbein and Fritze, "Hands-on Teaching," 72–73.

77. "Summer Seminars" (IA: 17/08/2000).

78. Gants, "Summer Seminar at Oxford's Humanities Computing Unit," *Humanist*, 2000, dhhumanist.org/Archives/Virginia/v14/subject.html.

79. "Participants at the Digital Humanities Summer Institute, 2001-Present," *Digital Humanities Summer Institute* (IA: 23/08/2017).

80. "UCREL Summer School" (IA: 19/07/2011).

81. "Lancaster Summer Schools" (IA: 16/03/2017).

82. "Digital History Summer School" (IA: 22/01/2018); "Digital Art History Summer School"(IA: 15/06/2017); "European Summer University" (IA: 01/04/2017); "Registration Still Open" (IA: 09/04/2017).

83. Trafford, "Databases for Historians" (IA: 22/06/2002); Archer, "Internet Data Course" (IA: 23/01/2003).

84. "Research Training" (IA: 28/04/2017).

85. "Digital History Seminar" (IA: 28/12/2017).

86. "Syllabus—Fall 2014" (IA: 22/01/2018).

87. "Registration," programming4humanists.tamu.edu/registration (IA: 22/01/2018).

88. "AHRC ICT Methods Network," methodsnetwork.ac.uk/index.html (IA: 06/03/2008).

89. "AHRC ICT Methods Network—Distributed Activities," methodsnetwork .ac.uk/activities/distributed.html (IA: 08/10/2008).

90. Methnet, "Text Mining for Historians - Forthcoming AHRC ICT," *Humanist*, 2007, dhhumanist.org/Archives/Converted_Text/humanist.2007–2008.txt; Ian Anderson and Bliss, "Report."

91. "Schedule," *THATCamp* (31 May–1 June 2008), thatcamp.org/schedule (IA: 24/07/2008).

92. Scheinfeldt, "Thoughts on THATCamp," foundhistory.org/2008/06/thoughts -on-thatcamp (IA: 23/12/2014); Scheinfeldt, "Invisible College" (IA: 20/12/2012).

93. Scheinfeldt, "Invisible College (IA: 20/12/2012); Mills Kelly, "The Future of the AHA (cont'd)," edwired.org/2008/06/04/the-future-of-the-aha-contd-2 (IA: 19/06/2013).

94. Scheinfeldt, "Digital Methods Training at Scale: Leveraging THATCamp through a Regional System," in *RRCHNM20*, 20.rrchnm.org/items/show/209 (IA: 22/01/2018); Scheinfeldt and French, "Sustaining Digital Humanities Training through THATCamp," in *RRCHNM20*, 20.rrchnm.org/items/show/212 (IA: 22/01/2018).

95. "THATCamps," thatcamp.org/camps; French, "How Long, How Much, How Many," *ThatCamp*, thatcamp.org/2013/04/24/how-long-how-much-how-many (IA: 23/04/2017).

96. Wilson, Landau, and McConnell, "What Should Computer Scientists Teach."

97. Jacobs, "What I Learned at Digital Summer Camp," theatlantic.com/technology/ archive/2012/06/what-i-learned-at-digital-summer-camp/258593 (IA: 04/06/2016).

98. LeBlanc, (@Zoe_Leblanc), *Twitter* (25 July 2017, 8:17am), twitter.com/Zoe_Leblanc/ status/889821876738023424 (IA: 22/01/2018).

99. Ayers, "Pasts and Futures."

Chapter 5. The Rise and Fall of the Scholarly Blog

1. McCutcheon, "Journal Des Scavans"; Atkinson, *Scientific Discourse*; Gross, Harmon, and Reidy, *Communicating Science*.

2. Luker, "Were There Blog Enough and Time," historians.org/publications-and -directories/perspectives-on-history/may-2005/were-there-blog-enough-and-time (IA: 27/03/2014); Holman, "Airminded at 10," airminded.org/2015/07/03/airminded-at -10 (IA: 22/07/2015); Goetz, "A Brief History of Blogging as Experienced by Yours Truly," historianess.wordpress.com/2015/06/18/a-brief-history-of-blogging-as-experienced -by-yours-truly (IA: 23/08/2015).

3. Burton, "Blogs as Infrastructure"; Terras, "The Verdict: Is Blogging or Tweeting about Research Papers Worth it?" eprints.lse.ac.uk/51970 (IA: 19/10/2015); Kjellberg, "I Am a Blogging Researcher," firstmonday.org/article/view/2962/2580 (IA: 23/11/2012).

4. Kelty, "This Is Not an Article."

5. American Historical Association, "Perspectives on History | AHA"; Canadian Historical Association, "Bulletin—Canadian Historical Association."

6. Bessinger and Robinson, "Old English Newsletter."

7. Conner, "ANSAXNET"; O'Donnell, "History of Humanist-L, Medtext-l, Ansax-l, etc. (i.e. early scholarly communities online)," *Humanist*, 2017, dhhumanist.org/ Archives/Current/Humanist.vol30.txt.

8. Hyman, "Twenty Years of ListServ."

9. McCarty, "HUMANIST," 207.

10. Ayers, "Pasts and Futures."

11. Middleton and Wardley, "Annual Review," 379; Jensen, "H-Net Announces 13 New Scholarly Lists in History," *Humanist* 1993, dhhumanist.org/Archives/Virginia/v06/subject.html.

12. Conner, "Notes from ANSAXNET"; McCarty, "HUMANIST."

13. The joke can be read at McCarty, "Not Me . . .," *X-Humanist*, 1987, dhhumanist .org/Archives/Converted_Text/humanist.1987–1988.txt; McCarty, "HUMANIST," 210; Conner, "Networking," 196.

14. McCarty, "HUMANIST," 209–10; Conner, "Networking," 196.

15. Matzat, "Academic Communication," 227.

16. Conner, "Networking," 196; McCarty, "HUMANIST," 207.

17. Matt Burton ascribes the first historical blog post to danah boyd in 1997, though she was neither a historian nor writing about history at that point in her life: danah boyd, [no title], zephoria.org/thoughts/archives/1997/06/09/1.html (IA: 12/02/2010). Noted in Burton, "Blogs as Infrastructure," 100. Ralph Luker instead attributes Kevin Murphy as the first history blogger. Murphy published a scant comment about a historian's view of Bill Clinton on 21 February 2000, but Murphy was not a historian or a history student at the time, and instead worked indirectly for Clinton: Murphy, "2/21/00," ghostinthemachine.net/weblog2100.html (IA: 01/09/2001); Luker, "Were There Blog Enough."

18. MacDougall, "1.25.2001," robmacdougall.org/blogger/index.html#2122836 (IA: 15/05/2008); MacDougall, "1.12.2001," robmacdougall.org/blogger/index.html #1950506 (IA: 15/05/2008); MacDougall, "She's My Rushmore, Max," robmacdougall .org/blogger/index.html#3086492 (IA: 15/05/2008).

19. With thanks to Rob MacDougall for directing me to these: McCallum-Stewart, *Break of Day*, whatalovelywar.co.uk/war (IA: 05/06/2002); Goetz, *Historianess*, rebecca-goetz.blogspot.com (IA: 25/09/2002).

20. McDaniel, "Blogging in the Early Republic."

21. Quoted in ibid.

22. Black, "How Far Have We Come in the Digital Humanities?" parezcoydigo .wordpress.com/2010/10/14/how-far-have-we-come-in-the-digital-humanities (IA: 15/10/2010).

23. McCarty, "HUMANIST," 210; Terras, "Stats and the Digital Humanities," melissa terras.blogspot.co.uk/2011/11/stats-and-digital-humanities.html (IA: 19/05/2012); For a detailed analysis of user behavior in the early days of *Humanist*, see Burnard, "The Numbers Game, Again," louburnard.wordpress.com/2011/12/05/the-numbers -game-again (IA: 21/01/2018).

24. Coppa, "Brief History"; Eichhorn, *Archival Turn*; for an archive of Zines, see Lastufka and Sandler, *ZineWiki*; Rauch, "Hands-on Communication."

25. Kjellberg, "I Am a Blogging Researcher."

26. Burton, "Blogs as Infrastructure," 8, 185.

27. Greenberg interview, 2017; Findlen, Edelstein, and Coleman, *Mapping* (IA: 10/05/2012); Garrioch, "Female Epistolary Friendships."

28. Ayers, "A Historian in Cyberspace," *American Heritage*.

29. Hitchcock, *Historyonics*, historyonics.blogspot.co.uk (IA: 06/05/2012).

30. Luker, "Were There Blog Enough."

31. "Ralph Luker: Reflects on HIS Fast to Protest Denial of Tenure," historynews network.org/article/35682 (IA: 24/05/2017).

32. McCarty interview, 2017.

33. Tribble, "Bloggers Need Not Apply," chronicle.com/article/Bloggers-Need-Not -Apply/45022 (IA: 10/06/2010).

34. Fitzpatrick, "Bloggers Need Not Apply," plannedobsolescence.net/bloggers -need-not-apply (IA: 07/10/2008).

35. Cohen, "Professors, Start Your Blogs," dancohen.org/2006/08/21/professors -start-your-blogs (IA: 23/08/2007).

36. The quotation concerned a disagreement between Ruth Glynn of Oxford Electronic Publishing and Sebastian Rahtz of Southampton University over the cost of a new digital edition of Shakespeare's works. Rahtz, "Bards and Mallards," *X-Humanist*, 1989, dhhumanist.org/Archives/Converted_Text/humanist.1988–1989.txt; Glynn, "Shakespeare: Compete Works, OUP," *X-Humanist*, 1989, dhhumanist.org/Archives/ Converted_Text/humanist.1988–1989.txt; Goerwitz, untitled, *X-Humanist*, 1989, dh humanist.org/Archives/Converted_Text/humanist.1988–1989.txt.

37. CC Rider, "Re: Bloggers Need Not Apply << Reply #9," chronicle.com/forums/ index.php/topic,20188.msg292837.html#msg292837 (IA: 05/05/2011).

38. Herring, "Gender and Participation"; Herring, "Gender and Democracy"; Herring, "Posting in a Different Voice"; Herring, "Rhetorical Dynamics"; Herring, "Gender Differences"; Johnson, "#FemFuture," dh.jmjafrx.com/2013/04/12/femfuture -history-loving-each-other-harder-2 (cannot be archived).

39. Habermas, *Structural Transformation*.

40. "Yet Another Me-Zine?" invisibleadjunct.com/archives/2003_02.html (IA: 20/07/2003).

41. "Signing Off," invisibleadjunct.com/archives/000498.html (IA: 16/03/2006).

42. Burke, "Cliopatria's Hall of Fame," historynewsnetwork.org/blog/29664 (12/09/2015).

43. Luker, [original post lost], *Cliopatria* (March 2004): hnn.us/blogs/entries/4313 .html (IA: 02/04/2004); Wolfson, "Invisible Adjunct," topicexchange.com/t/invisible _adjunct/about (IA: 13/02/2005).

44. Based on calculations of citations of articles in *Past and Present* 182 (2004) [192 citations, 7 articles], and *American History Review* 109, no. 1 (2004) [147 citations, 3 articles] using *Google Scholar*'s "cited by" metrics, taken 13 December 2016: scholar. google.co.uk. These "cited by" counts are not perfect and are derived automatically by Google's algorithms, but they provide a reasonable count of the number of citations found in the scholarly literature for a given article.

45. "When the Best Give Up," heartofcanada.typepad.com/randomthoughts/2004/03/ when_the_best_g.html; quoted from Greenberg, "When the Best Give Up," blog .epistemographer.com/archives/2004_03.html (IA: 31/08/2004).

46. May, "Investigation"; Brownlee, "Contract Faculty."

47. Cebula, "Open Letter to My Students," northwesthistory.blogspot.com/2011/11/ open-letter-to-my-students-no-you.html (IA: 16/1/2011).

48. Shenkman, "Bill Clinton's Legacy," historynewsnetwork.org/articles/article
.html?id=82 (IA: 14/09/2001); Shenkman, "Bio," rickshenkman.com/bio (IA:
22/12/2016).

49. Milligan et al., *Active History.ca.*

50. "About Us," *History News Network,* historynewsnetwork.org/custom/aboutus
.html (IA: 14/09/2001); Mollett and Rainford, "Impact of Social Sciences Blog," *LSE
Impact Blog,* blogs.lse.ac.uk/impactofsocialsciences (IA: 03/04/2011); *The Conversation* (IA: 27/09/2016).

51. The original Cliopatria group blog included contributions from Timothy Burke,
Oscar Chamberlain, Kenneth Heineman, Robert "KC" Johnson, Mary Catherine Mo-
ran, and Ralph E. Luker: Luker, "Transblogrification: (Inactive) Welcome to My World,"
(4 December 2003), historynewsnetwork.org/article/1368 (IA: 19/01/2006); Luker et
al., "Cliopatria: A Group Blog," historynewsnetwork.org/article/1829 (IA: 17/12/2014);
Luker, "Farewell to Cliopatria," historynewsnetwork.org/blog/144952 (IA: 27/09/2015).

52. Josh Greenberg, "Blogging and Other Literary Forms," blog.epistemographer
.com (IA: 07/07/2003).

53. Josh Greenberg, "Big News . . .," blog.epistemographer.com/archives/2004_05
.html (IA: 02/09/2004).

54. Boggs, "New Domain, New Design," clioweb.org (IA: 31/08/2004); Leon, "Here
We Go," 6floors.org/bracket/2005/07/22/here-we-go (cannot be archived); Mills Kelly,
"Students Using Websites," edwired.org/2005/10/18/students-using-websites (IA:
06/09/2010); Cohen, "Welcome to My Blog," dancohen.org/2005/11/14/welcome-to
-my-blog (IA: 21/09/2007); Scheinfeldt, "Finding History," foundhistory.org/2005/12/
finding-history (IA: 23/09/2014); Owens, "First Post," trevorowens.org/2006/07/first
-post (IA: 23/04/2016); "Blogs + Podcasts," *Roy Rosenzweig Center for History and
New Media* (n.d.), chnm.gmu.edu/blogs-podcasts (IA: 08/02/2011).

55. Cohen, "Welcome to My Blog."

56. Cohen, *Equations from God.*

57. Cohen, "Digital Campus Podcast Launches," dancohen.org/2007/03/07/digital
-campus-podcast-launches (IA: 29/08/2008); Cohen et al., *Digital Campus* (IA:
11/03/2007).

58. Derakhshan, *Editor* (IA: 29/10/2008).

59. Derakhshan, "The Web We Have to Save," medium.com/matter/the-web-we
-have-to-save-2eb1fe15a426 (IA: 14/07/2015).

60. *Facebook* (2005-present), facebook.com (IA: 06/04/2005); *Twitter* (2006–present), twitter.com (IA: 06/10/2006); *Instagram* (2011-present), instagram.com (IA:
29/04/2011).

61. Crogan and Kinsley, "Paying Attention."

62. Hölzle, "A Second Spring of Cleaning," googleblog.blogspot.co.uk/2013/03/a
-second-spring-of-cleaning.html (IA: 16/03/2013).

63. HNN Editor, "Clio's Blogroll: Part 1," historynewsnetwork.org/blog/9665
(IA: 08/10/2014); HNN Editor, "Clio's Blogroll: Part 2," historynewsnetwork.org/
blog/55068 (IA: 13/04/2015).

64. HNN Editor, "Clio's Blogroll: Part 1," historynewsnetwork.org/blog/9665 (IA: 08/10/2014).

65. *Internet Archive Wayback Machine*, archive.org/web (IA: 15/10/2013).

66. Howard, "History Carnival #1," earlymodernnotes.wordpress.com/2005/01/14/history-carnival-1 (IA: 07/08/2014).

67. For example, see the "Calendar of Close Rolls," or "Calendar of State Papers," Tate et al., *British History Online* (version 5.0: 2015): british-history.ac.uk/catalogue/guides-and-calendars (24/01/2014).

68. Howard, "History Carnival #1," earlymodernnotes.wordpress.com/2005/01/14/history-carnival-1 (IA: 07/08/2014).

69. HNN Editor, "Clio's Blogroll: Part 1" (IA: 08/10/2014).

70. Luker, "The Cliopatria Awards," historynewsnetwork.org/blog/20359 (IA: 22/01/2018).

71. "DH Awards 2012, Nominations Committee," *Digital Humanities Awards*, dhawards .org (IA: 18/01/2013).

72. Cohen et al., *Digital Humanities Now*, digitalhumanitiesnow.org (IA: 09/07/2011); "Subscribed Feeds," digitalhumanitiesnow.org/subscribed-feeds (IA: 18/07/2015).

73. Adeline Koh, Roopika Risam, and Lisa Rhody were approached for interview. Koh did not respond, and Rhody declined to comment. Risam agreed to be interviewed, for which I am grateful.

74. "Reflections on the JDH Editorial Process," pressforward.org/2013/09/reflections -on-the-jdh-editorial-process (IA: 11/10/2013); Koh, "The Journal of Digital Humanities: Post-Publication Review or the Worst of Peer Review?" adelinekoh.org/blog/2013/08/29/journalofdigitalhumanitie (IA: 10/09/2013).

75. O'Sullivan, "Comment: The Journal of Digital Humanities: Post-Publication Review or the Worst of Peer Review?" adelinekoh.org/blog/2013/08/29/journalof digitalhumanitie (IA: 10/09/2013).

76. Cohen et al., "How This Works," *Digital Humanities Now*, digitalhumanities now.org/about (IA: 23/08/2013).

77. Koh, "The Journal of Digital Humanities: Post-Publication Review or the Worst of Peer Review?" adelinekoh.org/blog/2013/08/29/journalofdigitalhumanitie (IA: 10/09/2013); Koh, "Crowdsourcing Best Practices for Experimental Journals: Transparency," adelinekoh.org/blog/2013/08/31/crowdsourcing-best-practices-for -experimental-journals-transparency (IA: 11/09/2013); Hoffman, "Editor's Choice: Reviewing JDH Round-Up," digitalhumanitiesnow.org/2013/09/editors-choice -reviewing-jdh-round-up (IA: 24/10/2013).

78. Senier, "Comment: The Journal of Digital Humanities: Post-Publication Review or the Worst of Peer Review?" adelinekoh.org/blog/2013/08/29/journalofdigital humanitie (IA: 10/09/2013).

79. Moravec, "I Already Know What Happened and I Wasn't Even There," history inthecity.blogspot.com/2013/08/i-already-know-what-happened-and-i.html (IA: 11/09/2015).

80. "Reflections on the JDH Editorial Process," pressforward.org/2013/09/reflections-on-the-jdh-editorial-process (IA: 11/10/2013).

81. "The Journal of Digital Humanities Is Currently on Hiatus," journalofdigital humanities.org (IA: 27/04/2016).

82. Koh, "The Journal of Digital Humanities: Post-Publication Review or the Worst of Peer Review?" adelinekoh.org/blog/2013/08/29/journalofdigitalhumanitie (IA: 10/09/2013); Koh, "Crowdsourcing Best Practices for Experimental Journals: Transparency," adelinekoh.org/blog/2013/08/31/crowdsourcing-best-practices-for-experimental-journals-transparency (IA: 11/09/2013); Hoffman, "Editor's Choice: Reviewing JDH Round-up," digitalhumanitiesnow.org/2013/09/editors-choice-reviewing-jdh-round-up (IA: 24/10/2013).

83. Koh, @adelinekoh, *Twitter* (6 September 2013, 7:35am), twitter.com/adelinekoh/status/375990651005190144 (IA: 22/01/2018).

84. *Slashdot* (1997-present), Slashdot.org (IA: 13/01/1998); *Reddit* (2005-present), reddit.com (IA: 25/07/2005).

85. Jessifer, "The #DHThis Cat," dhthis.org/story.php?title=the-dhthis-cat (IA: 10/07/2015).

86. *Research Assessment Exercise*; *Research Excellence Framework*.

87. Williams et al., *Digital Miscellanies Index* (IA: 25/07/2011); Withington et al., *Intoxicants* (IA: 22/10/2014); Godfrey et al., *Digital Panopticon* (IA: 28/02/2015).

88. Crymble, "Analysis."

89. Inglis, *Georgian London*, lucyinglis.com (IA: 19/07/2012).

90. Hitchcock, "Doing It in Public: Impact, Blogging, Social Media and the Academy," historyonics.blogspot.co.uk/2014/07/doing-it-in-public-impact-blogging.html (IA: 25/11/2014); Schmidt, *Sapping Attention*, sappingattention.blogspot.com (IA: 09/08/2014); Evans, *Early Modern Medicine*, earlymodernmedicine.com (IA: 16/08/2014).

91. Burton, "Blogs as Infrastructure for Scholarly Communication."

92. Searched for "keynote" on Prescott, *Digital Riffs*, digitalriffs.blogspot.co.uk (IA: 10/08/2017). For example, see Hitchcock, "Big Data for Dead People: Digital Readings and the Conundrums of Positivism," historyonics.blogspot.co.uk/2013/12/big-data-for-dead-people-digital.html (IA: 25/02/2015); Hitchcock, "The Digital Humanities in Three Dimensions," historyonics.blogspot.co.uk/2016/07/the-digital-humanities-in-three.html (IA: 08/12/2016); Rock, "Criminal Skill: The Counterfeiter's Craft in the Long Eighteenth Century" (delivered 25 March 2014; published 30 March 2014), crimeandcoins.wordpress.com/2014/03/30/criminal-skill-the-counterfeiters-craft-in-the-long-eighteenth-century (IA: 14/05/2014).

93. Cebula, "In Which I Sit through a Conference Session," chronicle.com/forums/index.php/topic,115506.0.html (IA: 08/11/2012); Cebula, "We Know You Can Read. So Can We," chronicle.com/article/We-Know-You-Can-Read-So-Can/136607 (IA: 17/03/2013).

94. "Electronic Seminars in History" (last updated 28 May 1998), ihr.sas.ac.uk/ihr/esh/eshmnu.html (IA: 05/06/2000); "Apple Announces iTunes U" (IA: 10/12/2011);

"Conference & Workshop Archive" (2008–12), niche-canada.org/resources/conference
-workshop-archive (IA: 08/10/2015).

95. "Instructions for Contributors," *Transactions of the Royal Historical Society*
(last updated 2 September 2016), cambridge.org/core/journals/transactions-of-the
-royal-historical-society/information/instructions-contributors (IA: 22/01/2018).

96. McPherson, "Dynamic Vernaculars."

97. Hitchcock, "Doing It in Public."

Chapter 6. The Digital Past and the Digital Future

1. For example, Turkel, "A Naïve Bayesian in the Old Bailey, Part 1," digitalhistory
hacks.blogspot.ca/2008/05/naive-bayesian-in-old-bailey-part-1.html (IA: 21/01/2018).

2. Cosgrave (@mikecosgrave), *Twitter* (13 March 2017, 3:10pm), twitter.com/mike
cosgrave/status/841305479192158208 (IA: 22/01/2018).

3. Winters, "Digital History."

4. Noiret, "Digital History 2.0"; Brier, "Confessions."

5. Benedict Anderson, *Imagined Communities*.

6. Mintz and McNeil, *Digital History*.

7. Jørgensen (@Finnarne), *Twitter* (23 May 2018, 12:49am), twitter.com/finnarne/
status/999150306893221888.

8. There are a number of "digital humanities" initiatives that attempt to achieve
something similar. For example, see *TaDiRAH*.

9. Crymble, "The Five Lessons No One's Yet Written (But Need Writing),"
programminghistorian.org/posts/call-to-action (IA: 10/05/2017); Robertson, "Arguing with Digital History" (IA: 09/05/2017).

10. "Inaugural Conference" (IA: 02/05/2017); "Associate Professor/Professor" (IA:
23/01/2018).

11. Nkomo, "Seductive Power."

12. Rafols et al., "How Journal Rankings Can Suppress Interdisciplinary Research."

Appendix. Digital History Syllabus Corpus

1. These were gathered through a combination of targeted Google searches, browsing, and soliciting openly on Twitter.

2. Cutler interview, 2019.

3. Each syllabus was close read and manually classified by the author. All syllabi
were looked at in February 2017 so that the author could familiarize himself with the
material. All classifications were done on 30 July 2017 in an attempt to ensure consistency. Criteria for classifications are outlined in table 11. Where not enough detail
was available, a classification of "unknown" was used. The author acknowledges that
there is a degree of subjectivity to his decisions, so the counts and analysis should be
read with that in mind.

Bibliography

Interviews by the Author

Ayers, Edward, 23 November 2018.
Brier, Stephen, 25 November 2017.
Cutler, William, 15 February 2019.
French, Amanda, 18 July 2017.
Gaffield, Chad, 18 December 2018.
Greenberg, Josh, 27 April 2017.
MacDougall, Rob, 17 May 2017.
McCarty, Willard, 25 May 2017.
Mintz, Steven, 14 November 2018.
Reiff, Janice, 18 December 2018.
Risam, Roopika, 11 May 2017.
Schrum, Kelly, 28 November 2018.
Short, Harold, 25 January 2019.

Archival Materials

Tim Hitchcock. Private papers, 1991–96.
Roy Rosenzweig Papers. George Mason University, Special Collections Research
    Center, GMUSC C0038, 1934–2007.
Harold Short. Private papers, 1993.
John Styles. Private papers, 1987–88.

Born-Digital, Projects, and Multimedia

Date ranges represent periods cited, not periods of activity.
Afanador-Llach, Maria José, et al., eds. *Programming Historian*. London: Program-
    ming Historian Editorial Board, 2012. programminghistorian.org.

AHRC ICT Methods Network. 2005–8. methodsnetwork.ac.uk.

Aiden, Erez Lieberman, and Jean-Baptiste Michel. *Culturomics.* 2011. culturomics.org.

Allington, Daniel, Sarah Brouillette, and David Golumbia. *Los Angeles Review of Books.* 2016. lareviewofbooks.org.

American Historical Association Council. *AHA Today.* 2013. blog.historians.org.

American Historical Association Council. *Perspectives on History.* 1964-Present.

"American Memory." Library of Congress. 1994. memory.loc.gov/ammem/index .html.

Ancestry.com. 1996–present. ancestry.com.

Andrew W. Mellon Foundation's Grant Database. n.d. mellon.org/grants.

Appelbaum, Yoni. *Atlantic.* 2012. theatlantic.com.

"Apple Announces iTunes U on the iTunes Store." Apple Press Info. Press release. 2007. apple.com/uk/pr/library/2007/05/30Apple-Announces-iTunes-U-on-the -iTunes-Store.html.

Archer, Ian. "Internet Data Course." *Institute of Historical Research.* 2002. history.ac .uk/training/courses/internet.html.

"Associate Professor/Professor: Digital Humanities." *North-West University.* nwu.pnet. co.za/index.php?s=advert_view&g=11080&x=4230392&i=1192&pop=1.

Ayers, Edward. *American Heritage* 51, no. 6 (2000): 68–74.

———. *Chronicle of Higher Education* 2004. chronicle.com.

———, et al. *The Valley of the Shadow: Two Communities in the American Civil War.* [Charlottesville]: University of Virginia/Virginia Center for Digital History, 1993. valley.lib.virginia.edu.

Baker, James. "Digital Skills 2016/17 (provisional)." Google Drive Document. 2016.

———. *Library Carpentry.* 2015-present. librarycarpentry.github.io.

Banzi, Massimo, David Cuartielles, Tom Igoe, Gianluca Martino, and David Mellis. *Arduino.* 2005. arduino.cc.

Beals, M. H. "Digital History." *Sheffield Hallam University.* 2014.

———. *LSE Impact Blog.* 2013. blogs.lse.ac.uk/impactofsocialsciences.

Bender, Pennee, et al. *History Matters.* 1998. historymatters.gmu.edu.

Bessinger, Jess B., Jr., and Fred C. Robinson. "Old English Newsletter Volume 1, Nos. 1 & 2." Modern Language Association, 1986 (1967): 1–25. oenewsletter.org/OEN/ archive/OEN1_1–2.pdf.

Bhattacharyya, Anirudh. *Hindustan Times.* 2016. hindustantimes.com.

Binder, Natalie. *The Pixel and Page.* 2010. thebinderblog.com.

Black, Chad. *Parezco y Digo.* 2010. parezcoydigo.wordpress.com.

"Blogs + Podcasts." *Roy Rosenzweig Center for History and New Media.* n.d. chnm .gmu.edu.

Blevins, Cameron. "The Digital Historian's Toolkit: Studying the West in the Age of Big Data." *Cameron Blevins.* 2012. cameronblevins.org/teaching/dhtk2012.

Boggs, Jeremy. *Clioweb.* 2004. clioweb.org.

boyd, danah. *Apophenia.* 1997. zephoria.org.

Brennan, Sheila A., and T. Mills Kelly. *Center for History and New Media.* 2009. rrchnm.org/essay.

British Library Georeferencer. 2011-present. bl.uk/georeferencer/georefabout.html.

Brodman, James W. *H-Teach Discussion Log.* 1994. networks.h-net.org/h-teach.

Burke, Timothy. *History News Network.* 2009. historynewsnetwork.org.

Burnard, Lou. *Solipsism and Me.* 2011. louburnard.wordpress.com.

———, and Judith Proud. *Humanist.* 1989. dhhumanist.org.

Burns, Arthur, Kenneth Fincham, and Stephen Taylor. *Clergy of the Church of England Database.* 1999–present. theclergydatabase.org.uk.

Burns, Ken, dir. *The Civil War.* PBS documentary. 1990.

Busa, Robert. *Index Thomisticus.* 1974.

Caesar, Mathieu. "The Digital History of Religious Wars (1450–1750." *Academia. edu.* 2017? academia.edu/24281440/Syllabus_-_The_Digital_History_of_Religious_Wars.

Canadian Historical Association. Canadian Historical Association Bulletin. 1975–Present.

CC Rider. *Chronicle Forums.* 2005. chronicle.com/forums.

Cebula, Larry. *Chronicle Forums.* 2012. chronicle.com/forums.

———. *Chronicle of Higher Education.* 2013. chronicle.com.

———. *Northwest History.* 2011. northwesthistory.blogspot.com.

"CfP: Workshop & Tutorials for DH 2012 (University of Hamburg, Germany)." *European Association for Digital Humanities.* 2011. eadh.org/news-events/cfp-workshop-tutorials-dh-2012-university-hamburg-germany.

Civil War Hypermedia Project. CD-ROM. PBS. 1990.

Clifford, Jim, Josh MacFadyen, and Daniel Macfarlane. *Geospatial Historian: Open HGIS Lessons and Resources.* 2013. geospatialhistorian.wordpress.com.

Codecademy. 2011-present. codecademy.com.

Cohen, Dan. "Clio Wired." *Dan Cohen.* 2009. dancohen.org/clio-wired.

———. "Clio Wired." *Dan Cohen.* 2010. dancohen.org/clio-wired.

———. *Dan Cohen.* 2005–8. dancohen.org.

Cohen, Dan, Amanda French, Tom Scheinfeldt, Mills Kelly, et al. *Digital Campus.* Podcast. 2007–15. digitalcampus.tv.

Cohen, Dan, et al. *Digital Humanities Now.* 2009-present. digitalhumanitiesnow.org.

"Conference & Workshop Archive." *Network in Canadian History & Environment.* 2008–12. niche-canada.org/resources/conference-workshop-archive.

The Conversation. 2011. theconversation.com/global.

Corcoran, Frank, and Isobel Marks. *Canada's Visual History CD-ROM,* National Film Board. CD-ROM. 1997.

Cordell, Ryan. *Ryan Cordell.* 2015. ryancordell.org.

Cosgrave, Mike. @mikecosgrave, *Twitter.* 2017. twitter.com/mikecosgrave.

Crichton, Michael, dir. *Westworld*. Film. 1973.

Crymble, Adam. "Crowdsource Arcade." Lecture. British Library, London, 11 November 2015. youtube.com/watch?v=7MtNgc8-SmE.

———. "How to Write a Zotero Translator: A Practical Guide for Humanists." 2009.

———. "Intro to Digital History 2015." *Adam Crymble.org*. 2015. adamcrymble.org/intro-to-digital-history-2015.

———. *Programming Historian*. 2017. programminghistorian.org/posts.

———. *Thoughts on Public and Digital History*. 2013–14. adamcrymble.blogspot.ca.

Daunton, Martin. "Professor Martin Daunton: Interview Transcript." Interviewed by Danny Millum, London, 19 May 2008. history.ac.uk/makinghistory/resources/interviews/Daunton_Martin.html.

Davidson, Cathy. *Chronicle of Higher Education*. 2011. chronicle.com.

Derakhshan, Hossein. *Editor: Myself | Hossein Derakhshan's Weblog (Persian)*. 2001–8. i.hoder.com.

———. *Medium*. 2015. medium.com.

"DH2017 Call for Papers." *Digital Humanities 2017*. 2017. dh2017.adho.org/program/cfp.

"Digital Art History Summer School." *Departmento de Historia del Arte, Universidad de Málaga*. 2017. historiadelartemalaga.uma.es/dahss17/en.

"Digital History." *Umeå University*. 2016. umu.se/en/education/courses/digital-history/syllabus.

"Digital History Seminar." *Institute of Historical Research*. 2012-present. history.ac.uk/events/seminar/digital-history.

"Digital History Summer School." *University of Lausanne*. 2017. infoclio.ch/fr/digital-history-summer-school-registration-now-open.

Digital Humanities at Oxford Summer School. 2017. dhoxss.net.

Digital Humanities Awards. 2012–17. dhawards.org.

Digital Humanities Summer Institute. 2001–17. dhsi.org/archive.php.

Do, Brian, Luda Zhao, and Karen Wang. *British Library Labs*. 2016. labs.bl.uk.

Dubnick, Melvin J. *H-Survey*. 1999. networks.h-net.org/h-survey.

Dunning, Alastair. "List of Digitisation Projects by UK's JISC (Joint Information Systems Committee) up to 2011." 2011. hdl.handle.net/10760/17520.

———. "List of Digitisation Projects Funded Under UK's AHRC Resource Enhancement Scheme." 2011. hdl.handle.net/10760/17517.

———. "List of Projects Funded Under UK New Opportunities Fund." 2011. hdl.handle.net/10760/17518.

Düring, Marten. "Assignments." *Hist 980–005 Digital History*. 2014. digitalhistory.web.unc.edu/assignments.

"Electronic Seminars in History." *Institute of Historical Research* 1998. ihr.sas.ac.uk/ihr/esh.

Europeana. 2008–present. europeana.eu.

"European Summer University in Digital Humanities." *Universität Leipzig*. 2017. culingtec.uni-leipzig.de/ESU_C_T.

Evans, Jennifer. *Early Modern Medicine.* 2012–17. earlymodernmedicine.com.

Facebook. 2005–present. facebook.com.

Farquhar, Adam, et al. *British Library Labs.* 2013. labs.bl.uk.

Findlen, Paula, Dan Edelstein, and Nicole Coleman. *Mapping the Republic of Letters.* 2013. republicofletters.stanford.edu.

Fitzgerald, Brendan. *The Morning News.* 2012. themorningnews.org.

Fitzpatrick, Kathleen. *Planned Obsolescence.* 2005. plannedobsolescence.net.

Floud, Roderick. "Professor Sir Roderick Floud: Interview Transcript." Interviewed by Danny Millum, London. 2 May 2008. history.ac.uk/makinghistory/resources/interviews/Floud_Roderick.html.

Fontana, Lynn. "Lynn Fontana, Ph.D." *LinkedIn.* 2017. linkedin.com.

French, Amanda. *ThatCamp* 2013. thatcamp.org.

Friedman, Matthew. "New Viewpoints in American History: Digital History Theory and Practice." *Rutgers University.* 2016. ncas.rutgers.edu/digital-history-theory-and-practice.

Fusco, Joseph, Jr. *H-Edtech Discussion Log.* 1994. networks.h-net.org/edtech.

"Gale Leads to Advance Academic Research by Offering Content for Data Mining and Textual Analysis." Gale Cengage. Press release. 2014. news.cengage.com/higher-education/gale-leads-to-advance-academic-research-by-offering-content-for-data-mining-and-textual-analysis.

Gants, David L. *Humanist.* 2000. dhhumanist.org.

Garrioch, David. "Female Epistolary Friendships." Keynote address. *British Society of Eighteenth Century Studies*, Oxford, 2017.

"Getting Started in Digital History 2017: Schedule." *American Historical Association.* 2017. historians.org/teaching-and-learning/digital-history-resources/resources-for-getting-started-in-digital-history/getting-started-in-digital-history-2017.

Gibbs, Fred. "Digital Mapping + Geospatial Humanities." *Fredgibbs.* 2014. redgibbs.net/courses/digital-mapping.

———. *Fredgibbs.* 2011. fredgibbs.net.

Glynn, Ruth. *X-Humanist.* 1989. dhhumanist.org.

Godfrey, Barry, et al. *The Digital Panopticon.* 2013–17. digitalpanopticon.org.

Goerwitz, Richard. *X-Humanist.* 1989. dhhumanist.org.

Goetz, Rebecca. *Historianess.* 2002–15. rebecca-goetz.blogspot.com.

Goldstone, Andrew. *Andrew Goldstone.* 2017. andrewgoldstone.com.

Google N-gram Viewer. 2013. books.google.com/ngrams.

Google Scholar. 2016. scholar.google.co.uk.

Gorman, Michael John. "The Wired Historian." *Stanford University.* 2002. stanford.edu/group/STS/230.html.

Grafton, Anthony. *Perspectives on History.* 2011. historians.org/publications-and-directories/perspectives-on-history.

Graham, Shawn. "hist3907b-winter2015/syllabus/exercise_assessment_guidelines.md." *Github.com.* 2015. github.com/hist3907b-winter2015/syllabus.

Gravois, John. *Chronicle of Higher Education.* 2007. chronicle.com.

Greenberg, Josh. *Epistemographer.* 2003–4. blog.epistemographer.com.

Greenberg, Saul. *Phidgets.* 2001. phidgets.com.

Haahr, Mads. *Haunted Planet.* 2010–18. hauntedplanet.com.

———. "The Vampire in the Machine." Lecture. *Universitat Oberta de Catalunya,* Barcelona, 21 December 2015. youtube.com/watch?v=TFxmKF6ujrc.

"Hacks." *O'Reilly Publishing.* 2005–17. Shop.oreilly.com/category/series/hacks.do.

H-Amstdy Comoderator. *H-Amstdy Discussion Log.* 1994. networks.h-net.org/h -amstdy.

Harford, Tim. *Tim Harford.* 2017. timharford.com.

Hart, Michael. *Project Gutenberg.* 1971. gutenberg.org.

———. *Project Gutenberg Wiki.* 1992. gutenberg.org/wiki.

Hatfield_visitor. *TripAdvisor.co.uk.* 2017. tripadvisor.co.uk.

Hathi Trust Digital Library. 2008. hathitrust.org.

Hawtin, Abigail. *ESRC Centre for Corpus Approaches to Social Science (CASS).* 2015. cass.lancs.ac.uk.

Hazen, Margaret. *H-Edtech Discussion Log.* 1991. networks.h-net.org/edtech.

Heart of Canada. 2004. heartofcanada.typepad.com.

Heppler, Jason. *Jason Heppler.* 2010. jasonheppler.org.

———, and Gabriel Wolfenstein. *The American Historian* 2015. tah.oah.org.

Hersh, Gemma. *Elsevier Connect.* 2014. elsevier.com/connect.

History News Network. 2007. historynewsnetwork.org.

Historypin. 2010. historypin.org.

Hitchcock, Tim. *Digital Connections.* 2011. sas-space.sas.ac.uk.

———. *Historyonics.* 2007–16. historyonics.blogspot.co.uk.

———. *Making History.* 2008. history.ac.uk/makinghistory.

———. "The Old Bailey Online: Democratising Access to Social History." *REF2014 Impact Case Studies.* 2014. impact.ref.ac.uk/CaseStudies/CaseStudy.aspx?Id=44489.

———, Robert Shoemaker, Clive Emsley, Sharon Howard, Jamie McLaughlin, et al. *The Old Bailey Proceedings Online, 1674–1913.* 2003–17. oldbaileyonline.org.

———, Robert Shoemaker, Jane Winters, et al. *Connected Histories.* 2011. connected histories.org.

HNN Editor. *Cliopatria.* 2011. historynewsnetwork.org/blog.

Hoffman, Sasha. *Digital Humanities Now.* 2013. digitalhumanitiesnow.org.

Holman, Brett, *Airminded.* 2015. airminded.org.

Hölzle, Urs. *Google Official Blog.* 2013. googleblog.blogspot.com.

Hopkin, Deian. *Humanist.* 1990. dhhumanist.org.

Horbinski, Andrea. *Day of DH 2014.* 2014. dayofdh2014.matrix.msu.edu.

Horowitz, Mark. *American Heritage.* 1995. americanheritage.com.

House of Commons Parliamentary Papers. Database. Proquest. n.d.

Howard, Sharon. *Early Modern Notes.* 2005. earlymodernnotes.wordpress.com.

Howe, Jeff. *Wired.* 2006. wired.com.

Humanist. 1996. dhhumanist.org.

Ide, Nancy. *The Computing Curriculum in the Arts and Humanities.* 2001. web.viu
.ca/siemensr/HCCurriculum.

"Inaugural Conference of the Digital Humanities Association of Southern Africa
(DHASA)." 2017. nwu.ac.za/unit-languages-and-literature-south-african-context
-digital-humanities-south-africa.

Inglis, Lucy. *Georgian London.* 2009–14. lucyinglis.com.

Instagram. 2011-present. instagram.com.

"Instructions for Contributors." *Transactions of the Royal Historical Society.* 2016.
Cambridge.org.

Internet Archive Wayback Machine. 2001-present. archive.org/web.

Invisible Adjunct. 2003–4. invisibleadjunct.com.

Jacobs, Alan. *Atlantic.* 2012. theatlantic.com.

Jane. *The Last American Pirate.* 2008. lastamericanpirate.net.

Jensen, Richard. *Humanist.* 1993. dhhumanist.org.

Jessifer. *DHThis.* 2013. dhthis.org.

Johnson, Jessica Marie. *Diaspora Hypertext.* 2013. dh.jmjafrx.com.

Johnston, Leslie. *The Signal: Library of Congress.* 2012. blogs.loc.gov/thesignal.

Johnston, Penny. *Day of DH 2014.* 2014. dayofdh2014.matrix.msu.edu.

Jørgensen, Finn Arne. @Finnarne, *Twitter.* 2018. twitter.com/finnarne.

Journal for the Association for History and Computing. 1998–2010. quod.lib.umich
.edu/j/jahc.

Journal of Digital Humanities 2011–14. journalofdigitalhumanities.org.

Kelly, Mills. "Lying about the Past: History 389-08/ver. 1.2." *George Mason University.*
2008. chnm.gmu.edu/history/faculty/kelly/blogs/h389.

———. *Mills Kelly.* 2005–13. edwired.org.

———. "Teaching and Learning in the Digital Age." *George Mason University.* 2006.
chnm.gmu.edu:80/history/faculty/kelly/courses/clio3/f06syl.pdf.

Kirsch, Adam. *New Republic.* 2014. newrepublic.com.

Kjellberg, Sara. *First Monday.* 2010. firstmonday.org.

Koh, Adeline. *AdelineKoh.* 2013. adeliinekoh.org.

———. @adelinekoh, *Twitter.* 2013. twitter.com/adelinekoh.

Kowal, Kimberley. *Maps and Views Blog.* 2014. blogs.bl.uk/magnificentmaps.

Kreibich, Christian. *Medium.* 2015. medium.com.

Lancashire, Ian. *Humanist.* 1989. dhhumanist.org.

"Lancaster Summer Schools in Corpus Linguistics and other Digital methods (#Lancs
SS17)." *University of Lancashire.* 2017. ucrel.lancs.ac.uk/summerschool.

Lane, Abigail. *Guardian.* 2013. theguardian.com.

Langer, Adina. "Hist 8885 Syllabus." *Digital History Class Blog.* 2015. sites.gsu.edu/
mhp-digital-history/syllabus.

Lastufka, Alan, and Kate Sandler. *ZineWiki.* 2006. zinewiki.com (dead).

LeBlanc, Zoe. @Zoe_LeBlanc, *Twitter.* 2017. twitter.com/Zoe_LeBlanc.

Leon, Sharon. *[Bracket].* 2005. 6floors.org/bracket.

———, and Sheila Brennan. *Scholars as Students: Introductory Digital History Training for Mid-Career Historians.* Roy Rosenzweig Center for History and New Media. 2015. history2014.doingdh.org/wp-content/uploads/sites/2/2014/07/RRCHNM_DoingDH_WhitePaper_8-31-2015.pdf.

"Living Headstones." monuments.com/living-headstones.

Luker, Ralph. *History News Network.* 2003. historynewsnetwork.org.

———. *Perspectives on History.* 2005. historians.org/publications-and-directories/perspectives-on-history.

———, et al. *Cliopatria.* 2004-12. historynewsnetwork.org/blog/20359.

MacDougall, Rob. *Roblog.* 2001. robmacdougall.org/blogger.

MacEachern, Alan, et al. *Network in Canadian History & Environment* 2008-12. niche-canada.org.

Madsen-Brooks, Leslie. "Hist 381-001/581-001: Digital History." *Digital History.* 2014. digitally.doinghistory.com/syllabus.

Marche, Stephen. *Los Angeles Review of Books.* 2012. lareviewofbooks.org.

Martin, Tamar. *Digital Humanities Q&A.* 2014. digitalhumanities.org/answers.

McCallum-Stewart, Esther. *Break of Day in the Trenches.* 2002. whatalovelywar.co.uk/war.

McCarty, Willard. *X-Humanist.* 1987. dhhumanist.org.

McClurken, Jeffrey. "Hist 471C3: Digital History." *Adventures in Digital History 3.0.* 2012. dh2012.umwblogs.org/syllabus.

———. "Syllabus." *Digital History.* 2008. digitalhistory.umwblogs.org/syllabus.

McDaniel, Caleb. "Syllabus." *Digital History @ Rice.* 2014. digitalhistory.blogs.rice.edu/syllabus.

———. *W. Caleb McDaniel.* 2012. wcm1.web.rice.edu.

McGillivray, Murray. *The Computing Curriculum in the Arts and Humanities.* 2001. web.viu.ca/siemensr/HCCurriculum.

McPherson, Tara. "Dynamic Vernaculars: Emergent Digital Forms in Contemporary Scholarship." Lecture. *HUMlab*, Umeå Universitet, Sweden. 3 March 2008. stream.humlab.umu.se/index.php?streamName=dynamicVernaculars.

Methnet. *Humanist.* (2007. dhhumanist.org.

Mhobbs. *Clio Wired (History 696) A Weblog for Students in Clio Wired (History 696) at George Mason University.* 2005. chnm.gmu.edu:80/history/faculty/Kelly/blogs/h696f05.

Michalove, Sharon. *H-Albion Discussion Log.* 1993. networks.h-net.org/h-albion.

Milligan, Ian. "HIST 303: Digital History." *Ian Milligan.* 2014. ianmilli.files.wordpress.com/2014/01/w2014-hist-303.pdf.

———, Christine McLaughlin, Jason Young, Jim Clifford, and Thomas Peace. *Active History.ca.* 2008-present. activehistory.ca.

Mintz, Steven, and Sara McNeil. *Digital History.* 1990s. digitalhistory.uh.edu.

Mollett, Amy, and Paul Rainford. *LSE Impact Blog.* 2011. blogs.lse.ac.uk/impactofsocialsciences.

Moravec, Michelle. *History in the City.* 2013. historyinthecity.blogspot.com.
———. *HT.* 2016. medium.com/on-archivy.
Morgan, John. *Times Higher Education.* 2014. timeshighereducation.com.
Mueller, Phil. *H-Latam Discussion Log.* 1994. networks.h-net.org/h-latam.
Mühlberger, Günter, et al. *Transkribus.* 2016. transkribus.eu.
Mullen, Lincoln. "Clio 3: Programming for Historians." *Lincolnmullen.com.* 2014. lincolnmullen.com/files/clio3.syllabus.hist698.2014f.pdf.
———. *Computational Historical Thinking with Applications in R.* 2017-ongoing. dh-r .lincolnmullen.com.
Murphy, Kevin. *Ghost in the Machine.* 2000. ghostinthemachine.net.
Nowviskie, Bethany. *Bethany Nowviskie.* 2010–14. nowviskie.org.
O'Donnell, Daniel. *Humanist.* 2017. dhhumanist.org.
Old Weather. 2010. classic.oldweather.org.
O'Reilly, Tim. *O'Reilly.* 2005. oreilly.com.
O'Sullivan, James. *AdelineKoh.* 2013. adelinekoh.org/blog.
Owens, Trevor. *Trevor Owens.* 2006. trevorowens.org.
Parry, Marc. *Chronicle of Higher Education.* 2013. chronicle.com.
Peters, Emily. *Chronicle of Higher Education.* 2002. chronicle.com.
Petrik, Paula. "Clio II: History & New Media." *George Mason University.* 2012. archiva .net/pdf/hist697ay12.pdf.
Posner, Miriam. *Miriam Posner's Blog.* 2013. miriamposner.com.
Prelinger, Rick, George Oates, Tracey Jaquith, et al. *Understanding 9/11: A Television News Archive.* 2001–11. archive.org/details/911.
Prescott, Andrew. *Digital Riffs.* 2012–15. digitalriffs.blogspot.co.uk.
PressForward. 2013. pressforward.org.
"Registration." *Programming 4 Humanists.* 2018. Programming4humanists.tamu.edu.
"Qeepr." 2013. qeepr.com.
Rahtz, Sebastian. *X-Humanist.* 1989. dhhumanist.org.
Reddit. 2005-present. reddit.com.
Reddit. 2013. as.reddit.com.
"Registration Still Open: Enhancing Digital Skills for Historians, Humanities, and Beyond." *Northwestern University.* 2016. nwu.ac.za/eresearch/registration-still -open-enhancing-digital-skills-historians-humanities-and-beyond
"Research Training." *Institute of Historical Research.* 2017. history.ac.uk/research -training/browse.
Robertson, Stephen. "Arguing with Digital History: Workshop to Address a Central Problem in Digital History." *Roy Rozensweig Center for History and New Media.* 2017. rrchnm.org/news/arguing-with-digital-history-workshop-to-address-a-central -problem-in-digital-history.
———. *Stephen Robertson.* 2014. drstephenrobertson.com.
Rock, Robert. *Coins, Crime and History.* 2014. crimeandcoins.wordpress.com.
Rosenzweig, Roy, et al. *Hurricane Digital Memory Bank.* 2005. hurricanearchive.org.

Rosenzweig, Roy, Stephen Brier, and Joshua Brown. *Who Built America? From the Centennial Celebration of 1876 to the Great War of 1914.* Voyager. CD-ROM. 1993.

RRCHNM20. 2014. 20.rrchnm.org.

di Santis, Francesco. *The Portrait-Story Project.* 2007. portraitstoryproject.org.

Scheinfeldt, Tom. "Digital Methods Training at Scale: Leveraging THATCamp through a Regional System." *RRCHNM20.* n.d.

———. *Found History.* 2005–10. foundhistory.org.

———. "Invisible College; THATCamp as Scholarly Society." Lecture. *Scholarly Communication Program,* Columbia University, New York, 5 April 2012. scholcomm .columbia.edu/2012/03/07/invisible-college-thatcamp-as-scholarly-society.

———, and Amanda French. "Sustaining Digital Humanities Training through THAT-Camp." RRCHNM20. n.d.

———, Greg Umbach, Pennee Bender, Joshua Brown, et al. *The September 11 Digital Archive.* 2002–5. 911digitalarchive.org.

Schmidt, Ben. *Sapping Attention.* 2009-present. sappingattention.blogspot.com.

Seaward, Louise. *Transcribe Bentham.* 2017. blogs.ucl.ac.uk/transcribe-bentham.

Seefeldt, Douglas. "Hist 470: Digital History." *Digital History, UNL.* 2009. digital history.unl.edu/syllabi/seefeldt_470_fo9.pdf.

Senier, Siobhan. *AdelineKoh.* 2013. adelinekoh.org/blog.

17th and 18th Century Burney Collection Newspapers. Gale Cengage. n.d.

Shenkman, Rick. *History News Network.* 2001. historynewsnetwork.org.

———. *Rick Shenkman.* n.d. richshenkman.com.

Shevlin, Eleanor. *Early Modern Online Bibliography.* 2010. earlymodernonlinebib .wordpress.com.

Siemens, Ray. *The Computing Curriculum in the Arts and Humanities.* 2001. web.viu .ca/siemensr/HCCurriculum.

Sinclair, Stéfan, and Geoffrey Rockwell. *Voyant Tools: Reveal Your Texts.* 2003. voyeur tools.org and voyanttools.org.

Sinkewicz, Robert E. *Humanist.* 1989. dhhumanist.org.

Slashdot. 1997-present. slashdot.org.

"Smart Love Lock." 2014. smartlovelock.com.

Smith, Lisa. "Digital Recipe Books Project." *University of Essex.* 2017.

———. "Supernatural Worlds." *University of Essex.* 2017.

Snapchat. 2011–present. snapchat.com.

Software Carpentry. 1998–present. https://software-carpentry.org/.

Spice, Byron, and Anne Watzman. *Carnegie Mellon University.* 2007. cmu.edu/news.

Street Museum, Museum of London. 2010.

Sullivan, Danny. *Search Engine Land.* 2010. searchengineland.com.

"Summer Seminars." *Humanities Computing Unit, University of Oxford.* 2000. hcu. ox.ac.uk/summer.

Swenson, Ewa. *Humanist.* 1987. dhhumanist.org.

"Syllabus—Fall 2014." *Programming for Humanists at TAMU.* 2014. programming 4humanists.tamu.edu/syllabus.

TaDiRAH—Taxonomy of Digital Research Activities in the Humanities. 2014. tadirah .dariah.eu/vocab.

Tate, Bruce, Jane Winters, Jonathan Blaney, Peter Webster, et al. *British History Online.* 2003. british-history.ac.uk.

Taycher, Leonid. *Google Book Search.* 2010. booksearch.blogspot.co.uk.

Teachers of History in the UK. 2017. history.ac.uk/history-online/teachers/institution.

TEI Text Encoding Initiative. 2014. tei-c.org.

Terras, Melissa. *LSE Impact Blog.* 2012. eprints.lse.ac.uk/51970.

———. *Melissa Terras' Blog.* 2011. melissaterras.blogspot.co.uk.

THATCamp. n.d.–2018. http://thatcamp.org/camps.

Thomas, Wayne. *Thomas and Collier Research.* 2014. thomasandcollier.com.

Time. 2014. time.com.

Tonra, Justin. *Day of DH 2014.* 2014. dayofdh2014.matrix.msu.edu.

Torget, Andrew J. "Course Syllabus." *Introduction to Digital Scholarship.* 2014. torget .us/HIST5100/syllabus.

Townsend, Robert B. *Perspectives on History* 2010. historians.org/publications-and -directories/perspectives-on-history.

Trafford, Simon. "Databases for Historians." *Institute of Historical Research.* 2002. history.ac.uk/training/courses/database.html.

Tribble, Ivan. *Chronicle of Higher Education.* 2005. chronicle.com.

Trove. National Library of Australia. (2009. trove.nla.gov.au.

"Try It Editor v1.3." *W3Schools.* 2002. w3schools/com/html/tryit.asp?filename=tryhtml _lists4.

Turkel, William J. *Digital History Hacks.* 2005–8. digitalhistoryhacks.blogspot.ca.

———. "Digital Humanities 1011B: Programming (Winter 2013)." *William J Turkel.* 2013. williamjturkel.net/teaching/digital-humanities-1011b-programming-winter -2013.

———. "History 513F Digital History: Methodology for the Infinite Archive." *University of Western Ontario.* 2006. digitalhistory.uwo.ca/h513f.

———. "History 9832B: Interactive Exhibit Design (Winter 2016)." *William J Turkel.* 2016. williamjturkel.net/teaching/history-9832b-interactive-exhibit-design-winter -2016.

———. "Interactive Exhibit Design." *William J Turkel.* 2012. williamjturkel.net/teaching/ history-9832b-interactive-exhibit-design-winter-2012.

———. "Max Programming: Happy Face Challenge." Demonstration. 2013. vimeo .com/86262980.

———. *William. J. Turkel.* 2013–15. williamjturkel.net.

Turkle, Sherry. *Chronicle of Higher Education.* 2004. chronicle.com.

Turovsky, Barak. *Google Blog.* 2016. blog.google/products/translate.

Twitter. 2006–present. twitter.com.

"UCREL Summer School in Corpus Linguistics." *Department of Linguistics and English Language, University of Lancaster.* 2011. ling.lancs.ac.uk/event/3622.

Virshup, Amy. *Wired.* 1998. wired.com.

Von Ahn, Luis. "Curriculum Vitae." *Carnegie Mellon University* (2012?), cs.cmu/edu.

Wakefield, Jane. *BBC News.* 2008. news.bbc.co.uk.

Wall, John N., David Hill, John Schofield, Joshua Stephens, et al. *Virtual St. Paul's Cross Project.* 2014. vpcp.chass.ncsu.edu.

Weingart, Scott. *The Scottbot Irregular.* 2013–16. scottbot.net.

Whisnant, Anne Mitchell. "History 671: Introduction to Public History." *History 671: Introduction to Public History.* 2015. publichistory.web.unc.edu:80/files/2010/06/20150819History671SyllabusWhisnant.pdf.

White, Richard. "What Is Spatial History?" Working paper. *Spatial History Project; Stanford University.* 2010. web.stanford.edu/group/spatialhistory/cgi-bin/site/pub.php?id=29.

Williams, Abigail, et al. *Digital Miscellanies Index.* 2010–16. digitalmiscellaniesindex.org.

Winters, Jane. *Digital History Seminar.* 2014. ihrdighist.blogs.sas.ac.uk.

Withington, Phil, et al. *Intoxicants and Early Modernity: England, 1580–1740.* 2013–16. intoxicantsproject.org.

Wolfson, Ben. "Invisible Adjunct." *TopicExchange.* 2004. topicexchange.com.

Young, Jeffrey R. *New York Times.* 2000. nytimes.com.

Published Sources

Aarseth, Espen. *Cybertext: Perspectives on Ergodic Literature.* Baltimore, Md.: Johns Hopkins University Press, 1997.

Aiden, Erez Lieberman, Jean-Baptist Michel, et al. "Quantitative Analysis of Culture Using Millions of Digitized Books." *Science* 331, no. 6014 (2011): 176–82.

American Historical Association. "Guidelines for the Professional Evaluation of Digital Scholarship by Historians." 2015. historians.org/teaching-and-learning/digital-history-resources/evaluation-of-digital-scholarship-in-history/guidelines-for-the-professional-evaluation-of-digital-scholarship-by-historians.

American Standard Code for Information Interchange: ASA Standard X3.4–1963. 1963. wordpowersystems.com/archives/codes/X3.4–1963/index.html.

Andersen, Deborah Lines. "Defining Digital History: Benchmarks." *Journal of the Association of History and Computing* 5, no. 1 (2002). hdl.handle.net/2027/spo.3310410.0005.103.

———. "September 11, Loss and Creation." *History and Computing* 4, no. 3 (2001). hdl.handle.net/2027/spo.3310410.0004.305.

Anderson, Benedict. *Imagined Communities.* Verso, 1983.

Anderson, Ian, and Zoe Bliss. *Report: Text Mining for Historians,* AHRC ICT Methods Network. 2007. methodsnetwork.ac.uk/redist/pdf/act25report.pdf.

Anderson, Margo. "Quantitative History." In *The SAGE Handbook of Social Science Methodology,* edited by William Outhwaite and Stephen Turner, 246–63. London: Sage, 2007.

Ankersmit, F. R. "Historiography and Postmodernism." *History and Theory* 28, no. 2 (1989): 137–53.

Anthony, Laurence. "AntConc: A Learner and Classroom Friendly, Multi-Platform Corpus Analysis Toolkit." *Proceedings of IWLeL 2004: An Interactive Workshop on Language e-Learning,* 7–14. 2005.

Antón, Carmen, Carmen Camarero, and María-José Garrido. "Exploring the Experience Value of Museum Visitors as a Co-Creation Process." *Current Issues in Tourism* (2017 preprint): 1–20.

Appleby, Joan, Lynn Hunt, and Margaret Jacob. *Telling the Truth about History.* New York: W. W. Norton, 1995.

Arkell, Thom. "Illuminations and Distortions: Gregory King's Scheme Calculated for the Year 1688 and the Social Structure of Later Stuart England." *Economic History Review* 59, no. 1 (2006): 32–69.

Armaselu, Florentina, Verónica Martins, and Catherine Emma Jones. "Materiality of TEI Encoding and Decoding: An Analysis of the Western European Union Archives on Armament Policy." *Selected Papers from the 2014 TEI Conference,* no. 9 (2016). jtei.revues.org/1463.

Arnold, Taylor, and Lauren Tilton. "Basic Text Processing in R." *The Programming Historian.* 2017. programminghistorian.org/lessons/basic-text-processing-in-r.

Atkinson, Dwight. *Scientific Discourse in Sociohistorical Context: The Philosophical Transactions of the Royal Society of London, 1675–1975.* Cambridge: Cambridge University Press, 1999.

Ayers, Edward. "Does Digital Scholarship Have a Future?" *EDUCASE Review* 48, no. 4 (2013). er.educause.edu/articles/2013/8/does-digital-scholarship-have-a-future

———. *In the Presence of Mine Enemies: War in the Heart of America, 1859–1863.* New York: W. W. Norton, 2003.

———. "Lincoln's America 2.0." *Journal of American History* 96 (2009): 441–46.

———. "The Pasts and Futures of Digital History." *History News* 56, no. 4 (2001): 5–9.

———. *Vengeance and Justice, Crime and Punishment in the 19th century American South.* Oxford: Oxford University Press, 1984.

———. *What Caused the Civil War? Reflections on the South and Southern History.* New York: Norton, 2005.

Ayres, Marie-Louise. "Singing for Their Supper: Trove, Australian Newspapers, and the Crowd." *IFLA WLIC 2013.* Singapore (2013): 1–9.

Badke, William. "The Treachery of Keywords." *Online Searcher* 35, no. 2 (2011): 51–53.

Bain, Bob. "'They Thought the World Was Flat?' Applying the Principles of How People Learn in Teaching High School History." In *How Students Learn: History in the Classroom,* 179–214. Washington, D.C.: National Research Council, 2005.

Banks, Samuel L. "Review: Time on the Cross: The Economics of American Negro Slavery by Robert William Fogel; Stanley L. Engerman." *Journal of Negro Education* 44, no. 4 (1974): 557–60.

Banner, James M., Jr. *Being a Historian.* Cambridge: Cambridge University Press, 2012.

Beals, M. H. "Stuck in the Middle: Developing Research Workflows for a Multi-Scale Text Analysis." *Journal of Victorian Culture* 22, no. 2 (2017): 224–31.

Beattie, J. M. "The Pattern of Crime in England 1660–1800." *Past & Present* 62 (1974): 47–95.

Becker, Carl. "Everyman His Own Historian." *American Historical Review* 37, no. 2 (1932): 221–36.

Bederson, Benjamin B. "Audio Augmented Reality: A Prototype Automated Tour Guide." *CHI '95 Mosaic of Creativity.* Denver, 1995, 210–11.

Beichner, Robert J., Jeffrey M. Saul, David S. Abbott, Jeanne J. Morse, Duane Deardorff, Rhett J. Allain, Scott W. Bonham, Melissa H. Dancy, and John S. Risley. "The Student-Centred Activities for Large Enrollment Undergraduate Programs (SCALE-UP) Project." *Research-Based Reform of University Physics* 1, no. 1 (2007): 2–39.

Beichner, Robert J., Jeffrey M. Saul, Rhett J. Allain, Duane L. Deardorff, and David S. Abbott. "Introduction to SCALE-UP: Student-Centred Activities for Large Enrollment University Physics." Report ED459062. *Institute of Education Sciences*, 2000.

Blaney, Jonathan. "The Problem of Citation in the Digital Humanities." In *Proceedings of the Digital Humanities Congress 2012*, edited by Clare Mills, Michael Pidd, and Esther Ward. Sheffield: HRI Online Publications, 2014. hrionline.ac.uk/openbook/chapter/dhc2012-blaney.

Blaxill, Luke. "Quantifying the Language of British Politics, 1880–1910." *Historical Research* 86, no. 232 (2013): 313–41.

Blease, Derek. *Evaluating Educational Software.* London: Croom Helm, 1986.

Blevins, Cameron. "Digital History's Perpetual Future Tense." *Debates in the Digital Humanities.* Minneapolis: University of Minnesota Press, 2016. dhdebates.gc.cuny.edu/debates/text/77.

Bloch, Marc, *The Historian's Craft.* New York: Vintage, 1953.

Boggs, Jeremy. "Three Roles for Teachers Using Technology." In *Hacking the Academy: New Approaches to Scholarship and Teaching from Digital Humanities*, edited by Dan Cohen and Tom Scheinfeldt, 81–86. Ann Arbor: University of Michigan Press, 2013.

Bogue, Allan G. *Clio and the Bitch Goddess: Quantification in American Political History.* London: Sage, 1983.

Booth, Alan. *Teaching History at University: Enhancing Learning and Understanding.* London: Routledge, 2003.

———, and Paul Hyland. *The Practice of University History Teaching.* Manchester: Manchester University Press, 2000.

Börner, Katy. "Plug-and-Play Macroscopes." *Communications of the ACM* 54, no. 3 (2011): 60–69.

Bowen, William G. *1997 President's Report. The Andrew W. Mellon Foundation.* 1998. mellon.org:80/arpr97.html.

Braudel, Fernand. *On History.* Chicago: University of Chicago Press, 1982.

Brewer, John. *The Sinews of Power: War, Money and the English State, 1688–1783*. London: Unwin Hyman, 1989.

Brier, Stephen. "Confessions of a Premature Digital Humanist." *Journal of Interactive Educational Technology and Pedagogy* 11 (2017). jitp.commons.gc.cuny.edu/confessions-of-a-premature-digital-humanist.

———, Bruce Levine, Joshua B. Freeman, *Who Built America? Working People and the Nation's Economy, Politics, Culture, and Society*. New York: Pantheon, 1989.

Brown, Ann L., and Joseph C. Campione. "Guided Discovery in a Community of Learners." In *Classroom Lessons: Integrating Cognitive Theory and Classroom Practice*, edited by Kate McGilly, 229–70. Cambridge, Mass.: MIT Press, 1994.

Brownlee, Jamie. "Contract Faculty in Canada: Using Access to Information Requests to Uncover Hidden Academics in Canadian Universities." *Higher Education* 70, no. 5 (2015): 787–805.

Bruno, Robert A. "Review: Who Built America?" *Transformations: The Journal of Inclusive Scholarship and Pedagogy* 3, no. 1 (1992): 43–46.

Bryer, R. A. "Double-Entry Bookkeeping and the Birth of Capitalism: Accounting for the Commercial Revolution in Medieval Northern Italy." *Critical Perspectives on Accounting*, 4, no. 2 (1993): 113–40.

Burton, Matt. "Blogs as Infrastructure for Scholarly Communication." PhD diss., University of Michigan, 2015.

Carr, E. H. *What Is History?* Harmondsworth: Penguin, 1961.

Caswell, Michelle, Ricardo Punalan, and T-Kay Sangwand. "Critical Archival Studies: An Introduction." *Journal of Critical Library and Information Studies*, 1, no. 2 (2017): 1–8.

Cates, Ward M., Lynn A. Fontana, and Charles S. White. "Designing an Interactive Multimedia Instructional Environment: The Civil War Interactive." *ALT-J* 1, no. 2 (1993): 5–16.

Causer, Tim, and Valerie Wallace. "Building a Volunteer Community: Results and Findings from Transcribe Bentham." *Digital Humanities Quarterly* 6, no. 2 (2012): digitalhumanities.org:8081/dhq/vol/6/2/000125/000125.html.

Causer, Tim, Justin Tonra, and Valerie Wallace. "Transcription Maximized; Expense Minimized? Crowdsourcing and Editing *The Collected Works of Jeremy Bentham*." *Literary and Linguistic Computing* 27, no. 1 (2012): 119–37.

Cayley, Seth. "Digitization for the Masses: Taking Users Beyond Simple Searching in Nineteenth-Century Collections Online." *Journal of Victorian Culture* 22, no. 2 (2017): 248–55.

Charlesworth, Andrew, ed. *An Atlas of Rural Protest in Britain 1548–1900*. Beckenham, Kent: Croom Helm, 1983.

Clifford, Jim, Beatrice Alex, Colin M. Coates, Ewan Klein, and Andrew Watson. "Geoparsing History: Locating Commodities in Ten Million Pages of Nineteenth-Century Sources." *Historical Methods* 49, no. 3 (2016): 115–31.

Cockburn, J. S. "Early Modern Assize Records as Historical Evidence." *Journal of the Society of Archivists* 5, no. 4 (1975): 215–31.

Cohen, Dan. *Equations from God: Pure Mathematics and Victorian Faith*. Baltimore, Md.: Johns Hopkins University Press, 2007.

———. "History and the Second Decade of the Web." *Rethinking History: The Journal of Theory and Practice* 8, no. 2 (2004): 293–301.

———, and Roy Rosenzweig. *Digital History: A Guide to Gathering, Preserving, and Presenting the Past on the Web*. Philadelphia: University of Pennsylvania Press, 2005.

———, Frederick Gibbs, Tim Hitchcock, Geoffrey Rockwell, Jörg Sander, Robert Shoemaker, Stéfan Sinclair, Sean Takats, William J. Turkel, Cyril Briquet, Jamie McLaughlin, Milena Radzikowska, John Simpson, and Kirsten C. Uszkalo. *Data Mining with Criminal Intent: Final White Paper*. 2011. criminalintent.org/wp-content/uploads/2011/09/Data-Mining-with-Criminal-Intent-Final.pdf.

Collinson, Patrick. "The Elizabethan Church and the New Religion." In *Reign of Elizabeth I*, edited by Christopher Haigh, 169–94. Basingstoke: Macmillan, 1984.

Colson, Jean, Roger Middleton, and Peter Wardley. "Annual Review of Information Technology Developments for Economic and Social Historians, 1991." *The Economic History Review* 45, no. 2 (1992): 378–412.

Conner, Patrick W. "ANSAXNET: Telecommunications for Anglo-Saxonists." In *Old English Newsletter*, edited by Paul E. Szarmach. Vol. 20, no. 2 (1987): 25.

———. "Networking in the Humanities: Lessons from ANSAXNET." *Computers and the Humanities* 26, no. 3 (1992): 195–204.

———. "Notes from ANSAXNET, Again." In *Old English Newsletter*, edited by Paul E. Szarmach. Vol. 24, no. 1 (1990): 32–34.

Conrad, Alfred, and John Meyer. "The Economies of Slavery in the *Ante-Bellum* South." *Journal of Political Economy* 66, no. 2 (1958): 95–130.

Coppa, Francesca. "A Brief History of Media Fandom." In *Fan Fiction and Fan Communities in the Age of the Internet: New Essays*, edited by Karen Hellekson and Kristina Busse, 41–59. Jefferson, N.C.: McFarland, 2006.

The Copyright and Rights in Performances (Research, Education, Libraries and Archives) Regulations 2014. British Government. 2014. No. 1372.

Crane, Gregory. "What Do You Do with a Million Books?" *D-Lib Magazine* 12, no. 3 (2006): dlib.org/dlib/march06/crane/03crane.html.

Crogan, P., and S. Kinsley. "Paying Attention: Towards a Critique of the Attention Economy." *Culture Machine* 13 (2012): 1–29.

Crymble, Adam. "An Analysis of Twitter and Facebook Use by the Archival Community." *Archivaria* 70 (2010): 126–51.

———. "Digital History." In *A Companion to the History of Crime and Criminal Justice*, edited by Jo Turner, Paul Taylor, Sharon Morley, and Karen Corteen, 67–68. Bristol: Policy Press, 2017.

———, Fred Gibbs, Allison Hegel, Caleb McDaniel, Ian Milligan, Evan Taparata, Jeri Wieringa, Jeremy Boggs, and William J. Turkel, eds. *The Programming Histo-*

rian—Print Edition. London: Programming Historian Editorial Board, 2016. doi .org/10.5281/zenodo.49873.

Danniau, Fien. "Public History in a Digital Context: Back to the Future or Back to Basics?" *Low Countries Historical Review* 128, no. 4 (2013): 118–44.

Darcy, Robert, and Richard C. Rohrs. *A Guide to Quantitative History*. Westport, Conn.: Praeger, 1995.

Davies, W. M. "Groupwork as a Form of Assessment: Common Problems and Recommended Solutions." *Higher Education* 58, no. 4 (2009): 563–84.

de Groot, Jerome. *Consuming History*. London: Routledge, 2008.

Denley, Peter, and Deian Hopkin, eds. *History and Computing*. Manchester: Manchester University Press, 1987.

Deschamps, Ryan. "Correspondence Analysis for Historical Research with R." *The Programming Historian*. 2017. programminghistorian.org/lessons/correspondence -analysis-in-R.

Dollar, C. M., and R. J. Jensen. *Historian's Guide to Statistics: Quantitative Analysis and Historical Research*. Huntingdon, NY: Krieger, 1971.

Driscoll, M. J. "Encoding Old Norse/Icelandic Primary Sources Using TEI-Conformant SGML." *Literary and Linguistic Computing* 15, no. 1 (2000): 81–94.

Dunn, David, Roger Middleton, and Peter Wardley. "Annual Review of Information Technology Developments for Economic and Social Historians, 1992." *Economic History Review* 46, no. 2 (1993): 379–409.

Dunning, Alastair. *Digitising the Past: Next Steps for Public Sector Digitisation*, Joint Information Systems Committee. 2009. hdl.handle.net/10760/18048.

Earhart, Amy E. "Can Information Be Unfettered? Race and the New Digital Humanities Canon." In *Debates in Digital Humanities*, edited by Matthew K. Gold. Minneapolis: University of Minnesota Press, 2012. dhdebates.gc.cuny.edu/debates/ text/16.

———. *Traces of the Old, Uses of the New: The Emergence of Digital Literary Studies*. Ann Arbor: University of Michigan Press, 2015).

Eaton, Clement. "Review: Plain Folk of the Old South by Frank Lawrence Owsley." *American Historical Review* 55, no. 3 (1950): 617–18.

Eichhorn, Kate. *The Archival Turn in Feminism: Outrage in Order*. Philadelphia: Temple University Press, 2013.

Elliott, Devon, Robert MacDougall, and William J. Turkel. "New Old Things: Fabrication, Physical Computing, and Experiment in Historical Practice." *Canadian Journal of Communication* 37, no. 1 (2012): 121–28.

Elton, Geoffrey, *The Practice of History*. New York: Cromwell, 1967.

Endres, William. "More than Meets the Eye: Going 3D with an Early Medieval Manuscript." In *Proceedings of the Digital Humanities Congress 2012*, edited by Clare Mills, Michael Pidd, and Esther Ward. Sheffield: HRI Online Publications, 2014. hrionline.ac.uk/openbook/chapter/dhc2012-endres.

Eveleigh, Alexandra, Charlene Jennett, Stuart Lynn, and Anna L. Cox. "'I Want to Be a Captain! I Want to Be a Captain!': Gamification in the *Old Weather* Citizen

Science Project." *Proceedings of the First International Conference on Gameful Design, Research, and Applications.* 2013. 79–82.

Everett, James E. "Annual Review of Information Technology Developments for Economic and Social Historians, 1995." *Economic History Review* 49, no. 2 (1996): 377–81.

———. "Annual Review of Information Technology Developments for Economic and Social Historians, 1996." *Economic History Review* 50, no. 3 (1997): 543–55.

———. "Annual Review of Information Technology Developments for Economic and Social Historians, 1997." *Economic History Review* 51, no. 2 (1998): 382–97.

Exceptions to Copyright: Research. Intellectual Property Office, British Government. 2014. gov.uk/government/uploads/system/uploads/attachment_data/file/375954/Research.pdf.

Feinstein, Charles H., and Mark Thomas. *Making History Count: A Primer in Quantitative Methods for Historians.* Cambridge: Cambridge University Press, 2002.

Fiormonte, Dominco, "Digital Humanities from a Global Perspective." 2014. 10.12862/ispf14L203.

Fish, Stanley, "What Is Stylistics and Why Are They Saying Such Terrible Things about it?: Part II" *boundary 2* 8, no. 1 (1976): 129–46.

Flanagan, David. *JavaScript: the Definitive Guide.* Sebastopol: O'Reilly, 1996.

Fleming, N. D. "I'm Different; Not Dumb. Modes of Presentation (VARK) in the Tertiary Classroom." In *Proceedings of the 1995 Annual Conference of the Higher Education and Research Development Society of Australasia (HERDSA)*, 18 (1995): 308–13.

Floud, Roderick. *An Introduction to Quantitative Methods for Historians.* London: Routledge, 1973.

Fogel, Robert. "The New Economic History: I. Its Findings and Methods." *Economic History Review* 19, no. 3 (1966): 642–56.

———, and Stanley Engerman. *Time on the Cross: The Economics of American Negro Slavery.* Boston: Little, Brown, 1974.

Fouh, Eric, Daniel A. Breakiron, Sally Hamouda, Mohammed F. Farghally, and Clifford A. Shaffer. "Exploring Students Learning Behavior with an Interactive Etextbook in Computer Science Course." *Computers in Human Behavior* 41 (2014): 478–85.

Fraistat, Neil, Steven Jones, and Carl Stahmer. "The Canon, the Web, and the Digitization of Romanticism." *Romanticism on the Net* 10 (1998). dx.doi.org/10.7202/005801ar.

Frisch, Michael. *A Shared Authority: Essays on the Craft and Meaning of Oral and Public History.* Albany: SUNY Press, 1990.

Froehlich, Heather. "Corpus Analysis with Antconc." *Programming Historian*, 2015. programminghistorian.org/lessons/corpus-analysis-with-antconc.

Gaddis, John Lewis. *The Landscape of History: How Historians Map the Past.* Oxford: Oxford University Press, 2002.

Gaffield, Chad. "Words, Words, Words: How the Digital Humanities Are Integrating Diverse Research Fields to Study People." *Annual Review of Statistics and its Application* 5 (2018): 119–39.

Gardner, Howard. *Multiple Intelligences: The Theory in Practice.* New York: Basic Books, 1993.

Giacometti, Alejandro. "Evaluating Multispectral Imaging Processing Methodologies for Analysing Cultural Heritage Documents." PhD diss., University College London, 2014.

Goislard De Monsabert, Ben, D. Edwards, D. Shah, and A. Kedgley. "Importance of Consistent Datasets in Musculoskeletal Modelling: A Study of the Hand and Wrist." *Annals of Biomedical Engineering* 46, no. 1 (2018): 71–85.

Goodman, David, and Shane White. "'Who Built America?': The Interview." *Australasian Journal of American Studies* 14, no. 2 (1995): 121–29.

Gordon, Scott. *The History and Philosophy of Social Science.* London: Routledge, 1991.

Graham, Shawn, Ian Milligan, and Scott Weingart. *Exploring Big Historical Data: The Historian's Macroscope.* London: Imperial College Press, 2016.

Graham, Shawn, Scott Weingart, and Ian Milligan. "Getting Started with Topic Modeling and MALLET." *Programming Historian,* 2012. programminghistorian.org/lessons/topic-modeling-and-mallet.

Grief, Avner. "Cliometrics After 40 Years: Micro Theory and Economic History." *American Economic Review.* 87, no. 2 (1997): 400–403.

Gross, Alan G., Joseph E. Harmon, and Michael Reidy. *Communicating Science: The Scientific Article from the 17th Century to the Present.* Oxford: Oxford University Press, 2001.

Guildi, Jo, and David Armitage. *The History Manifesto.* Cambridge: Cambridge University Press, 2014.

Habermas, Jürgen. *The Structural Transformation of the Public Sphere.* Translated by Thomas Burger. Cambridge, U.K.: Polity, 1989.

Hackett Fisher, David. *Historians' Fallacies: Towards a Logic of Historical Thought.* New York: Harper & Row, 1970.

Hardman, Chris, "Walkmanology." *Drama Review* 27, no. 4 (1983): 43–46.

Hargreaves, Ian. *Digital Opportunity: A Review of Intellectual Property and Growth.* Independent report, United Kingdom. 2011.

Härtel, Reinhard. "To Treat or Not to Treat: the Historical Source Before the Input." *Historical Social Research* 14, no. 1 (1989): 25–38.

Haskins, Loren, and Kirk Jeffrey. *Understanding Quantitative History.* Cambridge, Mass.: MIT Press, 1990.

Hay, Douglas. "War, Dearth and Theft in the Eighteenth Century: The Record of the English Courts." *Past and Present* 95 (1982): 117–60.

Hedge, Alan. "The Open-Plan Office: A Systematic Investigation of Employee Reactions to Their Work Environment." *Environment and Behavior* 14, no. 5 (1982): 519–42.

Herring, S. "Gender and Democracy in Computer-Mediated Communication." *Electronic Journal of Communication* 3, no. 2 (1993). cios.org/ejcpublic/003/2/00328.html.

———. "Gender and Participation in Computer-Mediated Linguistic Discourse." *ERIC Clearninghouse on Language and Linguistics.* 1992. Doc. no. ED345552.

———. "Gender Differences in CMC: Findings and Implications." *CPSR Newsletter* 18 no. 1 (2000). cpsr.org/issues/womenintech/herring.

———. "Posting in a Different Voice: Gender and Ethics in Computer-Mediated Communication." In *Philosophical Perspectives on Computer-Mediated Communication*, edited by C. Ess, 115–45. Albany: SUNY Press, 1996.

———. "The Rhetorical Dynamics of Gender Harassment On-Line." *Information Society* 15, no. 3 (1999): 151–67.

Hirsch, Brett D. "</Parentheses>: Digital Humanities and the Place of Pedagogy." In *Digital Humanities Pedagogy: Practices, Principles and Politics*, edited by Brett D. Hirsch, 3–30. Cambridge, U.K.: Open Book Publishers, 2012.

———, ed. *Digital Humanities Pedagogy: Practices, Principles and Politics*. Cambridge, U.K.: Open Book Publishers, 2012.

"Historical Computation Noticeboard." *Social History* 12, no. 2 (1987): 237–40.

Hitchcock, Tim, and Robert Shoemaker. *London Lives: Poverty, Crime and the Making of a Modern City, 1690–1800*. Cambridge: Cambridge University Press, 2015).

Hitchcock, Tim, and Robert Shoemaker. "Making History Online." *Transactions of the Royal Historical Society* 25 (2015): 75–93.

Hitchcock, Tim, and William J. Turkel. "The *Old Bailey Proceedings, 1674–1913*: Text Mining for Evidence of Court Behavior." *Law and History Review* 34, no. 4 (2016): 929–55.

Hockey, Susan. "The History of Humanities Computing." In *A Companion to Digital Humanities*, edited by Susan Schreibman, Ray Siemens, and John Unsworth, 3–19. Oxford: Blackwell, 2004.

Holley, Rose. "How Good Can It Get? Analysing and Improving OCR Accuracy in Large Scale Historic Newspaper Digitisation Programs." *D-Lib Magazine* 15, no. 3/4 (2009). dlib.org/dlib/march09/holley/03holley.html

Huber, Magnus. "The *Old Bailey Proceedings*, 1674–1834: Evaluating and Annotating a Corpus of 18th- and 19th-Century Spoken English." *Varieng* 1 (2007). helsinki.fi/varieng/series/volumes/01/huber.

Hudson, Pat. *History by Numbers: an Introduction to Quantitative Approaches*. London: Oxford University Press, 2000.

Hulden, Vilja. "Supervised Classification: The Naive Bayesian Returns to the Old Bailey." *Programming Historian*, 2014. programminghistorian.org/lessons/naive-bayesian.

Hyman, Avi. "Twenty Years of ListServ as an Academic Tool." *Internet and Higher Education* 6, no. 1 (2003): 17–24.

Inglis, Lucy. *Georgian London: Into the Streets*. London: Penguin, 2013.

Irving, Gemma Louise. "Collaboration in Open-Plan Offices." PhD diss., University of Queensland, 2016.

Jarausch, Konrad, and Kenneth Hardy. *Quantitative Methods for Historians*. Chapel Hill: University of North Carolina Press, 1991).

Jockers, Matthew L. *Macroanalysis*. Urbana: University of Illinois Press, 2013.

Jordanova, Ludmilla. "Historical Vision in a Digital Age." *Cultural and Social History* 11, no. 3 (2014): 343–48.

———. *History in Practice*. London: Arnold, 1999.

Kedgley, Angela. "Development of a Fluoroscopic Radiostereometric Analysis System with an Application to Glenohumeral Joint Kinematics." PhD diss., University of Western Ontario, 2009.

Kelly, John. *The Text and Data Mining Copyright Exception: Benefits and Implications for UK Higher Education*. JISC. 2016. jisc.ac.uk/guides/text-and-data-mining-copyright-exception.

Kelly, Mills T. *Teaching History in the Digital Age*. Ann Arbor: University of Michigan Press, 2013.

Kelty, Christopher M. "This Is Not an Article: Model Organism Newsletters and the Question of 'Open Science.'" *BioSocieties* 7 (2012): 140–68.

Kenney, Anne R., Katherine P. Speiss, Spencer R. Crew, Abby Smith, and Bernard Reilly. "Collections, Content, and the Web." *Council on Library and Information Resources*. Washington, D.C.: 2000.

King, Alison. "From Sage on the Stage to Guide on the Side." *College Teaching* 41, no. 1 (1993): 30–35.

King, Edmund. "Digitisation of Newspapers at the British Library." *Serials Librarian* 49, no. 1–2 (2005): 165–81.

Koeser, Rebecca Sutton. "Trusting Others to 'Do the Math.'" *Interdisciplinary Science Reviews* 40, no. 4 (2015): 376–92.

Kolb, David. *Learning Style Inventory*. Boston: McBer, 1976.

Kousser, J. Morgan. "The State of Social Science History in the Late 1980s." *Historical Methods* 22, no. 1 (1989): 13–20.

Kracauer, Siegfried, and Paul Oskar Kristeller. *History: The Last Things Before the Last*. Oxford: Oxford University Press, 1969.

Ladd, John, Jessica Otis, Christopher N. Warren, and Scott Weingart. "Exploring and Analyzing Network Data with Python." *Programming Historian*, 2017. programminghistorian.org/lessons/exploring-and-analyzing-network-data-with-python.

Lage, Maureen J., Glenn J. Platt, and Michael Treglia. "Inverting the Classroom: A Gateway to Creating an Inclusive Learning Environment." *Journal of Economic Education* 31 (2000): 30–43.

Lancioni, Judith. "The Rhetoric of the Frame Revisioning Archival Photographs in *The Civil War*." *Western Journal of Communication* 60, no. 4 (1996): 397–414.

Landau, Norma. "The Laws of Settlement and the Surveillance of Immigration in Eighteenth Century Kent." *Continuity and Change* 3, no. 3 (1988): 391–420.

Lane, Richard. *The Big Humanities: Digital Humanities/Digital Laboratories*. London: Routledge, 2016.

Lawson, John, and Harold Silver. *A Social History of Education in England*. London: Methuen, 1973.

Lenstra, Noah, and Abdul Alkalimat. "eBlack Studies as Digital Community Archives: A Proof of Concept Study in Champaign-Urbana, Illinois." *Fire!!!* 1, no. 2 (2012): 151–84.

Lewis, M. J., and Roger Lloyd-Jones. *Using Computers in History: A Practical Guide.* London: Routledge, 1996.

Leydier, Yann, Frank Lebourgeois, and Hubert Emptoz. "Text Search for Medieval Manuscript Images." *Pattern Recognition* 40, no. 12 (2007): 3552–67.

Libin, Laurence. *American Musical Instruments in the Metropolitan Museum of Art.* New York: Metropolitan Museum of Art, 1985.

Lieberman, Mark. "Text on Tap: The ACL/DCI." In *Proceedings of the Workshop on Speech and Natural Language*, 1989, 173–88.

Lowenthal, David. *The Past Is a Foreign Country.* Cambridge: Cambridge University Press, 1985.

Magdy, Walid, and Kareem Darwish. "Arabic OCR Error Correction Using Character Segment Correction, Language Modelling, and Shallow Morphology." In *EMNLP '06 Proceedings of the 2006 Conference on Empirical Methods in Natural Language Processing*, Sydney, 2006, 408–14.

Mahony, Simon, and Elena Pierazzo. "Teaching Skills or Teaching Methodology?" In *Digital Humanities Pedagogy*, edited by Brett D. Hirsch, 215–27. Cambridge, U.K.: Open Book Publishers, 2012.

Marsh, C. "Sacred Space in England 1560–1640: The View from the Pew." *Journal of Ecclesiastical History* 53, no. 2 (2002): 286–311.

Matzat, Uwe. "Academic Communication and Internet Discussion Groups: Transfer of Information or Creation of Social Contacts?" *Social Networks* 26, no. 3 (2004): 221–55.

Mawdsley, Evan, and Thomas Munck. *Computing for Historians: An Introductory Guide.* Manchester: Manchester University Press, 1993.

May, Robyn Lee. "An Investigation of the Casualisation of Academic Work in Australia." PhD diss., Griffith University, Australia, 2013.

Mayer, John, and Alfred Conrad. "Economic Theory, Statistical Inference and Economic History." *Journal of Economic History* 17, no. 4 (1957): 524–44.

McCarty, Willard. "HUMANIST: Lessons from a Global Electronic Seminar." *Computers and the Humanities* 26, no. 3 (1992): 205–22.

McClurken, Jeffrey. "Teaching and Learning with Omeka: Discomfort, Play, and Creating Public, Online, Digital Collections." In *Learning through Digital Media: Experiments in Technology and Pedagogy*, edited by Trebor Shultz, 137–47. New York: New School and the Macarthur Foundation, 2011.

———, and Jerry Slezak. "Research-Based Web Sites: Students Creating Online Scholarship." *Journal of the Association of History and Computing* 9, no. 2 (2006).

———, Jeremy Boggs, Adrianne Wadewitz, Anne Ellen Geller, and Jon Beasley-Murray. "Digital Literacy and the Undergraduate Curriculum." In *Hacking the Academy: New Approaches to Scholarship and Teaching from Digital Humanities*, edited by Dan Cohen and Tom Scheinfeldt, 80–86. Ann Arbor: University of Michigan Press, 2011.

McCutcheon, Roger Philip. "The 'Journal Des Scavans' and the 'Philosophical Transactions of the Royal Society.'" *Studies in Philology* 21, no. 4 (1924): 626–28.

McDaniel, Caleb. "Blogging in the Early Republic: Why Bloggers Belong in the History of Reading." *Common-Place* 5, no. 4 (2005).

McEnery, A. M., and R. Z. Xiao. "Character Encoding in Corpus Construction." In *Developing Linguistic Corpora: A Guide to Good Practice*, edited by Martin Wynne. Oxford: Oxbow Books, 2005. ota.ox.ac.uk/documents/creating/dlc/chapter4.htm.

McEnery, Anthony, and Helen Baker. *Corpus Linguistics and 17th-Century Prostitution*. London: Bloomsbury, 2017.

Merriman, Scott. "The View from Here: The First Ten Years of the JAHC." *Journal of the Association of History and Computing* 12, no. 1 (2009). hdl.handle.net/2027/spo.3310410.0012.104.

Middleton, Roger. "Annual Review of Information Technology Developments for Economic and Social Historians, 1994." *Economic History Review* 48, no. 2 (1995): 370–95.

———, and Peter Wardley. "Annual Review of Information Technology Developments for Economic and Social Historians, 1990." *Economic History Review* 44, no. 2 (1991): 343–72.

———, and Peter Wardley. "Annual Review of Information Technology Developments for Economic and Social Historians, 1993." *Economic History Review* 47, no. 2 (1994): 374–407.

Milligan, Ian. "Automated Downloading with Wget." *Programming Historian*, 2012. programminghistorian.org/lessons/automated-downloading-with-wget.

———. "Lost in the Infinite Archive: The Promise and Pitfalls of Web Archives." *International Journal of Humanities and Arts Computing* 10, no. 1–2 (2016): 87–94.

———. "Mining the Internet Graveyard: Rethinking the Historian's Toolkit." *Journal of the Canadian Historical Association* 23, no. 2 (2012): 21–64.

Mitschele, Anna. "Identity and Opportunity in Early Modern Politics: How Job Vacancies Induced Witch Persecutions in Scotland, 1563–1736." In *Analytical Sociology*, edited by Gianluca Manzo, 149–68. Chichester: Wiley, 2014.

Molesworth, Mike, Elizabeth Nixon, and Richard Scullion. "Having, Being and Higher Education: The Marketization of the University and the Transformation of the Student into Consumer." *Teaching in Higher Education* 14, no. 3 (2009): 277–87.

Moretti, Franco. "Conjectures on World Literature." *New Left Review* 1 (2000): 54–68.

Morse, Samuel. *Improvements in the Mode of Communicating by Signals by the Application of Electro-Magnetism*. U.S. Patent 1,647, issued 20 June 1840.

Morton, A. Q. "Once. A Test of Authorship Based on Words Which Are Not Repeated in the Sample." *Literary and Linguistic Computing* 1, no. 1 (1986): 1–8.

Munslow, Alun. *A History of History*. Hoboken, N.J.: Taylor and Francis, 2012.

Murray, Janet H. *Hamlet on the Holodeck: The Future of Narrative in Cyberspace*. Cambridge, Mass.: MIT Press, 1997.

Navickas, Katrina, and Adam Crymble. "From Chartist Newspaper to Digital Map of Grass-roots Meetings, 1841–44: Documenting Workflows." *Journal of Victorian Culture* 22, no. 2 (2017): 232–47.

Nicholson, Bob. "The Digital Turn: Exploring the Methodological Possibilities of Digital Newspaper Archives." *Media History* 19, no. 1 (2011): 59–73.

———. "The Victorian Meme Machine: Remixing the Nineteenth-Century Archive." *Interdisciplinary Studies in the Long Nineteenth Century* 21 (2015). doi.org/10.16995/ntn.738.

Nkomo, Stella M. "The Seductive Power of Academic Journal Rankings." *Academy of Management Learning and Education* 8, no. 1 (2009): 106–12.

Noiret, Serge. "Digital History 2.0." In *L'Histoire Contemporaine à l'Ère Numérique*, edited by Frédéric Clavert and Serge Noiret, 155–90. Brussels: Peter Lang, 2013.

Nora, Pierre. *Realms of Memory.* New York: Columbia University Press, 1996.

North, Douglass C. "Cliometrics—40 Years Later." *American Economic Review* 87, no. 2 (1997): 412–14.

Novick, Peter. *That Noble Dream: The "Objectivity Question" and the American Historical Profession.* Cambridge: Cambridge University Press, 1988.

Nowviskie, Bethany. "On the Origin of 'Hack' and 'Yack.'" *Journal of Digital Humanities* 3, no. 2 (2014). journalofdigitalhumanities.org/3-2/on-the-origin-of-hack-and-yack-by-bethany-nowviskie.

Nyhan, Julianne, and Andrew Flinn. *Computation and the Humanities.* London: Springer, 2016.

Organisciak, Peter, and Boris Capitanu. "Text Mining in Python through the HTRC Feature Reader." *Programming Historian*, 2016. programminghistorian.org/lessons/text-mining-with-extracted-features.

Orwell, George. *1984.* London: Secker & Walburg, 1949.

Owsley, Frank Lawrence. *Plain Folk of the Old South.* Baton Rouge: Louisiana State University Press, 1949.

Pittman, Matthew, and Kim Sheehan. "Amazon's Mechanical Turk as a Digital Sweatshop? Transparency and Accountability in Crowdsourced Online Research." *Journal of Media Ethics* 32, no. 4 (2016): 260–62.

Posner, Miriam. "Think Talk Make Do: Power and the Digital Humanities." *Journal of Digital Humanities* 1, no. 2 (2012).

Price, Kenneth M. "Digital Scholarship, Economics, and the American Literary Canon." *Literature Compass* 6 (2009): 274–90.

Purvis, Keith. "The Teacher as Moderator: A Technique for Interactional Learning." *ELT Journal* 37 (1983): 221–28.

Putnam, Lara. "The Transnational and the Text Searchable: Digitized Sources and the Shadows They Cast." *American Historical Review* 121, no. 2 (2016): 377–402.

Raddick, M. Jordan, Georgia Bracey, Pamela L. Gay, Chris J. Lintott, Phil Murray, Kevin Schawinski, Alexander S. Szalay, and Jan Vandenberg. "Galaxy Zoo: Exploring the Motivations of Citizen Science Volunteers." *Astronomy Education Review* 9, no. 1 (2010).

Rafols, Ismael, Loet Leydesdorff, Alice O'Hare, Paul Nightingale, and Andy Stirling. "How Journal Rankings Can Suppress Interdisciplinary Research." *Research Policy*, 41, no. 7 (2012): 1262–82.

Rahtz, Sebastian. "The Processing of Words." In *Information Technology in the Humanities: Tools, Techniques and Applications*, edited by Sebastian Rahtz, 69–79. London: John Wiley, 1987.

———, ed. *Information Technology in the Humanities: Tools, Techniques and Applications*. London: John Wiley, 1987.

Ramsay, Stephen. "The Hermeneutics of Screwing Around; or What You Do with a Million Books." In *Pastplay: Teaching and Learning History with Technology*, edited by Kevin Kee. Ann Arbor: University of Michigan Press, 2014. dx.doi.org/10.3998/dh.12544152.0001.001.

Rauch, Jennifer. "Hands-on Communication: Zine Circulation Rituals and the Interactive Limitations of Web Self-Publishing." *Popular Communication: The International Journal of Media and Culture* 2, no. 3 (2004): 153–69.

Ravenstein, E. G. "The Laws of Migration." *Journal of the Statistical Society* 52, no. 2 (1889): 241–305.

Rehbein, Malte, and Christiane Fritze. "Hands-on Teaching Digital Humanities: A Didactic Analysis of a Summer School Course on Digital Editing." In *Digital Humanities Pedagogy: Practices, Principles and Politics*, edited by Brett D. Hirsch, 47–78. Cambridge, U.K.: Open Book Publishers, 2012.

Reiff, Janice L. *Structuring the Past: The Use of Computers in History*. Washington, D.C.: American Historical Association, 1991.

Research Assessment Exercise. England and Wales. 2008.

Research Excellence Framework. England and Wales. 2014.

Reynolds, Graham. "Making Canadian History More Inclusive Through the Multi-Media: The Peopling of Atlantic Canada CD ROM." *Canadian Social Studies* 36, no. 1 (2001).

Reynolds, John. "Do Historians Count Anymore? The Status of Quantitative Methods in History, 1975–1995." *Historical Methods* 31, no. 4 (1998): 141–48.

Risam, Roopika. "Navigating the Global Digital Humanities: Insights from Black Feminism." In *Debates in the Digital Humanities,* edited by Matthew Gold and Lauren Klein, chapter 29. Minneapolis: University of Minnesota Press, 2016. dhdebates.gc.cuny.edu/read/65be1a40-6473-4d9e-ba75-6380e5a72138/section/4316ff92-bad0-45e8-8f09-90f493c6f564#ch29.

Rockwell, Geoffrey, and Stéfan Sinclair. "Acculturation and the Digital Humanities Community." In *Digital Humanities Pedagogy,* edited by Brett D. Hirsch, 177–212. Cambridge, U.K.: Open Book Publishers, 2012.

Rockwell, Geoffrey, Peter Organisciak, Megan Meredith-Lobay, Kamal Ranaweera, Stan Ruecker, and Julianne Nyhan. "The Design of an International Social Media Event: A Day in the Life of the Digital Humanities." *Digital Humanities Quarterly* 6, no. 2 (2012). digitalhumanities.org/dhq/vol/6/2/000123/000123.html.

Roediger, David. "Review: What Was So Great about Herbert Gutman?" *Labour / Le Travail* 23 (1989): 255–61.

Rosenzweig, Roy. "'So, What's Next for Clio?' CD-ROM and Historians." *Journal of American History* 81, no. 4 (1995): 1621–40.

——, and Steve Brier. "Why Read a History Book on a Computer? Putting *Who Built America?* on CD-ROM." *History Microcomputer Review* 9 no. 2 (1993): 9–14.

Samaha, Joel. *Law and Order in Historical Perspective: The Case of Elizabethan Essex.* New York: Academic Press, 1974.

di Santis, Francesco. *The Post-Katrina Portraits: Written and Narrated by Hundreds.* New Orleans: Francesco di Santis, 2007.

Schön, Donald. *The Reflective Practitioner: How Professionals Think in Action.* London: Temple Smith, 1983.

Schreibman, Susan, Ray Siemens, and John Unsworth, eds. *A Companion to Digital Humanities.* Oxford, U.K.: Blackwell, 2004.

Sharpe, J. A. *Crime in Early Modern England 1550–1750.* 2d ed. London: Routledge, 1999.

Sheldon, James L. "The Extended Museum: Production and Design of the Harold Tovish: Scultpr and Eadweard Muybridge: Motion Studies Videodisc." MSc thesis, Massachusetts Institute of Technology, 1989.

Shorter, Edward. *The Historian and the Computer: A Practical Guide.* New York: Norton, 1971.

Sichani, Anna-Maria, James Baker, Maria José Afanador Llach, and Brandon Walsh. "Diversity and Inclusion in Digital Scholarship and Pedagogy: The Case of the *Programming Historian.*" *Insights* 32, no. 1 (2019). doi.org/10.1629/uksg.465.

Smith, Abby. "New-Model Scholarship: How Will it Survive?" *Council on Library and Information Resources.* Washington, D.C.: 2003.

Smith, G. G., C. Sorensen, A. Gump, A. J. Heindel, M. Caris, and C. D. Martinez. "Overcoming Student Resistance to Group Work: Online vs Face-to-Face." *Internet and Higher Education* 14, no. 2 (2011): 121–28.

Smith Rumsey, Abby. "Creating Value and Impact in the Digital Age through Translational Humanities." *Council on Library and Information Resources.* Washington, D.C.: 2013.

——. "Strategies for Building Digitized Collections." *Council on Library and Information Resources.* Washington, D.C.: 2001.

Solberg, Janine. "Googling the Archive: Digital Tools and the Practice of History." *Advances in the History of Rhetoric* 15, no. 1 (2012): 53–76.

Speck, W. A. "Introduction." *Social History* 9 (1984): 412–14.

Sperberg-McQueen, C. M. "Text in the Electronic Age: Textual Study and Textual Study and Text Encoding, with Examples from Medieval Texts." *Literary and Linguistic Computing* 6, no. 1 (1991): 34–46.

Sridhar, M. S. "User Participation in Collection Building in a Special Library: A Case Study." *IASLIC Bulletin* 28, no. 3 (1983): 117–22.

Steedman, Carolyn. *Dust.* Manchester: Manchester University Press, 2001.

Stoler, Ann Laura. *Along the Archival Grain: Epistemic Anxieties and Colonial Common Sense.* Princeton, N.J.: Princeton University Press, 2009.

——. "The Pulse of the Archive." *Ab Imperio* 3 (2007): 225–64.

Sweet, Richard. *An Analysis of the Australian Labour Market for Typists, Stenographers and Secretaries.* New South Wales Department of TAFE, 1983.

Tebeau, Mark. "Listening to the City: Oral History and Place in the Digital Era." *Oral History Review* 40, no. 1 (2013): 25–35.

———. "Pursuing e-Opportunities in the History Classroom." *Journal of American History* 89, no. 4 (2003): 1489–94.

———, Erin J. Bell, and Mark J. Souther. "Strategies for Mobile Interpretive Projects for Humanists and Cultural Organizations." *Mobile Historical* 1 (2013).

TEI P1 Guidelines for the Encoding and Interchange of Machine Readable Texts First Draft 16 July 1990; Draft Version 1.1, Text Encoding Initiative. 1990. tei-c.org/Vault/Vault-GL.html.

Terras, Melissa, and Paul Robertson. "Downs and Acrosses: Textual Markup on a Stroke Level." *Literary and Linguistic Computing* 19, no. 3 (2004): 397–414.

Thomas, William G. "Computing and the Historical Imagination." In *A Companion to Digital Humanities,* edited by Susan Schreibman, Ray Siemens, and John Unsworth, 56–68. Oxford, U.K.: Blackwell, 2004.

Thompson, E. P. *The Making of the English Working Class.* London: Victor Gollancz, 1963.

Thompson, Willie. *Postmodernism and History.* Basingstoke, U.K.: Palgrave Macmillan, 2004.

Tomasek, Kathryn, and Syd Bauman. "Encoding Financial Records for Historical Research." *Journal of the Text Encoding Initiative* 6 (2013).

Tomlinson, Roger. *Introduction to the Geo-Information System and the Canadian Land Inventory.* Ottawa, Canada ARDA, 1967.

Toplin, Robert Brent, ed. *Ken Burns's* The Civil War: *Historians Respond.* New York: Oxford University Press, 1996.

Torabi, Katayoun, Jessica Durgan, and Bryan Tarpley. "Early Modern OCR Project (eMOP) at Texas A&M University: Using Aletheia to Train Tesseract." *DocEng '13: Proceedings of the 2013 ACM Symposium on Document Engineering.* Florence, 2013. 23–26.

Townsend, Rob. *History's Babel.* Chicago: University of Chicago Press, 2013.

Trouillot, Michel-Rolph. *Silencing the Past: Power and the Production of History.* Boston: Beacon, 1995.

Turkel, William J. *The Archive of Place: Unearthing the Pasts of the Chilcotin Plateau.* Vancouver: University of British Columbia Press, 2007.

———, and Alan MacEachern. *The Programming Historian.* 1st ed. London, Ont.: Network in Canadian History and Environment, 2008. niche-canada.org/wp-content/uploads/2013/09/programming-historian-1.pdf.

Turnbull, Paul. "Historians, Computing and the World-Wide-Web." *Australian Historical Studies* 41, no. 2 (2010): 131–48.

Tyrrell, Ian. *Historians in Public: The Practice of American History 1890–1970.* Chicago: University of Chicago Press, 2005.

Vincent, Annette, and Dianne Ross. "Learning Style Awareness." *Journal of Research on Computing in Education* 33, no. 5 (2001): 1–10.

von Ahn, Luis, Benjamin Mauer, Colin McMillen, David Abraham, and Manuel Blum. "reCAPTCHA: Human-Based Character Recognition via Web Security Measures." *Science* 321 (2008): 1465–68.

Wallach Scott, Joan. *Gender and the Politics of History.* New York: Columbia University Press, 1989.

Ward, Geoffrey C., Ric Burns, and Ken Burns. *The Civil War: An Illustrated History.* New York: Knopf, 1990.

Weller, Toni, *History in the Digital Age.* Abingdon, U.K.: Routledge, 2013.

Wells, H. G. *The Time Machine.* London: William Heinemann, 1895.

Whaples, Robert. "A Quantitative History of the Journal of Economic History and the Cliometric Revolution." *Journal of Economic History* 51, no. 2 (1991): 289–301.

White, Susan, Raymond Chu, and Roman Czujko. *The 2012–13 Survey of Humanities Departments at Four-Year Institutions: Full Technical Report.* Statistical Research Center, American Institute of Physics. 2014.

Williams, Kenneth H. "Review: *Ken Burns's The Civil War: Historians Respond.*" *Public Historian* 20, no. 2 (1998): 95–96.

Wilson, G. V., R. H. Landau, and S. McConnell. "What Should Computer Scientists Teach to Physical Scientists and Engineers." *IEEE Computational Science and Engineering* 3, no. 2 (2002): 46–65.

Wineburg, Sam. "Crazy for History." *Journal of American History* 90, no. 4 (2004): 1401–14.

———. "Historical Thinking and Other Unnatural Acts: Charting the Future of Teaching the Past." *Phi Delta Kappan* 92, no. 4 (2010): 81–94.

Winters, Jane. "Digital History." In *Debating New Approaches in History*, edited by Peter Burk and Marek Tamm. London: Bloomsbury, 2019.

Wrigley, E. A., and R. S. Schofield. *The Population History of England 1541–1871.* London: Edward Arnold, 1981.

Young, Margaret Levine. *The Internet for Windows for Dummies: Starter Kit.* Foster City, Calif.: IDG Books, 1994.

Young, Michael, and Peter Willmott. *The Symmetrical Family.* Harmondsworth: Penguin, 1975.

Zampolli, A. "Introduction to the Special Section on Machine Translation." *Literary and Linguistic Computing* 4, no. 3 (1989): 182–84.

Zephyr, Frank. "Layers, Flows and Intersections: Jeronymo José de Mello and Artisan Life in Rio de Janeiro, 1840s-1880s." *Journal of Social History* 41, no. 2 (2007): 307–28.

Index

Aarseth, Espen, 9, 54
Afanador-Llach, Maria-José, 168
Aiden, Erez Lieberman, 38
algorithmic thinking, 18–28, 37–40, 99, 119, 151–53
Alkalimat, Abdul, 66
Andersen, Deborah Lines, 65
Ankersmith, F.R., 162
Anthony, Laurence, 39
archives and collections: Ancestry.com, 61; born-digital, 42, 65–67; collection management, 40, 65–67; curation, 52–54, 60, 65–67, 151–55; database software, 92, 113–16; digital and archival theory, 44, 47, 57–59; digital challenges of, 33–36, 40, 123; digital creation of, 47, 51–53, 57–59, 62–67, 92; digital potential of, 32, 40–44, 123; Europeana, 64; Google Books, 34, 38, 61, 64; historical: 46, 51, 58, 61–63; invented archive, 47, 57–59, 62, 67, 174; Old Bailey Online, 35–36, 40, 62–63, 124; Omeka, 91–92, 97; *Valley of the Shadow*, 57–60, 62, 78; *Who Built America?*, 51–52, 55–56
Austin, Jane, 39
Ayers, Edward, 47, 57–59, 136, 139

Baker, Helen, 39, 162
Baker, James, 134
Bauman, Syd, 29
Beals, M. H., 33–37

Beattie, John, 25
Bederson, Benjamin, 73–74
Bender, Pennee, 60
Bentham, Jeremy, 70–71
Blaney, Jonathan, 33
Blaxill, Luke, 39
Blease, Derek, 114
Blevins, Cameron, 102–3
Boggs, Jeremy, 80, 149
Booth, Alan, 82, 105
Börner, Katy, 32
Bowen, William G., 60
Brennan, Sheila, 130
Bridenbaugh, Carl, 17
Brier, Steve, 50–57
British Library Labs, 36–37
Burke, Timothy, 146, 153
Burnard, Lou, 80
Burns, Arthur, 87, 103
Burns, Ken, 52–53
Busa, Robert, 17–19, 27–30, 42–44

Caesar, Mathieu, 103
Cambridge Group for the History of Population and Social Structure (Campop), 24, 26
capitalism: difficulties of, 36, 56, 103, 123; influence of, 89, 97, 151; partnerships with businesses, 36, 55, 61; projects by businesses, 61

Caswell, Michelle, 48
Cebula, Larry, 147, 158
Clifford, Jim, 37, 128
Cockburn, J. S., 25, 33, 39, 43–44, 85
Cohen, Dan, 49, 91, 122–23, 149–56, 163–65
Conner, Patrick, W., 139–40
conservativism, influence of, 55
copyright, 36–37, 48
Cordell, Ryan, 102
Cosgrave, Mike, 96
Crane, Gregory, 27, 32, 38, 44
Cummings, James, 153
Cutler, William, 82

data: acquisition, 36–37, 123–26; analysis, 33–36, 85–87, 116, 125, 132, 174; big, 32, 38–39, 83, 98–99, 105; cleaning, 37, 46, 111, 118, 122–26, 174; learning about, 83, 85–87, 111, 121–26, 131; quality, 25, 34–37, 38, 85–86, 162
data mining. See data: analysis
Daunton, Martin, 26
Day of Digital Humanities, 49
Denley, Peter, 113–14
Derakhshan, Hossein, 151
digital history turns: cliometrics, 22–27, 30–31, 44, 101, 127, 174; culturomics, 38–39, 43–44; distant reading, 27–40, 99, 126
digital tools. See software
digitization: approaches to, 34–35, 47, 68–69, 99; challenges of, 28, 31–37, 50–51, 68; history of, 47, 50–51, 61; learning about, 92, 116, 132; motivation for, 48, 61–64, 77–78, 92; potential for research, 19, 27, 31–32, 38–42, 45; as public history, 48, 54–56; three dimensional, 40–41, 94. See also funding
discipline (not history): corpus linguistics, 31, 35–44, 125, 131, 162; engineering, 37, 41, 57, 93–95; humanities computing, 27–32, 38–45, 115, 120, 129–31; information science, 40, 46, 62, 65; library and archive science, 43–44, 47–51, 58, 64–65, 78; linguistics, 18–19, 27–31, 39–43, 99–101, 120–30; literature studies, 27–31, 39, 54, 131; social sciences, 17–27, 42–44, 109–13, 125, 135; sociology, 21, 76, 84–85; user studies, 49, 54–55, 68–77, 80–81
D'Sena, Peter, 63
Dunning, Alastair, 61

Eaton, Clement, 22
encoding: applied, 59; history of, 28–30, 46; learning, 89, 131–32, 135
Endres, William, 40–41
engagement strategies: cool, being, 89, 94, 97, 133; gamification, 69–72, 76, 120; participatory web, 54, 64–78, 89
Engerman, Stanley, 23–25

Fitzgerald, Mark, 89
Fitzpatrick, Kathleen, 144
Fleming, Neil, 81
Floud, Roderick, 109–11, 113, 118, 127
Fogel, Robert, 23, 25
Frische, Michael, 66
Fritze, Christiane, 131
Froehlich, Heather, 125
funding: challenges of, 86; granting agencies, 50, 60–62, 132, 156; influence on scholarly agendas, 50, 60, 63, 156; private partnerships, 61, 89

Gaffield, Chad, 18, 42
Gardner, Howard, 81
Gayol, Victor, 168
Giacometti, Alejandro, 41
Gibbs, Fred, 93, 118, 127
global and local digital history: in Africa, 131, 166–68; in Asia, 151–52, 169; in Britain, 50, 63, 84–88, 103–4, 156, 171–74; in continental Europe, 130–31, 152, 166–68; in Ireland, 76, 96; in Latin America, 166–69; in North America, 50–52, 56, 63, 90–93, 171–74; in Oceania, 34, 64, 68; regional differences, 48, 63, 104, 118, 133, 161. See also privilege
Goetz, Rebecca, 138, 141
Goldstone, Andrew, 102
Gorman, Michael John, 89
Grafton, Anthony, 38
Graham, Shawn, 32, 91, 124–25, 164
Greenberg, Josh, 90, 143, 149
Gutman, Herbert, 51–52

Haahr, Mads, 76
Hardman, Chris, 73
Hart, Michael, 47
Hay, Douglas, 25, 93
Heppler, Jason, 67, 128
Herring, Susan, 145

Hirsch, Brett, 82
historiography: influences on, 27, 43–44, 150, 162; teaching of, 94, 104, 135, 174
history subfield: cultural, 19, 27–28, 32, 38–39, 41–42; demographic, 21–26; economic, 20–32, 85–87, 111–12, 116; family, 61, 63; gender, 33, 49, 118, 155, 165; geography, 21–24, 41, 69–76, 128, 132; intellectual, 70; local, 24, 92–93; political, 19–22, 24, 36, 39, 71; post-colonial, 47–50, 153–55 166–69; public, 47, 51–53, 64–67, 70–76, 89–94; quantitative, 17–27, 39–45, 83–87, 99–105, 108–11; social, 20–27, 50–52, 57–63, 85, 88
Hitchcock, Tim, 38, 50, 62–63, 77, 87–88, 143
Hobsbawm, Eric, 52
Holley, Rose, 34
Hopkin, Deian, 113–14
Horbinski, Andrea, 43
Howard, Sharon, 152–53
Huber, Magnus, 39
Hulden, Vilja, 125

Ide, Nancy, 100, 118
image analysis, 40–41, 70–72, 102
Index Thomisticus, 17–19, 27–30
Institute of Historical Research, 104, 131, 135, 140
interactive media: CD-ROM, 46, 53–57, 59, 63–65, 77; mobile computing, 51, 72–78, 99, 162; physical computing, 72–76, 93–95; virtual reality, 40–42, 72–77
interdisciplinary, 18, 38–43, 87–102, 108, 139, 150, 168
internet, 18, 27–42, 47–64, 88–89, 116–23. See also web development
invisible college, 81–82, 107–36, 140–46, 162, 170

Jensen, Richard, 128, 130
Johnson, Jessica Marie, 145
Jordanova, Ludmilla, 162
Jørgensen, Finn Arne, 166

Kelly, Mills, 82–83, 91–93, 105, 149–50
King, Alison, 80
Kirsch, Adam, 28
Kjellberg, Sara, 138, 143
Koeser, Rebecca Sutton, 101, 112
Koh, Adeline, 153–54
Kolb, David, 80

Laslett, Peter, 24
LeBlanc, Zoe, 108, 126, 135
Lehuu, Isabelle, 56
Lenstra, Noah, 66
Leon, Sharon, 130, 149
Lieberman, Mark, 30–31
Luker, Ralph, 137, 144–49, 152

MacDougall, Rob, 141–45, 153
machine learning, 40, 71–72, 77, 99, 108
Madsen-Brooks, Leslie, 93
Mahony, Simon, 118
Marche, Stephen, 28–29
markup. See encoding
Mawdsley, Evan, 115
McCallum-Stewart, Esther, 141
McCarty, Willard, 139–40, 144
McClurken, Jeffrey, 90–93, 98
McDaniel, Caleb, 90–91, 141
McEnery, Anthony, 39, 162
McLuhan, Marshall, 140, 170
McNeil, Sara, 59, 165
methodology: applying, 22; developing, 19, 21, 28–32, 37–41, 122; ignoring, 33, 39, 43; learning, 99, 103–4, 108–11, 118, 129–35; publishing, 26, 124, 157
Meyer, John, 22–23, 25, 86
Michel, Jean-Baptiste, 38
Middleton, Roger, 85–88, 104, 116
Milligan, Ian, 32, 42, 102, 125, 164
Mintz, Steven, 59, 165
Moravec, Michelle, 33, 155
Moretti, Franco, 32, 99
Mullen, Lincoln, 100, 128
Munck, Thomas, 115

Navickas, Katrina, 36, 71
Nicholson, Bob, 33, 37, 103–4
Noiret, Serge, 47, 50, 164
Novick, Peter, 21–23, 161
Nowviskie, Bethany, 117

O'Reilly, Tim, 65, 119, 122
O'Sullivan, James, 154
Owsley, Frank, 17–19, 22–23, 44

Petrik, Paula, 93
Phillips, U. B., 23
Pierazzo, Elena, 118
Posner, Miriam, 118, 128

Prescott, Andrew, 157–58
privilege: access to, 36, 38, 106, 118; canonicity, 47–48; lack of, 107, 138, 144–46, 155, 168; power to influence because of, 48, 60–61, 144, 151–55, 168; resourcing available through, 56, 86, 130
programming, 99–102, 108, 113–28, 132, 174
Programming Historian, 43, 100–101, 123–28, 135, 166–69
Purvis, Keith, 80
Putnam, Lara, 33

race and ethnicity, 17, 22–23, 153–55, 166–69
Rahtz, Sebastian, 114
Ramsdell, C. W., 23
Ravenstein, E. G., 21
Rehbein, Malte, 131
Reiff, Janice, 82, 115
research: historical, 18–19, 32, 58, 102–4, 162–65; meta, 32, 42, 49, 70, 157
Reynolds, John, 109
Risam, Roopika, 153–54
Robertson, Stephen, 30–31
Rockwell, Geoffrey, 39, 118
Rojas Castro, Antonio, 168
Rosenzweig, Roy, 49, 54–57, 65–67, 91, 122, 164–65
Ross, Dianne, 81
Roy Rosenzweig Center for History and New Media, 43, 133, 149–50, 153
Rudé, George, 52
Rumsey, Abby Smith, 48, 67

Santis, Francesco de, 66
Scheinfeldt, Tom, 43, 133, 149–50
Schmidt, Benjamin, 48, 125, 157
Schofield, R. S., 24
scholarly communication: approaches to, 157, 168; Cliopatria, 147–49, 152–53; DH Now, 153–55; DHThis, 155; History News Network, 148–50; Humanist, 128, 139, 141, 144–45; Invisible Adjunct, 145–47; journals, 26, 30–31, 149, 153, 159; newsletters, 121–22, 130, 137–39; ranting, 141–48, 159–60, 162; reflective practice, 81–82, 90–91, 137, 157–58. See also invisible college
scholarly society: ADHO (Alliance of Digital Humanities Organizations), 30, 129, 150; AHA (American Historical Association), 17, 30, 83, 130, 139; CHA (Canadian Historical Association), 83, 139; RHS (Royal Historical Society), 83, 158
Schön, Donald, 90
Senier, Siobhan, 155
Shakespeare, William, 39, 48, 60
Shenkman, Rick, 148
Shoemaker, Robert, 36, 62–63
Siemens, Ray, 131
Sinclair, Stéfan, 39, 118
Smith, Lisa, 103–4
socialism, influence of, 22, 50–52, 56, 63, 77
social media: blogging, 90–91, 94, 117, 137–60, 174; Facebook, 89, 151; Instagram, 99, 151, 159; Listservs, 128, 137–45; Twitter, 108, 126, 135, 151–55, 159
software, 37–40, 69–71, 99–102, 112–22, 132–34, 164–66
statistics: faith in, 23, 101, 112; learning, 84–85, 101, 109–16, 130; using, 21, 25, 40, 125
Steedman, Carolyn, 47
Stein, Bob, 55
Stoler, Ann Laura, 47–48
Styles, John, 86–87
sustainability, 62, 113, 120–21, 124

teaching: classroom design, 79–80, 86–88, 95–98; curriculum development, 63, 130; Digital Humanities at Oxford Summer School, 131, 135; educational theory, 79–83, 110–11, 126; flipped classroom, 95–96, 105, 162; primary source based, 52–56, 59–60, 78, 162; project-based learning, 84–88, 92–94; short courses and workshops, 82, 128–34, 162; student centred learning, 79–81, 90–96, 105; syllabus, 82, 102, 164, 171–74; ThatCamp, 133–34. See also data; encoding; historiography; methodology
Tebeau, Mark, 75, 90
technical writing, 100–101, 122–27
Terras, Melissa, 138
Text Encoding Initiative, 29–30, 131–32
Thomas, William, III, 17, 22
Thomas Acquinas, Saint, 18
Thompson, E. P., 22, 50–52, 63, 77
Tomasek, Kathryn, 29
Tomlinson, Roger, 24
Tribble, Ivan (pseudonym), 144–45
Trouillot, Michel-Rolph, 47

Turkel, William J., 40, 74–75, 90–100, 122–26, 135

Underwood, Ted, 135

Vincent, Annette, 81

ways of working: co-creation, 65–67, 71; collaboration, 70–71, 91, 95–98; crowdsourcing, 49, 65–72

web development, 33, 89–93, 100–102, 120–21
Weingart, Scott, 30–32, 43, 125, 164
Whisnant, Anne Mitchell, 93
Winters, Jane, 18, 36, 42, 49, 163–64
Wrigley, E. A., 24, 26

Zephyr, Frank, 24

ADAM CRYMBLE is an editor of *Programming Historian* and a lecturer of digital humanities at University College London.

TOPICS IN THE DIGITAL HUMANITIES

From Papyrus to Hypertext: Toward the Universal Digital Library
 *Christian Vandendorpe, translated from the French by Phyllis Aronoff
 and Howard Scott*
Reading Machines: Toward an Algorithmic Criticism   *Stephen Ramsay*
Macroanalysis: Digital Methods and Literary History   *Matthew L. Jockers*
Digital Critical Editions   *Edited by Daniel Apollon, Claire Bélisle, and Philippe Régnier*
Teaching with Digital Humanities: Tools and Methods for Nineteenth-Century
 American Literature   *Edited by Jennifer Travis and Jessica DeSpain*
Critical Digital Humanities: The Search for a Methodology   *James E. Dobson*
Technology and the Historian: Transformations in the Digital Age   *Adam Crymble*

The University of Illinois Press
is a founding member of the
Association of University Presses.

University of Illinois Press
1325 South Oak Street
Champaign, IL 61820-6903
www.press.uillinois.edu

Printed by Printforce, United Kingdom